D1882604

HISTORY OF BURMA

HISTORY OF BURMA

INCLUDING

BURMA PROPER, PEGU, TAUNGU, TENASSERIM, AND ARAKAN.

LIEUT-GENERAL SIR ARTHUR P. PHAYRE,

GYAN

Published by

Gyan Publishing House
5, Ansari Road
Daryaganj, New Delhi-110002
Phone: 011-47034999, 9811692060
E-mail: books@gyanbooks.com

Distribution Network
gyanbooks.com
India, USA, Canada, UK, Australia, France

© Publisher

All rights reserved. No part of this work may be reproduced, stored, adapted, or transmitted in any form or by any means, electronic, mechanical, photocopying, micro-filming, recording or otherwise, or translated in any language, without the prior written permission of the copyright owner and the publisher.

ISBN : 978-81-212-9606-9 (PB)
First Published, 1883

2nd Impression 2023

Printed at: Gyan Press, Delhi.

The book is sold subject to the condition that it shall not, by way of trade or otherwise, be lent, resold, hired out, or otherwise circulated without the prior publisher's written consent.

HISTORY OF BURMA
Author: LIEUT-GENERAL SIR ARTHUR P. PHAYRE,

TRÜBNER'S ORIENTAL SERIES.

"A knowledge of the commonplace, at least, of Oriental literature, philosophy, and religion is as necessary to the general reader of the present day as an acquaintance with the Latin and Greek classics was a generation or so ago. Immense strides have been made within the present century in these branches of learning; Sanskrit has been brought within the range of accurate philology, and its invaluable ancient literature thoroughly investigated; the language and sacred books of the Zoroastrians have been laid bare; Egyptian, Assyrian, and other records of the remote past have been deciphered, and a group of scholars speak of still more recondite Accadian and Hittite monuments; but the results of all the scholarship that has been devoted to these subjects have been almost inaccessible to the public because they were contained for the most part in learned or expensive works, or scattered throughout the numbers of scientific periodicals. Messrs. TRÜBNER & Co., in a spirit of enterprise which does them infinite credit, have determined to supply the constantly-increasing want, and to give in a popular, or, at least, a comprehensive form, all this mass of knowledge to the world."—*Times.*

Second Edition, post 8vo, pp. xxxii.—748, with Map, cloth, price 21s.

THE INDIAN EMPIRE: ITS PEOPLE, HISTORY, AND PRODUCTS.

By the HON. SIR W. W. HUNTER, K.C.S.I., C.S.I., C.I.E., LL.D.

Member of the Viceroy's Legislative Council,

Director-General of Statistics to the Government of India.

Being a Revised Edition, brought up to date, and incorporating the general results of the Census of 1881.

"It forms a volume of more than 700 pages, and is a marvellous combination of literary condensation and research. It gives a complete account of the Indian Empire, its history, peoples, and products, and forms the worthy outcome of seventeen years of labour with exceptional opportunities for rendering that labour fruitful. Nothing could be more lucid than Sir William Hunter's expositions of the economic and political condition of India at the present time, or more interesting than his scholarly history of the India of the past."—*The Times.*

THE FOLLOWING WORKS HAVE ALREADY APPEARED:—

Third Edition, post 8vo, cloth, pp. xvi.—428, price 16s.

ESSAYS ON THE SACRED LANGUAGE, WRITINGS, AND RELIGION OF THE PARSIS.

BY MARTIN HAUG, PH.D.,

Late of the Universities of Tübingen, Göttingen, and Bonn; Superintendent of Sanskrit Studies, and Professor of Sanskrit in the Poona College.

EDITED AND ENLARGED BY DR. E. W. WEST.

To which is added a Biographical Memoir of the late Dr. HAUG by Prof. E. P. EVANS.

I. History of the Researches into the Sacred Writings and Religion of the Parsis, from the Earliest Times down to the Present.
II. Languages of the Parsi Scriptures.
III. The Zend-Avesta, or the Scripture of the Parsis.
IV. The Zoroastrian Religion, as to its Origin and Development.

"'Essays on the Sacred Language, Writings, and Religion of the Parsis,' by the late Dr. Martin Haug, edited by Dr. E. W. West. The author intended, on his return from India, to expand the materials contained in this work into a comprehensive account of the Zoroastrian religion, but the design was frustrated by his untimely death. We have, however, in a concise and readable form, a history of the researches into the sacred writings and religion of the Parsis from the earliest times down to the present—a dissertation on the languages of the Parsi Scriptures, a translation of the Zend-Avesta, or the Scripture of the Parsis, and a dissertation on the Zoroastrian religion, with especial reference to its origin and development."—*Times.*

Post 8vo, cloth, pp. viii.—176, price 7s. 6d.

TEXTS FROM THE BUDDHIST CANON

COMMONLY KNOWN AS "DHAMMAPADA."

With Accompanying Narratives.

Translated from the Chinese by S. BEAL, B.A., Professor of Chinese, University College, London.

The Dhammapada, as hitherto known by the Pali Text Edition, as edited by Fausböll, by Max Müller's English, and Albrecht Weber's German translations, consists only of twenty-six chapters or sections, whilst the Chinese version, or rather recension, as now translated by Mr. Beal, consists of thirty-nine sections. The students of Pali who possess Fausböll's text, or either of the above-named translations, will therefore needs want Mr. Beal's English rendering of the Chinese version; the thirteen above-named additional sections not being accessible to them in any other form; for, even if they understand Chinese, the Chinese original would be unobtainable by them.

"Mr. Beal's rendering of the Chinese translation is a most valuable aid to the critical study of the work. It contains authentic texts gathered from ancient canonical books, and generally connected with some incident in the history of Buddha. Their great interest, however, consists in the light which they throw upon everyday life in India at the remote period at which they were written, and upon the method of teaching adopted by the founder of the religion. The method employed was principally parable, and the simplicity of the tales and the excellence of the morals inculcated, as well as the strange hold which they have retained upon the minds of millions of people, make them a very remarkable study."—*Times.*

"Mr. Beal, by making it accessible in an English dress, has added to the great services he has already rendered to the comparative study of religious history."—*Academy.*

"Valuable as exhibiting the doctrine of the Buddhists in its purest, least adulterated form, it brings the modern reader face to face with that simple creed and rule of conduct which won its way over the minds of myriads, and which is now nominally professed by 145 millions, who have overlaid its austere simplicity with innumerable ceremonies, forgotten its maxims, perverted its teaching, and so inverted its leading principle that a religion whose founder denied a God, now worships that founder as a god himself."—*Scotsman.*

Second Edition, post 8vo, cloth, pp. xxiv.—360, price 10s. 6d.

THE HISTORY OF INDIAN LITERATURE.

By ALBRECHT WEBER.

Translated from the Second German Edition by JOHN MANN, M.A., and THÉODOR ZACHARIAE, Ph.D., with the sanction of the Author.

Dr. BUHLER, Inspector of Schools in India, writes:—"When I was Professor of Oriental Languages in Elphinstone College, I frequently felt the want of such a work to which I could refer the students."

Professor COWELL, of Cambridge, writes:—"It will be especially useful to the students in our Indian colleges and universities. I used to long for such a book when I was teaching in Calcutta. Hindu students are intensely interested in the history of Sanskrit literature, and this volume will supply them with all they want on the subject."

Professor WHITNEY, Yale College, Newhaven, Conn., U.S.A., writes:—"I was one of the class to whom the work was originally given in the form of academic lectures. At their first appearance they were by far the most learned and able treatment of their subject; and with their recent additions they still maintain decidedly the same rank."

"Is perhaps the most comprehensive and lucid survey of Sanskrit literature extant. The essays contained in the volume were originally delivered as academic lectures, and at the time of their first publication were acknowledged to be by far the most learned and able treatment of the subject. They have now been brought up to date by the addition of all the most important results of recent research."—*Times.*

Post 8vo, cloth, pp. xii.—198, accompanied by Two Language Maps, price 7s. 6d.

A SKETCH OF THE MODERN LANGUAGES OF THE EAST INDIES.

By ROBERT N. CUST.

The Author has attempted to fill up a vacuum, the inconvenience of which pressed itself on his notice. Much had been written about the languages of the East Indies, but the extent of our present knowledge had not even been brought to a focus. It occurred to him that it might be of use to others to publish in an arranged form the notes which he had collected for his own edification.

"Supplies a deficiency which has long been felt."—*Times.*

"The book before us is then a valuable contribution to philological science. It passes under review a vast number of languages, and it gives, or professes to give, in every case the sum and substance of the opinions and judgments of the best-informed writers."—*Saturday Review.*

Second Corrected Edition, post 8vo, pp. xii.—116, cloth, price 5s.

THE BIRTH OF THE WAR-GOD.

A Poem. By KALIDASA.

Translated from the Sanskrit into English Verse by RALPH T. H. GRIFFITH, M.A.

"A very spirited rendering of the *Kumárasambhava,* which was first published twenty-six years ago, and which we are glad to see made once more accessible."—*Times.*

"Mr. Griffith's very spirited rendering is well known to most who are at all interested in Indian literature, or enjoy the tenderness of feeling and rich creative imagination of its author."—*Indian Antiquary.*

"We are very glad to welcome a second edition of Professor Griffith's admirable translation. Few translations deserve a second edition better."—*Athenæum.*

Post 8vo, pp. 432, cloth, price 16s.

A CLASSICAL DICTIONARY OF HINDU MYTHOLOGY AND RELIGION, GEOGRAPHY, HISTORY, AND LITERATURE.

By JOHN DOWSON, M.R.A.S.,
Late Professor of Hindustani, Staff College.

"This not only forms an indispensable book of reference to students of Indian literature, but is also of great general interest, as it gives in a concise and easily accessible form all that need be known about the personages of Hindu mythology whose names are so familiar, but of whom so little is known outside the limited circle of *savants*."—*Times.*

"It is no slight gain when such subjects are treated fairly and fully in a moderate space; and we need only add that the few wants which we may hope to see supplied in new editions detract but little from the general excellence of Mr. Dowson's work." —*Saturday Review.*

Post 8vo, with View of Mecca, pp. cxii.—172, cloth, price 9s.

SELECTIONS FROM THE KORAN.

By EDWARD WILLIAM LANE,
Translator of "The Thousand and One Nights;" &c., &c.

A New Edition, Revised and Enlarged, with an Introduction by
STANLEY LANE POOLE.

". . . Has been long esteemed in this country as the compilation of one of the greatest Arabic scholars of the time, the late Mr. Lane, the well-known translator of the 'Arabian Nights.' . . . The present editor has enhanced the value of his relative's work by divesting the text of a great deal of extraneous matter introduced by way of comment, and prefixing an introduction."—*Times.*

"Mr. Poole is both a generous and a learned biographer. . . . Mr. Poole tells us the facts . . . so far as it is possible for industry and criticism to ascertain them, and for literary skill to present them in a condensed and readable form."—*Englishman, Calcutta.*

Post 8vo, pp. vi.—368, cloth, price 14s.

MODERN INDIA AND THE INDIANS,

BEING A SERIES OF IMPRESSIONS, NOTES, AND ESSAYS.

By MONIER WILLIAMS, D.C.L.,
Hon. LL.D. of the University of Calcutta, Hon. Member of the Bombay Asiatic Society, Boden Professor of Sanskrit in the University of Oxford.

Third Edition, revised and augmented by considerable Additions, with Illustrations and a Map.

"In this volume we have the thoughtful impressions of a thoughtful man on some of the most important questions connected with our Indian Empire. . . . An enlightened observant man, travelling among an enlightened observant people, Professor Monier Williams has brought before the public in a pleasant form more of the manners and customs of the Queen's Indian subjects than we ever remember to have seen in any one work. He not only deserves the thanks of every Englishman for this able contribution to the study of Modern India—a subject with which we should be specially familiar—but he deserves the thanks of every Indian, Parsee or Hindu, Buddhist and Moslem, for his clear exposition of their manners, their creeds, and their necessities."—*Times.*

Post 8vo, pp. xliv.—376, cloth, price 14s.

METRICAL TRANSLATIONS FROM SANSKRIT WRITERS.

With an Introduction, many Prose Versions, and Parallel Passages from Classical Authors.

By J. MUIR, C.I.E., D.C.L., LL.D., Ph.D.

". . . An agreeable introduction to Hindu poetry."—*Times.*

". . . A volume which may be taken as a fair illustration alike of the religious and moral sentiments and of the legendary lore of the best Sanskrit writers."—*Edinburgh Daily Review.*

Second Edition, post 8vo, pp. xxvi.—244, cloth, price 10s. 6d.

THE GULISTAN;

OR, ROSE GARDEN OF SHEKH MUSHLIU'D-DIN SADI OF SHIRAZ.

Translated for the First Time into Prose and Verse, with an Introductory Preface, and a Life of the Author, from the Atish Kadah,

BY EDWARD B. EASTWICK, C.B., M.A., F.R.S., M.R.A.S.

"It is a very fair rendering of the original."—*Times.*

"The new edition has long been desired, and will be welcomed by all who take any interest in Oriental poetry. The *Gulistan* is a typical Persian verse-book of the highest order. Mr. Eastwick's rhymed translation . . . has long established itself in a secure position as the best version of Sadi's finest work."—*Academy.*

"It is both faithfully and gracefully executed."—*Tablet.*

In Two Volumes, post 8vo, pp. viii.—408 and viii.—348, cloth, price 28s.

MISCELLANEOUS ESSAYS RELATING TO INDIAN SUBJECTS.

BY BRIAN HOUGHTON HODGSON, ESQ., F.R.S.,

Late of the Bengal Civil Service; Corresponding Member of the Institute; Chevalier of the Legion of Honour; late British Minister at the Court of Nepal, &c., &c.

CONTENTS OF VOL. I.

SECTION I.—On the Kocch, Bódó, and Dhimál Tribes.—Part I. Vocabulary.—Part II. Grammar.—Part III. Their Origin, Location, Numbers, Creed, Customs, Character, and Condition, with a General Description of the Climate they dwell in.—Appendix.

SECTION II.—On Himalayan Ethnology.—I. Comparative Vocabulary of the Languages of the Broken Tribes of Népál.—II. Vocabulary of the Dialects of the Kiranti Language.—III. Grammatical Analysis of the Váyu Language. The Váyu Grammar.—IV. Analysis of the Báhing Dialect of the Kiranti Language. The Báhing Grammar.—V. On the Váyu or Háyu Tribe of the Central Himaláya.—VI. On the Kiranti Tribe of the Central Himaláya.

CONTENTS OF VOL. II.

SECTION III.—On the Aborigines of North-Eastern India. Comparative Vocabulary of the Tibetan, Bódó, and Gáró Tongues.

SECTION IV.—Aborigines of the North-Eastern Frontier.

SECTION V.—Aborigines of the Eastern Frontier.

SECTION VI.—The Indo-Chinese Borderers, and their connection with the Himalayans and Tibetans. Comparative Vocabulary of Indo-Chinese Borderers in Arakan. Comparative Vocabulary of Indo-Chinese Borderers in Tenasserim.

SECTION VII.—The Mongolian Affinities of the Caucasians.—Comparison and Analysis of Caucasian and Mongolian Words.

SECTION VIII.—Physical Type of Tibetans.

SECTION IX.—The Aborigines of Central India.—Comparative Vocabulary of the Aboriginal Languages of Central India.—Aborigines of the Eastern Ghats.—Vocabulary of some of the Dialects of the Hill and Wandering Tribes in the Northern Sircars.—Aborigines of the Nilgiris, with Remarks on their Affinities.—Supplement to the Nilgirian Vocabularies.—The Aborigines of Southern India and Ceylon.

SECTION X.—Route of Nepalese Mission to Pekin, with Remarks on the Water-Shed and Plateau of Tibet.

SECTION XI.—Route from Káthmándú, the Capital of Nepâl, to Darjeeling in Sikim.—Memorandum relative to the Seven Cosis of Nepâl.

SECTION XII.—Some Accounts of the Systems of Law and Police as recognised in the State of Nepâl.

SECTION XIII.—The Native Method of making the Paper denominated Hindustan, Népálese.

SECTION XIV.—Pre-eminence of the Vernaculars; or, the Anglicists Answered; Being Letters on the Education of the People of India.

"For the study of the less-known races of India Mr. Brian Hodgson's 'Miscellaneous Essays' will be found very valuable both to the philologist and the ethnologist."

Third Edition, Two Vols., post 8vo, pp. viii.—268 and viii.—326, cloth, price 21s.

THE LIFE OR LEGEND OF GAUDAMA,

THE BUDDHA OF THE BURMESE. With Annotations.

The Ways to Neibban, and Notice on the Phongyies or Burmese Monks.

BY THE RIGHT REV. P. BIGANDET,

Bishop of Ramatha, Vicar-Apostolic of Ava and Pegu.

"The work is furnished with copious notes, which not only illustrate the subject-matter, but form a perfect encyclopædia of Buddhist lore."—*Times.*

"A work which will furnish European students of Buddhism with a most valuable help in the prosecution of their investigations."—*Edinburgh Daily Review.*

"Bishop Bigandet's invaluable work."—*Indian Antiquary.*

"Viewed in this light, its importance is sufficient to place students of the subject under a deep obligation to its author."—*Calcutta Review.*

"This work is one of the greatest authorities upon Buddhism."—*Dublin Review.*

Post 8vo, pp. xxiv.—420, cloth, price 18s.

CHINESE BUDDHISM.

A VOLUME OF SKETCHES, HISTORICAL AND CRITICAL.

BY J. EDKINS, D.D.

Author of "China's Place in Philology," "Religion in China," &c., &c.

"It contains a vast deal of important information on the subject, such as is only to be gained by long-continued study on the spot."—*Athenæum.*

"Upon the whole, we know of no work comparable to it for the extent of its original research, and the simplicity with which this complicated system of philosophy, religion, literature, and ritual is set forth."—*British Quarterly Review.*

"The whole volume is replete with learning. . . . It deserves most careful study from all interested in the history of the religions of the world, and expressly of those who are concerned in the propagation of Christianity. Dr. Edkins notices in terms of just condemnation the exaggerated praise bestowed upon Buddhism by recent English writers."—*Record.*

Post 8vo, pp. 496, cloth, price 10s. 6d.

LINGUISTIC AND ORIENTAL ESSAYS.

WRITTEN FROM THE YEAR 1846 TO 1878.

BY ROBERT NEEDHAM CUST,

Late Member of Her Majesty's Indian Civil Service; Hon. Secretary to the Royal Asiatic Society; and Author of "The Modern Languages of the East Indies."

"We know none who has described Indian life, especially the life of the natives, with so much learning, sympathy, and literary talent."—*Academy.*

"They seem to us to be full of suggestive and original remarks."—*St. James's Gazette.*

"His book contains a vast amount of information. The result of thirty-five years of inquiry, reflection, and speculation, and that on subjects as full of fascination as of food for thought."—*Tablet.*

"Exhibit such a thorough acquaintance with the history and antiquities of India as to entitle him to speak as one having authority."—*Edinburgh Daily Review.*

"The author speaks with the authority of personal experience. . . . . It is this constant association with the country and the people which gives such a vividness to many of the pages."—*Athenæum.*

Post 8vo, pp. civ.—348, cloth, price 18s.

BUDDHIST BIRTH STORIES; or, Jataka Tales.

The Oldest Collection of Folk-lore Extant:

BEING THE JATAKATTHAVANNANA,

For the first time Edited in the original Pāli.

By V. FAUSBOLL;

And Translated by T. W. Rhys Davids.

Translation. Volume I.

"These are tales supposed to have been told by the Buddha of what he had seen and heard in his previous births. They are probably the nearest representatives of the original Aryan stories from which sprang the folk-lore of Europe as well as India. The introduction contains a most interesting disquisition on the migrations of these fables, tracing their reappearance in the various groups of folk-lore legends. Among other old friends, we meet with a version of the Judgment of Solomon."—*Times.*

"It is now some years since Mr. Rhys Davids asserted his right to be heard on this subject by his able article on Buddhism in the new edition of the 'Encyclopædia Britannica.'"—*Leeds Mercury.*

"All who are interested in Buddhist literature ought to feel deeply indebted to Mr. Rhys Davids. His well-established reputation as a Pali scholar is a sufficient guarantee for the fidelity of his version, and the style of his translations is deserving of high praise."—*Academy.*

"No more competent expositor of Buddhism could be found than Mr. Rhys Davids. In the Jātaka book we have, then, a priceless record of the earliest imaginative literature of our race; and . . . it presents to us a nearly complete picture of the social life and customs and popular beliefs of the common people of Aryan tribes, closely related to ourselves, just as they were passing through the first stages of civilisation."—*St. James's Gazette.*

Post 8vo, pp. xxviii.—362, cloth, price 14s.

A TALMUDIC MISCELLANY;

Or, A THOUSAND AND ONE EXTRACTS FROM THE TALMUD THE MIDRASHIM, AND THE KABBALAH.

Compiled and Translated by PAUL ISAAC HERSHON,

Author of "Genesis According to the Talmud," &c.

With Notes and Copious Indexes.

"To obtain in so concise and handy a form as this volume a general idea of the Talmud is a boon to Christians at least."—*Times.*

"Its peculiar and popular character will make it attractive to general readers. Mr. Hershon is a very competent scholar. . . . Contains samples of the good, bad, and indifferent, and especially extracts that throw light upon the Scriptures."—*British Quarterly Review.*

"Will convey to English readers a more complete and truthful notion of the Talmud than any other work that has yet appeared."—*Daily News.*

"Without overlooking in the slightest the several attractions of the previous volumes of the 'Oriental Series,' we have no hesitation in saying that this surpasses them all in interest."—*Edinburgh Daily Review.*

"Mr. Hershon has . . . thus given English readers what is, we believe, a fair set of specimens which they can test for themselves."—*The Record.*

"This book is by far the best fitted in the present state of knowledge to enable the general reader to gain a fair and unbiassed conception of the multifarious contents of the wonderful miscellany which can only be truly understood—so Jewish pride asserts—by the life-long devotion of scholars of the Chosen People."—*Inquirer.*

"The value and importance of this volume consist in the fact that scarcely a single extract is given in its pages but throws some light, direct or refracted, upon those Scriptures which are the common heritage of Jew and Christian alike."—*John Bull.*

"It is a capital specimen of Hebrew scholarship; a monument of learned, loving, light-giving labour."—*Jewish Herald.*

Post 8vo, pp. xii.—228, cloth, price 7s. 6d.

THE CLASSICAL POETRY OF THE JAPANESE.

BY BASIL HALL CHAMBERLAIN,
Author of "Yeigo Heñkaku Shirañ."

"A very curious volume. The author has manifestly devoted much labour to the task of studying the poetical literature of the Japanese, and rendering characteristic specimens into English verse."—*Daily News.*

"Mr. Chamberlain's volume is, so far as we are aware, the first attempt which has been made to interpret the literature of the Japanese to the Western world. It is to the classical poetry of Old Japan that we must turn for indigenous Japanese thought, and in the volume before us we have a selection from that poetry rendered into graceful English verse."—*Tablet.*

"It is undoubtedly one of the best translations of lyric literature which has appeared during the close of the last year."—*Celestial Empire.*

"Mr. Chamberlain set himself a difficult task when he undertook to reproduce Japanese poetry in an English form. But he has evidently laboured *con amore*, and his efforts are successful to a degree."—*London and China Express.*

Post 8vo, pp. xii.—164, cloth, price 10s. 6d.

THE HISTORY OF ESARHADDON (Son of Sennacherib), KING OF ASSYRIA, B.C. 681–668.

Translated from the Cuneiform Inscriptions upon Cylinders and Tablets in the British Museum Collection; together with a Grammatical Analysis of each Word, Explanations of the Ideographs by Extracts from the Bi-Lingual Syllabaries, and List of Eponyms, &c.

BY ERNEST A. BUDGE, B.A., M.R.A.S.,
Assyrian Exhibitioner, Christ's College, Cambridge.

"Students of scriptural archæology will also appreciate the 'History of Esarhaddon.'"—*Times.*

"There is much to attract the scholar in this volume. It does not pretend to popularise studies which are yet in their infancy. Its primary object is to translate, but it does not assume to be more than tentative, and it offers both to the professed Assyriologist and to the ordinary non-Assyriological Semitic scholar the means of controlling its results."—*Academy.*

"Mr. Budge's book is, of course, mainly addressed to Assyrian scholars and students. They are not, it is to be feared, a very numerous class. But the more thanks are due to him on that account for the way in which he has acquitted himself in his laborious task."—*Tablet.*

Post 8vo, pp. 448, cloth, price 21s.

THE MESNEVI

(Usually known as THE MESNEVIYI SHERIF, or HOLY MESNEVI)
OF
MEVLANA (OUR LORD) JELALU 'D-DIN MUHAMMED ER-RUMI.
Book the First.

Together with some Account of the Life and Acts of the Author, of his Ancestors, and of his Descendants.

Illustrated by a Selection of Characteristic Anecdotes, as Collected by their Historian,
MEVLANA SHEMSU-'D-DIN AHMED, EL EFLAKI, EL 'ARIFI.

Translated, and the Poetry Versified, in English,
BY JAMES W. REDHOUSE, M.R.A.S., &c.

"A complete treasury of occult Oriental lore."—*Saturday Review.*

"This book will be a very valuable help to the reader ignorant of Persia, who is desirous of obtaining an insight into a very important department of the literature extant in that language."—*Tablet.*

Post 8vo, pp. xvi.—280, cloth, price 6s.

EASTERN PROVERBS AND EMBLEMS

ILLUSTRATING OLD TRUTHS.

BY REV. J. LONG,

Member of the Bengal Asiatic Society, F.R.G.S.

"We regard the book as valuable, and wish for it a wide circulation and attentive reading."—*Record.*

"Altogether, it is quite a feast of good things."—*Globe.*

"It is full of interesting matter."—*Antiquary.*

Post 8vo, pp. viii.—270, cloth, price 7s. 6d.

INDIAN POETRY;

Containing a New Edition of the "Indian Song of Songs," from the Sanscrit of the "Gita Govinda" of Jayadeva; Two Books from "The Iliad of India" (Mahabharata), "Proverbial Wisdom" from the Shlokas of the Hitopadesa, and other Oriental Poems.

BY EDWIN ARNOLD, C.S.I., Author of "The Light of Asia."

"In this new volume of Messrs. Trübner's Oriental Series, Mr. Edwin Arnold does good service by illustrating, through the medium of his musical English melodies, the power of Indian poetry to stir European emotions. The 'Indian Song of Songs' is not unknown to scholars. Mr. Arnold will have introduced it among popular English poems. Nothing could be more graceful and delicate than the shades by which Krishna is portrayed in the gradual process of being weaned by the love of

'Beautiful Radha, jasmine-bosomed Radha,'

from the allurements of the forest nymphs, in whom the five senses are typified."—*Times.*

"No other English poet has ever thrown his genius and his art so thoroughly into the work of translating Eastern ideas as Mr. Arnold has done in his splendid paraphrases of language contained in these mighty epics."—*Daily Telegraph.*

"The poem abounds with imagery of Eastern luxuriousness and sensuousness; the air seems laden with the spicy odours of the tropics, and the verse has a richness and a melody sufficient to captivate the senses of the dullest."—*Standard.*

"The translator, while producing a very enjoyable poem, has adhered with tolerable fidelity to the original text."—*Overland Mail.*

"We certainly wish Mr. Arnold success in his attempt 'to popularise Indian classics,' that being, as his preface tells us, the goal towards which he bends his efforts."—*Allen's Indian Mail.*

Post 8vo, pp. xvi.—296, cloth, price 10s. 6d.

THE MIND OF MENCIUS;

OR, POLITICAL ECONOMY FOUNDED UPON MORAL PHILOSOPHY.

A SYSTEMATIC DIGEST OF THE DOCTRINES OF THE CHINESE PHILOSOPHER MENCIUS.

Translated from the Original Text and Classified, with Comments and Explanations,

By the REV. ERNST FABER, Rhenish Mission Society.

Translated from the German, with Additional Notes,

By the REV. A. B. HUTCHINSON, C.M.S., Church Mission, Hong Kong.

"Mr. Faber is already well known in the field of Chinese studies by his digest of the doctrines of Confucius. The value of this work will be perceived when it is remembered that at no time since relations commenced between China and the West has the former been so powerful—we had almost said aggressive—as now. For those who will give it careful study, Mr. Faber's work is one of the most valuable of the excellent series to which it belongs."—*Nature.*

Post 8vo, pp. 336, cloth, price 16s.

THE RELIGIONS OF INDIA.

By A. BARTH.

Translated from the French with the authority and assistance of the Author.

The author has, at the request of the publishers, considerably enlarged the work for the translator, and has added the literature of the subject to date; the translation may, therefore, be looked upon as an equivalent of a new and improved edition of the original.

"Is not only a valuable manual of the religions of India, which marks a distinct step in the treatment of the subject, but also a useful work of reference."—*Academy.*

"This volume is a reproduction, with corrections and additions, of an article contributed by the learned author two years ago to the 'Encyclopédie des Sciences Religieuses.' It attracted much notice when it first appeared, and is generally admitted to present the best summary extant of the vast subject with which it deals."—*Tablet.*

"This is not only on the whole the best but the only manual of the religions of India, apart from Buddhism, which we have in English. The present work . . . shows not only great knowledge of the facts and power of clear exposition, but also great insight into the inner history and the deeper meaning of the great religion, for it is in reality only one, which it proposes to describe."—*Modern Review.*

"The merit of the work has been emphatically recognised by the most authoritative Orientalists, both in this country and on the continent of Europe, But probably there are few Indianists (if we may use the word) who would not derive a good deal of information from it, and especially from the extensive bibliography provided in the notes."—*Dublin Review.*

"Such a sketch M. Barth has drawn with a master-hand."—*Critic (New York).*

Post 8vo, pp. viii.—152, cloth, price 6s.

HINDU PHILOSOPHY.

THE SĀNKHYA KĀRIKA OF IS'WARA KRISHNA.

An Exposition of the System of Kapila, with an Appendix on the Nyāya and Vais'eshika Systems.

By JOHN DAVIES, M.A. (Cantab.), M.R.A.S.

The system of Kapila contains nearly all that India has produced in the department of pure philosophy.

"The non-Orientalist . . . finds in Mr. Davies a patient and learned guide who leads him into the intricacies of the philosophy of India, and supplies him with a clue that he may not be lost in them. In the preface he states that the system of Kapila is the 'earliest attempt on record to give an answer, from reason alone, to the mysterious questions which arise in every thoughtful mind about the origin of the world, the nature and relations of man and his future destiny,' and in his learned and able notes he exhibits 'the connection of the Sankhya system with the philosophy of Spinoza,' and 'the connection of the system of Kapila with that of Schopenhauer and Von Hartmann.'"—*Foreign Church Chronicle.*

"Mr. Davies's volume on Hindu Philosophy is an undoubted gain to all students of the development of thought. The system of Kapila, which is here given in a translation from the Sānkhya Kārikā, is the only contribution of India to pure philosophy. . . . Presents many points of deep interest to the student of comparative philosophy, and without Mr. Davies's lucid interpretation it would be difficult to appreciate these points in any adequate manner."—*Saturday Review.*

"We welcome Mr. Davies's book as a valuable addition to our philosophical library."—*Notes and Queries.*

Post 8vo, pp. x.—130, cloth, price 6s.

A MANUAL OF HINDU PANTHEISM. VEDÂNTASÂRA.

Translated, with copious Annotations,

BY MAJOR G. A. JACOB,

Bombay Staff Corps; Inspector of Army Schools.

The design of this little work is to provide for missionaries, and for others who, like them, have little leisure for original research, an accurate summary of the doctrines of the Vedânta.

"The modest title of Major Jacob's work conveys but an inadequate idea of the vast amount of research embodied in his notes to the text of the Vedantasara. So copious, indeed, are these, and so much collateral matter do they bring to bear on the subject, that the diligent student will rise from their perusal with a fairly adequate view of Hindû philosophy generally. His work . . . is one of the best of its kind that we have seen."—*Calcutta Review.*

Post 8vo, pp. xii.—154, cloth, price 7s. 6d.

TSUNI—| | GOAM:

THE SUPREME BEING OF THE KHOI-KHOI.

BY THEOPHILUS HAHN, Ph.D.,

Custodian of the Grey Collection, Cape Town; Corresponding Member of the Geogr. Society, Dresden; Corresponding Member of the Anthropological Society, Vienna, &c., &c.

"The first instalment of Dr. Hahn's labours will be of interest, not at the Cape only, but in every University of Europe. It is, in fact, a most valuable contribution to the comparative study of religion and mythology. Accounts of their religion and mythology were scattered about in various books; these have been carefully collected by Dr. Hahn and printed in his second chapter, enriched and improved by what he has been able to collect himself."—*Prof. Max Müller in the Nineteenth Century.*

"It is full of good things."—*St. James's Gazette.*

In Four Volumes. Post 8vo, Vol. I., pp. xii.—392, cloth, price 12s. 6d., Vol. II., pp. vi.—408, cloth, price 12s. 6d., Vol. III., pp. viii.—414, cloth, price 12s. 6d., Vol. IV., pp. viii.—340, cloth, price 10s. 6d.

A COMPREHENSIVE COMMENTARY TO THE QURAN.

TO WHICH IS PREFIXED SALE'S PRELIMINARY DISCOURSE, WITH ADDITIONAL NOTES AND EMENDATIONS.

Together with a Complete Index to the Text, Preliminary Discourse, and Notes.

By Rev. E. M. WHERRY, M.A., Lodiana.

"As Mr. Wherry's book is intended for missionaries in India, it is no doubt well that they should be prepared to meet, if they can, the ordinary arguments and interpretations, and for this purpose Mr. Wherry's additions will prove useful."—*Saturday Review.*

Post 8vo, pp. vi.—208, cloth, price 8s. 6d.

THE BHAGAVAD-GÎTÂ.

Translated, with Introduction and Notes.

By JOHN DAVIES, M.A. (Cantab.)

"Let us add that his translation of the Bhagavad Gîtâ is, as we judge, the best that has as yet appeared in English, and that his Philological Notes are of quite peculiar value."—*Dublin Review.*

Post 8vo, pp. 96, cloth, price 5s.

THE QUATRAINS OF OMAR KHAYYAM.

Translated by E. H. WHINFIELD, M.A.,

Barrister-at-Law, late H.M. Bengal Civil Service.

Post 8vo, pp. xxxii.—336, cloth, price 10s. 6d.

THE QUATRAINS OF OMAR KHAYYAM.

The Persian Text, with an English Verse Translation.

By E. H. WHINFIELD, late of the Bengal Civil Service.

"Mr. Whinfield has executed a difficult task with considerable success, and his version contains much that will be new to those who only know Mr. Fitzgerald's delightful selection."—*Academy.*

"The most prominent features in the Quatrains are their profound agnosticism, combined with a fatalism based more on philosophic than religious grounds, their Epicureanism and the spirit of universal tolerance and charity which animates them."—*Calcutta Review.*

Post 8vo, pp. xxiv.—268, cloth, price 9s.

THE PHILOSOPHY OF THE UPANISHADS AND ANCIENT INDIAN METAPHYSICS.

As exhibited in a series of Articles contributed to the *Calcutta Review.*

By ARCHIBALD EDWARD GOUGH, M.A., Lincoln College, Oxford; Principal of the Calcutta Madrasa.

"For practical purposes this is perhaps the most important of the works that have thus far appeared in 'Trübner's Oriental Series.' . . . We cannot doubt that for all who may take it up the work must be one of profound interest."—*Saturday Review.*

In Two Volumes. Vol. I., post 8vo, pp. xxiv.—230, cloth, price 7s. 6d.

A COMPARATIVE HISTORY OF THE EGYPTIAN AND MESOPOTAMIAN RELIGIONS.

By Dr. C. P. TIELE.

Vol. I.—History of the Egyptian Religion.

Translated from the Dutch with the Assistance of the Author.

By JAMES BALLINGAL.

"It places in the hands of the English readers a history of Egyptian Religion which is very complete, which is based on the best materials, and which has been illustrated by the latest results of research. In this volume there is a great deal of information, as well as independent investigation, for the trustworthiness of which Dr. Tiele's name is in itself a guarantee; and the description of the successive religions under the Old Kingdom, the Middle Kingdom, and the New Kingdom, is given in a manner which is scholarly and minute."—*Scotsman.*

Post 8vo, pp. xii.—302, cloth, price 8s. 6d.

YUSUF AND ZULAIKHA.

A Poem by JAMI.

Translated from the Persian into English Verse.

By RALPH T. H. GRIFFITH.

"Mr. Griffith, who has done already good service as translator into verse from the Sanskrit, has done further good work in this translation from the Persian, and he has evidently shown not a little skill in his rendering the quaint and very oriental style of his author into our more prosaic, less figurative, language. . . . The work, besides its intrinsic merits, is of importance as being one of the most popular and famous poems of Persia, and that which is read in all the independent native schools of India where Persian is taught."—*Scotsman.*

Post 8vo, pp. viii.—266, cloth, price 9s.

LINGUISTIC ESSAYS.

By CARL ABEL.

"An entirely novel method of dealing with philosophical questions and impart a real human interest to the otherwise dry technicalities of the science."—*Standard.*

"Dr. Abel is an opponent from whom it is pleasant to differ, for he writes with enthusiasm and temper, and his mastery over the English language fits him to be a champion of unpopular doctrines."—*Athenæum.*

Post 8vo, pp. ix.—281, cloth, price 10s. 6d.

THE SARVA-DARSANA-SAMGRAHA;

OR, REVIEW OF THE DIFFERENT SYSTEMS OF HINDU PHILOSOPHY.

By MADHAVA ACHARYA.

Translated by E. B. COWELL, M.A., Professor of Sanskrit in the University of Cambridge, and A. E. GOUGH, M.A., Professor of Philosophy in the Presidency College, Calcutta.

This work is an interesting specimen of Hindu critical ability. The author successively passes in review the sixteen philosophical systems current in the fourteenth century in the South of India; and he gives what appears to him to be their most important tenets.

"The translation is trustworthy throughout. A protracted sojourn in India, where there is a living tradition, has familiarised the translators with Indian thought."—*Athenæum.*

Post 8vo, pp. lxv.—368, cloth, price 14s.

TIBETAN TALES DERIVED FROM INDIAN SOURCES.

Translated from the Tibetan of the Kah-Gyur.

By F. ANTON VON SCHIEFNER.

Done into English from the German, with an Introduction,

By W. R. S. RALSTON, M.A.

"Mr. Ralston, whose name is so familiar to all lovers of Russian folk-lore, has supplied some interesting Western analogies and parallels, drawn, for the most part, from Slavonic sources, to the Eastern folk-tales, culled from the Kahgyur, one of the divisions of the Tibetan sacred books."—*Academy.*

"The translation . . . could scarcely have fallen into better hands. An Introduction . . . gives the leading facts in the lives of those scholars who have given their attention to gaining a knowledge of the Tibetan literature and language."—*Calcutta Review.*

"Ought to interest all who care for the East, for amusing stories, or for comparative folk-lore."—*Pall Mall Gazette.*

Post 8vo, pp. xvi.—224, cloth, price 9s.

UDÂNAVARGA.

A COLLECTION OF VERSES FROM THE BUDDHIST CANON.

Compiled by DHARMATRÂTA.

BEING THE NORTHERN BUDDHIST VERSION OF DHAMMAPADA.

Translated from the Tibetan of Bkah-hgyur, with Notes, and Extracts from the Commentary of Pradjnavarman,

By W. WOODVILLE ROCKHILL.

"Mr. Rockhill's present work is the first from which assistance will be gained for a more accurate understanding of the Pali text; it is, in fact, as yet the only term of comparison available to us. The 'Udanavarga,' the Thibetan version, was originally discovered by the late M. Schiefner, who published the Tibetan text, and had intended adding a translation, an intention frustrated by his death, but which has been carried out by Mr. Rockhill. . . . Mr. Rockhill may be congratulated for having well accomplished a difficult task."—*Saturday Review.*

In Two Volumes, post 8vo, pp. xxiv.—566, cloth, accompanied by a Language Map, price 18s.

A SKETCH OF THE MODERN LANGUAGES OF AFRICA.

BY ROBERT NEEDHAM CUST,

Barrister-at-Law, and late of Her Majesty's Indian Civil Service.

"Any one at all interested in African languages cannot do better than get Mr. Cust's book. It is encyclopædic in its scope, and the reader gets a start clear away in any particular language, and is left free to add to the initial sum of knowledge there collected."—*Natal Mercury.*

"Mr. Cust has contrived to produce a work of value to linguistic students."—*Nature.*

Third Edition. Post 8vo, pp. xv.-250, cloth, price 7s. 6d.

OUTLINES OF THE HISTORY OF RELIGION TO THE SPREAD OF THE UNIVERSAL RELIGIONS.

BY C. P. TIELE,

Doctor of Theology, Professor of the History of Religions in the University of Leyden.

Translated from the Dutch by J. ESTLIN CARPENTER, M.A.

"Few books of its size contain the result of so much wide thinking, able and laborious study, or enable the reader to gain a better bird's-eye view of the latest results of investigations into the religious history of nations. As Professor Tiele modestly says, 'In this little book are outlines—pencil sketches, I might say—nothing more.' But there are some men whose sketches from a thumb-nail are of far more worth than an enormous canvas covered with the crude painting of others, and it is easy to see that these pages, full of information, these sentences, cut and perhaps also dry, short and clear, condense the fruits of long and thorough research."—*Scotsman.*

Post 8vo, pp. xii.—312, with Maps and Plan, cloth, price 14s.

A HISTORY OF BURMA.

Including Burma Proper, Pegu, Taungu, Tenasserim, and Arakan. From the Earliest Time to the End of the First War with British India.

BY LIEUT.-GEN. SIR ARTHUR P. PHAYRE, G.C.M.G., K.C.S.I., and C.B., Membre Correspondant de la Société Académique Indo-Chinoise de France.

"Sir Arthur Phayre's contribution to Trübner's Oriental Series supplies a recognised want, and its appearance has been looked forward to for many years. . . . . General Phayre deserves great credit for the patience and industry which has resulted in this History of Burma."—*Saturday Review.*

Third Edition. Post 8vo, pp. 276, cloth, price 7s. 6d.

RELIGION IN CHINA.

By JOSEPH EDKINS, D.D., PEKING.

Containing a Brief Account of the Three Religions of the Chinese, with Observations on the Prospects of Christian Conversion amongst that People.

"Dr. Edkins has been most careful in noting the varied and often complex phases of opinion, so as to give an account of considerable value of the subject."—*Scotsman.*

"As a missionary, it has been part of Dr. Edkins' duty to study the existing religions in China, and his long residence in the country has enabled him to acquire an intimate knowledge of them as they at present exist."—*Saturday Review.*

"Dr. Edkins' valuable work, of which this is a second and revised edition, has, from the time that it was published, been the standard authority upon the subject of which it treats."—*Nonconformist.*

"Dr. Edkins . . . may now be fairly regarded as among the first authorities on Chinese religion and language."—*British Quarterly Review.*

Post 8vo, pp. x.–274, cloth, price 9s.

THE LIFE OF THE BUDDHA AND THE EARLY HISTORY OF HIS ORDER.

Derived from Tibetan Works in the Bkah-hgyur and Bstan-hgyur. Followed by notices on the Early History of Tibet and Khoten.

Translated by W. W. ROCKHILL, Second Secretary U.S. Legation in China.

"The volume bears testimony to the diligence and fulness with which the author has consulted and tested the ancient documents bearing upon his remarkable subject."—*Times.*

"Will be appreciated by those who devote themselves to those Buddhist studies which have of late years taken in these Western regions so remarkable a development. Its matter possesses a special interest as being derived from ancient Tibetan works, some portions of which, here analysed and translated, have not yet attracted the attention of scholars. The volume is rich in ancient stories bearing upon the world's renovation and the origin of castes, as recorded in these venerable authorities."—*Daily News.*

Third Edition. Post 8vo, pp. viii.–464, cloth, price 16s.

THE SANKHYA APHORISMS OF KAPILA,

With Illustrative Extracts from the Commentaries.

Translated by J. R. BALLANTYNE, LL.D., late Principal of the Benares College.

Edited by FITZEDWARD HALL.

"The work displays a vast expenditure of labour and scholarship, for which students of Hindoo philosophy have every reason to be grateful to Dr. Hall and the publishers."—*Calcutta Review.*

In Two Volumes, post 8vo, pp. cviii.-242, and viii.-370, cloth, price 24s.
Dedicated by permission to H.R.H. the Prince of Wales.

BUDDHIST RECORDS OF THE WESTERN WORLD,

Translated from the Chinese of Hiuen Tsiang (A.D. 629).

BY SAMUEL BEAL, B.A.,

(Trin. Coll., Camb.); R.N. (Retired Chaplain and N.I.); Professor of Chinese, University College, London; Rector of Wark, Northumberland, &c.

An eminent Indian authority writes respecting this work:—"Nothing more can be done in elucidating the History of India until Mr. Beal's translation of the 'Si-yu-ki' appears."

"It is a strange freak of historical preservation that the best account of the condition of India at that ancient period has come down to us in the books of travel written by the Chinese pilgrims, of whom Hwen Thsang is the best known."—*Times.*

Post 8vo, pp. xlviii.-398, cloth, price 12s.

THE ORDINANCES OF MANU.

Translated from the Sanskrit, with an Introduction.

By the late A. C. BURNELL, Ph.D., C.I.E.

Completed and Edited by E. W. HOPKINS, Ph.D.,
of Columbia College, N.Y.

"This work is full of interest; while for the student of sociology ana the science of religion it is full of importance. It is a great boon to get so notable a work in so accessible a form, admirably edited, and competently translated."—*Scotsman.*

"Few men were more competent than Burnell to give us a really good translation of this well-known law book, first rendered into English by Sir William Jones. Burnell was not only an independent Sanskrit scholar, but an experienced lawyer, and he joined to these two important qualifications the rare faculty of being able to express his thoughts in clear and trenchant English. . . . We ought to feel very grateful to Dr. Hopkins for having given us all that could be published of the translation left by Burnell."—F. MAX MÜLLER in the *Academy.*

Post 8vo, pp. xii.-234, cloth, price 9s.

THE LIFE AND WORKS OF ALEXANDER CSOMA DE KOROS,

Between 1819 and 1842. With a Short Notice of all his Published and Unpublished Works and Essays. From Original and for most part Unpublished Documents.

By THEODORE DUKA, M.D., F.R.C.S. (Eng.), Surgeon-Major H.M.'s Bengal Medical Service, Retired, &c.

"Not too soon have Messrs. Trübner added to their valuable Oriental Series a history of the life and works of one of the most gifted and devoted of Oriental students, Alexander Csoma de Koros. It is forty-three years since his death, and though an account of his career was demanded soon after his decease, it has only now appeared in the important memoir of his compatriot, Dr. Duka."—*Bookseller.*

In Two Volumes, post 8vo, pp. xii.-318 and vi.-312, cloth, price 21s.

MISCELLANEOUS PAPERS RELATING TO INDO-CHINA.

Reprinted from "Dalrymple's Oriental Repertory" "Asiatic Researches," and the "Journal of the Asiatic Society of Bengal."

CONTENTS OF VOL. I.

I.—Some Accounts of Quedah. By Michael Topping.

II.—Report made to the Chief and Council of Balambangan, by Lieut. James Barton, of his several Surveys.

III.—Substance of a Letter to the Court of Directors from Mr. John Jesse, dated July 20, 1775, at Borneo Proper.

IV.—Formation of the Establishment of Poolo Peenang.

V.—The Gold of Limong. By John Macdonald.

VI.—On Three Natural Productions of Sumatra. By John Macdonald.

VII.—On the Traces of the Hindu Language and Literature extant amongst the Malays. By William Marsden.

VIII.—Some Account of the Elastic Gum Vine of Prince-Wales Island. By James Howison.

IX.—A Botanical Description of Urceola Elastica, or Caoutchouc Vine of Sumatra and Pulo-Pinang. By William Roxburgh, M.D.

X.—An Account of the Inhabitants of the Poggy, or Nassau Islands, lying off Sumatra. By John Crisp.

XI.—Remarks on the Species of Pepper which are found on Prince-Wales Island. By William Hunter, M.D.

XII.—On the Languages and Literature of the Indo-Chinese Nations. By J. Leyden, M.D.

XIII.—Some Account of an Orang-Outang of remarkable height found on the Island of Sumatra. By Clarke Abel, M.D.

XIV.—Observations on the Geological Appearances and General Features of Portions of the Malayan Peninsula. By Captain James Low.

XV.—Short Sketch of the Geology of Pulo-Pinang and the Neighbouring Islands. By T. Ware.

XVI.—Climate of Singapore.

XVII.—Inscription on the Jetty at Singapore.

XVIII.—Extract of a Letter from Colonel J. Low.

XIX.—Inscription at Singapore.

XX.—An Account of Several Inscriptions found in Province Wellesley. By Lieut.-Col. James Low.

XXI.—Note on the Inscriptions from Singapore and Province Wellesley. By J. W. Laidlay.

XXII.—On an Inscription from Keddah. By Lieut.-Col. Low.

XXIII.—A Notice of the Alphabets of the Philippine Islands.

XXIV.—Succinct Review of the Observations of the Tides in the Indian Archipelago.

XXV.—Report on the Tin of the Province of Mergui. By Capt. G. B. Tremenheere.

XXVI.—Report on the Manganese of Mergui Province. By Capt. G. B. Tremenheere.

XXVII.—Paragraphs to be added to Capt. G. B. Tremenheere's Report.

XXVIII.—Second Report on the Tin of Mergui. By Capt. G. B. Tremenheere.

XXIX.—Analysis of Iron Ores from Tavoy and Mergui, and of Limestone from Mergui. By Dr. A. Ure.

XXX.—Report of a Visit to the Pakchan River, and of some Tin Localities in the Southern Portion of the Tenasserim Provinces. By Capt. G. B. Tremenheere.

XXXI.—Report on a Route from the Mouth of the Pakchan to Krau, and thence across the Isthmus of Krau to the Gulf of Siam. By Capt. Al. Fraser and Capt. J. G. Forlong.

XXXII.—Report, &c., from Capt. G. B. Tremenheere on the Price of Mergui Tin Ore.

XXXIII.—Remarks on the Different Species of Orang-utan. By E. Blyth.

XXXIV.—Further Remarks. By E. Blyth.

MISCELLANEOUS PAPERS RELATING TO INDO-CHINA—continued.

CONTENTS OF VOL. II.

"The papers treat of almost every aspect of Indo-China—its philology, economy, geography, geology—and constitute a very material and important contribution to our accessible information regarding that country and its people."—*Contemporary Review.*

Post 8vo, pp. xii.–72, cloth, price 5s.

THE SATAKAS OF BHARTRIHARI.

Translated from the Sanskrit

By the Rev. B. HALE WORTHAM, M.R.A.S.,

Rector of Eggesford, North Devon.

"A very interesting addition to Trübner's Oriental Series."—*Saturday Review.*

"Many of the Maxims in the book have a Biblical ring and beauty of expression." —*St. James' Gazette.*

Post 8vo, pp. xii.–180, cloth, price 6s.

ANCIENT PROVERBS AND MAXIMS FROM BURMESE SOURCES;

OR, THE NITI LITERATURE OF BURMA.

BY JAMES GRAY,

Author of "Elements of Pali Grammar," "Translation of the Dhammapada," &c.

The Sanscrit-Pâli word Nîti is equivalent to "conduct" in its abstract, and "guide" in its concrete signification. As applied to books, it is a general term for a treatise which includes maxims, pithy sayings, and didactic stories, intended as a guide to such matters of every-day life as form the character of an individual and influence him in his relations to his fellow-men. Treatises of this kind have been popular in all ages, and have served as a most effective medium of instruction.

Post 8vo, pp. xxxii. and 330, cloth, price 7s. 6d.

MASNAVI I MA' NAVI:

THE SPIRITUAL COUPLETS OF MAULANA JALALU-'D-DIN MUHAMMAD I RUMI.

Translated and Abridged by E. H. WHINFIELD, M.A.,

Late of H.M. Bengal Civil Service.

Post 8vo, pp. viii. and 346, cloth, price 10s. 6d.

MANAVA-DHARMA-CASTRA: THE CODE OF MANU.

ORIGINAL SANSKRIT TEXT, WITH CRITICAL NOTES.

BY J. JOLLY, Ph.D.,

Professor of Sanskrit in the University of Wurzburg; late Tagore Professor of Law in the University of Calcutta.

The date assigned by Sir William Jones to this Code—the well-known Great Law Book of the Hindus—is 1250–500 B.C., although the rules and precepts contained in it had probably existed as tradition for countless ages before. There has been no reliable edition of the Text for Students for many years past, and it is believed, therefore, that Prof. Jolly's work will supply a want long felt.

Post 8vo, pp. 215, cloth, price 7s. 6d.

LEAVES FROM MY CHINESE SCRAP-BOOK.

BY FREDERIC HENRY BALFOUR.

Author of "Waifs and Strays from the Far East," "Taoist Texts, "Idiomatic Phrases in the Peking Colloquial," &c. &c.

Post 8vo, pp. xvi.–548, with Six Maps, cloth, price 21s.

LINGUISTIC AND ORIENTAL ESSAYS.

WRITTEN FROM THE YEAR 1847 TO 1887. *Second Series.*

BY ROBERT NEEDHAM CUST, LL.D.,

Barrister-at-Law; Honorary Secretary of the Royal Asiatic Society; Late Member of Her Majesty's Indian Civil Service.

In Two Volumes, post 8vo, pp. x.–308 and vi.–314, cloth, price 25s.

MISCELLANEOUS PAPERS RELATING TO INDO-CHINA.

Edited by R. ROST, Ph.D., &c. &c.,

Librarian to the India Office.

SECOND SERIES.

Reprinted for the Straits Branch of the Royal Asiatic Society from the Malayan "Miscellanies," the "Transactions and Journal" of the Batavian Society, and the "Journals" of the Asiatic Society of Bengal, and the Royal Geographical and Royal Asiatic Societies.

Post 8vo, pp. xii.–512, price 16s.

FOLK-TALES OF KASHMIR.

By the REV. J. HINTON KNOWLES, F.R.G.S., M.R.A.S, &c.

(C.M.S.) Missionary to the Kashmiris.

In Two Volumes, post 8vo, pp. xii.–336 and x.–352, cloth, price 21s.

MEDIÆVAL RESEARCHES FROM EASTERN ASIATIC SOURCES.

FRAGMENTS TOWARDS THE KNOWLEDGE OF THE GEOGRAPHY AND HISTORY OF CENTRAL AND WESTERN ASIA FROM THE THIRTEENTH TO THE SEVENTEENTH CENTURY.

BY E. BRETSCHNEIDER, M.D.,

Formerly Physician of the Russian Legation at Pekin.

THE FOLLOWING WORKS ARE IN PREPARATION:—

In Two Vols., post 8vo.

ALBERUNI'S INDIA:

AN ACCOUNT OF ITS RELIGION, PHILOSOPHY, LITERATURE, GEOGRAPHY, CHRONOLOGY, ASTRONOMY, CUSTOMS, LAW, AND ASTROLOGY (ABOUT A.D. 1031).

TRANSLATED INTO ENGLISH.

With Notes and Indices by Prof. EDWARD SACHAU, University of Berlin.

*** The Arabic Original, with an Index of the Sanskrit Words, Edited by Professor SACHAU, is in the press.

Post 8vo.

THE LIFE OF HIUEN TSIANG.

BY THE SHAMANS HWUI LI AND YEN-TSUNG.

With a Preface containing an account of the Works of I-TSING.

BY SAMUEL BEAL, B.A.

(Trin. Coll., Camb.); Professor of Chinese, University College, London; Rector of Wark, Northumberland, &c.
Author of "Buddhist Records of the Western World," "The Romantic Legend of Sakya Budda," &c.

When the Pilgrim Hiuen Tsiang returned from his travels in India, he took up his abode in the Temple of "Great Benevolence;" this convent had been constructed by the Emperor in honour of the Empress, Wen-te-hau. After Hiuen Tsiang's death, his disciple, Hwui Li, composed a work which gave an account of his illustrious Master's travels; this work when he completed he buried, and refused to discover its place of concealment. But previous to his death he revealed its whereabouts to Yen-tsung, by whom it was finally revised and published. This is "The Life of Hiuen Tsiang." It is a valuable sequel to the Si-yu-ki, correcting and illustrating it in many particulars.

Post 8vo.

A SKETCH OF THE MODERN LANGUAGES OF OCEANIA.

BY R. N. CUST, LL.D.

Author of "Modern Languages of the East," "Modern Languages of Africa," &c.

LONDON: TRÜBNER & CO., 57 AND 59 LUDGATE HILL.

500—21/6/88.

TRÜBNER'S

ORIENTAL SERIES.

HISTORY OF BURMA

INCLUDING

BURMA PROPER, PEGU, TAUNGU, TENASSERIM, AND ARAKAN.

From the Earliest Time to the End of the First War with British India.

BY

LIEUT.-GENERAL SIR ARTHUR P. PHAYRE,

G.C.M.G., K.C.S.I., AND C.B.

MEMBRE CORRESPONDANT DE LA SOCIÉTÉ ACADÉMIQUE INDO-CHINOISE DE FRANCE.

1883.

PREFACE.

Towards the end of last century, Dr. Francis Buchanan, who accompanied Colonel Symes on his mission to Ava, remarked that the histories of the Burmas might throw some light on a part of the world little known, and he hoped soon to be able to produce a translation of the Mahâ Râjâweng, or Great History of Kings.[1] Some years later, Dr. Leyden, in an essay on the languages and literature of the Indo-Chinese nations, which shows extensive knowledge of a subject then little regarded in Europe, mentioned the historical works to be found both in Arakan and Burma, on the importance of which he observed: "Supposing them to be strictly historical, it is needless to dilate."[2] Buchanan never carried out his intention, and though he had collected many Burmese manuscripts, it is not known what became of them. After his return to Europe, he published several papers on Burma in the "Edinburgh Philosophical Journal," but they referred only to the geography of the country. Colonel Henry Burney, who was Resident at the court of the king of Burma for several years up to 1837, published numerous papers, being translations of portions of the Mahâ Râjâweng, more particularly passages relating to the early kings and to the wars between Burma and China.[3] He observes that the Burmese

[1] See Buchanan on the religion and literature of the Burmas. Asiatic Researches, vol. vi. Calcutta.

[2] Asiatic Researches, vol. x.

[3] Journal of the Asiatic Society of Bengal, vols. iv., v., vi.

chronicles "bear strong internal marks of authenticity." The Rev. Father Sangermano, who was in Burma as a missionary from 1782 to 1806, has written an abridgment of Burmese history in his valuable work.[1] The Most Reverend Bishop Bigandet, Vicar Apostolic in Ava and Pegu, in his interesting "Legend of the Burmese Budha," recounts the salient points of history which concern the establishment of Buddhism in Burma. The Rev. Dr. Mason has contributed much to a knowledge of the history of Burma and of Pegu; and the late Captain Forbes, whose early death is a great loss to the cause of Burmese research, has published valuable observations on the history and language of the country.

Professor Lassen, who, more than any other of the great scholars of Europe, studied Burmese history, has observed: "The Burmese have lengthy historical writings, in which not only their own history, but that of Arakan, Pegu, Zimmay, Labang, and other neighbouring lands is given. These writings deserve on the whole the praise of credibility, as their authors relate not only the favourable events of their history, but also the unfavourable. Their inscriptions help to confirm their statements."[2]

Notwithstanding the many articles by competent authors which have appeared on the history of Burma, no one has yet published in any European language a continuous history of the country, whereby the rise and progress of the monarchy, and of the people, might be traced, and the succession of the events recorded, with their relation one to another, explained. In the Gazetteer of British Burma, lately published by authority at Rangoon, the full history has been narrated in a more connected form than had been done

[1] Description of the Burmese Empire. Translated into English by Tandy. Rome, 1833.

[2] Indische Alterthumskundé, vol. iv. p. 369. MS. translation into English.

before. But there still remain blanks to be filled in the history of Arakan, and the other countries which formed the empire of Burma up to the early part of the present century.

The chief authorities which have been followed in this little book are the Mahâ Râjâweng, a copy of which was obtained from the library of the king of Burma; a history of Arakan written by Maung Mi, a learned Arakanese Hsayâ; and a history of Pegu in the Mun language by Hsayâ dau Athwâ, a Talaing Buddhist monk, which was translated into Burmese. The last-named work is little more than a fragment, as the materials for a full history of the Mun people either do not exist, or are not now available in Pegu.

Early in the sixteenth century Europeans began to visit Burma in considerable numbers, and their narratives have been used to supplement or correct in some particulars the native histories. Colonel Michael Symes, in a historical memoir prefixed to his "Account of an Embassy to the Kingdom of Ava," gives a trustworthy account of events commencing from the re-establishment of the kingdom of Pegu under Binya Dâla in A.D. 1740 until the time of his own embassy in 1795. This narrative has evidently been chiefly derived from persons whom the writer met in Rangoon, some apparently Armenians in the Burmese service, who had been actors or eyewitnesses in most of the events described.

The general fulness of the national historical records of the countries which comprised the Burmese empire is remarkable. They present a marked contrast to the scantiness, or total absence of such writings, among the ancient Hindu kingdoms. For though, as remarked by Professor Horace Wilson, "genealogies and chronicles are found in various parts of India, recorded with some perseverance if not much skill," still they are few in comparison with the number and variety of states which have existed in India, and in value fall below what might be expected from the degree of civilisation and literary eminence which had been attained at an early period. The methodical writing of annals of events in the countries of Indo-China has probably resulted from the practical difference between Brahmanism and Buddhism which was gradually developed after the time of Goadamâ. While the former was exclusive, and sought to subordinate kings and rulers to the sacred race, the latter gave the first place in worldly affairs to the civil power, and held out honour and reward, secular and religious, to all who worshipped the three treasures and observed the moral law. Buddhism favoured the general extension of education, and appealed to the masses through the vernacular tongues; and thus, in spite of its tenets as to the worthlessness of worldly objects, and the inherent misery of being, induced a general interest in the affairs of life. The result is seen in the Râjâ Wanso of Ceylon, and, it may be added, in the Râjâ Taringiru of Cashmir. The latter, Wilson observes, is an exception to the total want of historical inquiry by the Hindus.[1] May not this work with probability be referred to a Buddhist original, adapted to Hindu readers after the triumph of Brahmanism?

The annals of Siam do not appear to have been kept with the same regularity and fulness as those of Burma, though they furnish an outline of prominent events. Of the ancient native histories of Anam, Cambodia, and Tonquin, we have as yet no detailed account available to the European student. But this deficiency is rapidly being supplied by the Société Académique Indo-Chinoise of France.

The chronicles of Burma are well supplemented by ancient stone inscriptions, generally those which record the building of pagodas, and include historical events

[1] Essay on the Hindu History of Cashmir, Asiatic Researches, vol. xv.

connected therewith. The inscriptions upon bells cast for religious purposes, and suspended in the precincts of monasteries and pagodas, in many instances furnish important historical information. Each principal pagoda has also a "Thamaing," which purports to give the history of the founder of the building, and of its subsequent benefactors. Such documents include notices of secular events.

In preparing the present little book, where the annals of the adjoining countries have been available, they have been compared with the statements as to contemporary events found in the chronicles of Burma. This is especially the case as regards China and Siam. The accounts of Burma and of Pegu in the narratives of European travellers, commencing with Marco Polo in the thirteenth century, have been summarised in a supplementary chapter. It is useful to compare their statements as to some historical facts, with those given in the native chronicles.

In order that the sequence of events may be as little confused as possible, all dates have been reduced to the eras B.C. and A.D. The attainment of Nirvâṇa by Goadama Buddha is assumed to have occurred B.C. 543, in accordance with Burmese chronology, though this date is now supposed to contain an error varying from sixty to the extent of a hundred and thirty-one years.[1] The present Burmese era commences in A.D. 639, at the time when the sun enters the sign Aries. It may at once be admitted that there are numerous events recorded in the histories of the countries that once formed the Burmese empire which no doubt are historically true, but which in the several chronicles have been hopelessly deranged in time.

In writing Burmese proper names, the rules proposed by Mr. H. L. St. Barbe, late Resident at Mandalay, for

[1] Mr. Rhys Davids in Ancient Coins and Medals of Ceylon. International Numismata Orientalia. London, 1877.

expressing in Roman characters the sounds of the spoken language, have been generally adopted.[1] But in the case of well-known places, as Rangoon, Pegu, Bassein, &c., the ordinary spelling has been followed. The vowel system as adopted is as follows:—

a	as in	woman.	ê	as a in	rate.
â	...	father.	è	as in	hair.
i	...	pin.	o	...	note.
î	...	pique.	oa	...	soar.
u	...	full.	ai	...	aisle.
û	...	mute.	au	...	sound.
e	...	met.			

In the Appendix full lists are given of the kings of Burma proper, Arakan, and Pegu, as found in the native chronicles.

[1] Journal of the Royal Asiatic Society, vol. x., New Series, p. 228.

ERRATA.

Page 47. *For* "Chittagong" *read* "Chittagaon."
" 133. *For* "Ibraham Khan" *read* "Ibrahîm Khan."
" 137. *For* "Momein" *read* "Momien."
" 172. *For* "Affghan" *read* "Afghan."
" 212. In Note, *for* "xvii." *read* "xviii."
" 216. *Omit* "Menam or."
" 225. *For* "Laknau" *read* "Lucknow."
" 226. *For* "khengbyan" *read* "khyengbyan."
" 243. *For* "by the kyî Wungyî" *read* "under the kyî Wungyî."

CONTENTS.

APPENDIX.

A.—LIST OF THE KINGS OF BURMA AS ENTERED IN THE MAHÂ RÂJAWENG.

B.—KINGS WHO REIGNED IN PEGU.

HISTORY OF BURMA.

CHAPTER I.

BURMA PROPER—LEGENDARY KINGS.

Country of the Burmese—Burmese people formed by union of Mongoloid tribes—Kshatriya settlers from India—Likeness between Burmese and neighbouring tribes — Probability of Kshatriya tribes having migrated from India—Opinion of Lassen—Names of ancient cities confirm tradition—Many tribes gradually become Mrâmmâ—Tribes in Tibet and Eastern Himâlaya kinsmen of the Burmese people—Opinion of Max Müller—Opinion of Hodgson—Tradition as to the first kings in Burmese history—First Arakanese king—Early Burmese monarchy destroyed by invaders from the east—Second monarchy established and overthrown—Legend of the preservation of the royal race—Monarchy established at Prome—New capital built—Irruption of the Tai or Shân people from the east—Probable cause of migration of Tai people into Burma—Remains at the ancient city of Tagaung support tradition.

THE people known to Europeans as Birman, Burman, or Burmese dwell in the western region of Indo-China, which is watered by the river Irâwadi. They are most numerous in the middle part of the river's course, which lies between the twenty-fourth degree of north latitude and the head of the delta. The mountains which bound the river valley on either side are inhabited by tribes belonging to the same great family as the Burmese. The Burman people many ages ago were formed into a nation by the union of Mongoloid tribes, who then occupied the land which is still the home of their

Country of the Burmese.

Burmese people formed by union of Mongoloid tribes.

race. Like the wild hill tribes of the present day, they probably had no worship but that of the invisible beings called Nât, whom they believed to rule over the woods, the hills, and the streams; who influenced their lives in hunting, fishing, and tilling; and when offended punished them with sickness, blight, or other calamity. The union of the tribes was accomplished, probably very gradually, under the influence of Aryan immigrants, chiefly, if we may trust the national traditions, Kshatriyas from Gangetic India, who introduced the softening influences of Buddhism, and probably those simple handicrafts, as spinning and weaving, the acquirement of which is, next to agriculture, of the greatest importance to a rude people. They also probably first taught the cultivation of the cotton plant, which is now universal among the wildest independent tribes. Only a few of the names by which the indigenous tribes were called in the remote past are now known; but the Indian settlers gave to them, and adopted themselves, the name of Brahmâ, which is that used in Buddhist sacred books for the first inhabitants of the world. This term, when used to designate the existing people, is now written Mrâmmâ, and generally pronounced Bamâ. Hence have been derived the words used by Europeans for this people.

Kshatriya settlers from India.

Likeness between Burmese and neighbouring tribes.

The race to which the Burmese belong may be traced by their physical resemblance to neighbouring tribes, especially those towards the north; and this evidence is confirmed by the similarity of their language to the tongues of those tribes. Neither history nor tradition gives much help in the inquiry into this kinship. The Buddhist religion, introduced in its simplest form probably two thousand years ago, has led the people to link their line of descent with that of their first teachers, or with those to whom the legends concerning Sakya Muni and his tribe referred. Thus the tradition as to the race from which their earliest kings sprung has made the whole people now bearing the name of Mrâmmâ, believe that they are descended from those Aryan settlers who reached the valley of the Irâwadi from Gangetic India.

Probability of Kshatriya tribes having migrated from India.

At first sight it appears improbable that any of the royal Kshatriya tribes of Northern India should, at the early period indicated, have left their homes and penetrated through the wild country of Eastern Bengal to the Upper Irâwadi. This, however, is what the Burmese chronicles, repeating an ancient tradition, assert, though no adequate cause for the movement is assigned. It would have appeared more probable had the migration been referred to the time when the Buddhists were being overwhelmed in Upper India by the revival of Brahmanical influence. But there is no trace in Burmese tradition of that revolution. The cause assigned in the Burmese Mahâ Râjâweng for the first migration of the Sâkya tribe, is the supposed conquest of that race in Kâpilavâstu by the king of Kosala, before the advent of Goadama. While it appears difficult to admit as a historical fact the alleged foundation of the Burmese monarchy by Kshatriya princes,—and no doubt the claim may have originated among the later kings, as flattering their vanity and upholding their dignity among the people,—still there are some existing facts which support the tradition. Professor Lassen,[1] after narrating the story as told in the chronicles, though rejecting the time assigned for it in the Burmese tradition, accepts as probably true that at a time which cannot be precisely determined a prince of Inner India, who had been expelled from his kingdom, passed over the border range which separates India proper from farther India with his forces, and there founded a dominion; that in favour of the credibility of the story we have the concordance of the geographical

Opinion of Lassen.

[1] Indische Alterthumskunde, vol. ii., second book (MS. translation into English).

information with existing localities; and that the Indian princes spoke Sanscrit may be most reasonably assumed, although the latest compiled records have come to us in a Pali form.[1] Such is the recorded opinion of the great scholar, after careful consideration of the subject. The route by which the Kshatriya princes arrived is indicated in the traditions as being through Manipûr, which lies within the basin of the Irâwadi. The northern part of the Kubo valley, which is the direct route from Manipûr towards Burma, is still called Mauriya or Maurira, said to be the name of the tribe to which King Asoka belonged. If we may accept the name Mareura, which occurs in Ptolemy, and is by him given as the name of a city in the country of the Upper Irâwadi, as referring either to this Maurira or to a city of the same name near Mweyen, east of the river, the building of which is attributed to Indian princes, and the ruins of which still exist, then we may conclude that this name has not been fancifully applied by the Burmese to the places indicated, later than the time when Ptolemy wrote, or the second century of the Christian era. The oldest city said in Burmese chronicles to have been built by Indian princes is Tagaung, on the east bank of the Upper Irâwadi. Colonel Yule is of opinion that it may be identified with the Tugma metropolis of Ptolemy. That cities such as those which have been mentioned, and of which there are existing remains, should have been founded independently by people in the rude condition of the Mongoloid tribes, even as we see them at the present day in remote places, is incredible. The

Names of ancient cities confirm tradition.

[1] For the occurrence of Sanscrit words in Burmese without any connection with Buddhism, see an interesting article by Mr. H. L. St. Barbe, B.C.S., in the Journal of the Asiatic Society of Bengal, vol. xlviii., N.S., p. 253. Max Müller has a suggestive remark on the same subject in Bunsen's Philosophy of Universal History, vol. i. p. 383, note. As to the language spoken by Goadama Buddha, see Oldenberg, English translation, p. 177.

tradition, therefore, as to the building of cities and the first commencement of the Burmese monarchy by Indian settlers, whether Kshatriya princes or others, may be accepted as probably true. That those Indians should have arrived by a northern or north-western route, and not have ascended from the delta of the Irâwadi, is rendered certain from the history of Pegu.

Many tribes gradually become Mrâmmâ.

The Indian settlers no doubt, in a few generations, became merged in the mass of Mongoloid tribes whom they found in the country. Only three names have been handed down as borne by original tribes, or the first conjunction of such tribes—that is, Kânrân, Pyû or Prû, and Sâk or Thek. The last, however, is not an original native term, but probably an abbreviation of Sâkya, and may have been retained by at least a portion of the earliest Indian settlers and their descendants for some time. But later, all who joined them were admitted to brotherhood, with the proud designation of Brahmâ. This term has, in the lapse of ages, included many tribes; and within the nineteenth century the great body of the Talaing people dwelling in the delta of the Irâwadi have assumed the name, and adopted, or insensibly received with it, the language of the Mrâmmâ.

Tribes in Tibet and the Eastern Himâlaya kinsmen of the Burmese people.

To find the true kinsmen of the ancestors of the Burmese people, that is, of the original Mongoloids before the arrival of Indian immigrants, we must look to the present neighbouring tribes, many of whom are still unaltered by Buddhism and have their languages unwritten. Through them the lineage of the existing Burmese people may be traced to tribes dwelling in the Eastern Himâlaya and the adjoining region of Tibet. Mr. Bryan Hodgson,[1] from the evidence of language and race, derives the whole of the Himâlayan tribes from the population beyond the snows, which

[1] Essays on the Aborigines of the Himâlaya, Journal of the Asiatic Society of Bengal for 1848, 1849, and 1853.

has in all time been one and the same, or Turanian, with subordinate distinctions equally found beyond and within the Himâlaya. The identity of some words for simple objects in the languages of Tibet, of some of the tribes of Nepâl, and of Burma, is very remarkable. A few words in those languages which show obvious similarity one to another will be found in a note at the end of this chapter. The Indo-Chinese, the Tibetans, and the Altaians form, Mr. Hodgson considers, but one ethnic family. The principal tribes now bordering on the south-east part of Tibet who may be considered as nearest akin to the Burmese are the Mishmi and the Abor. The former, says Robinson, occupy the ranges of low hills that form the north-east boundary of the valley of Asâm.[1] Dalton states that their country extended up the river Brahmaputra proper to the confines of Tibet.[2] Not far from the Mishmi on the south, though other little known tribes intervene, are now the Chingpaw or Singpho. They have advanced from the south into Asâm only from towards the end of last century. They extend through a long line of hilly country, north and south, along both banks of the Irâwadi and about the head waters of the Khyengdweng. They are the same race as the people known as Kakhyen, living in the hills east of Bamoa, where they appeared about two centuries ago coming from the north. Professor Max Müller has classed the languages of the Mishmi, Abor, Burmese, Singpho, and a few other tribes as a Lohitic subdivision of Bhotiya, now generally called Tibeto-Burman.[3] The Tai or Siamese branch of the Indo-Chinese peoples, called Shân by the Burmese, Max Müller considers were the first to

Opinion of Max Müller deduced from language.

[1] Descriptive Account of Asâm. Calcutta, 1841.

[2] Descriptive Ethnology of Bengal. Calcutta, 1872.

[3] Essay on the Turanian Family of Languages in Bunsen's Philosophy of Universal History, vol. i. pp. 357-402. See also Grammatical Sketch of the Kakhyen Language, by Cushing, Journal of the Royal Asiatic Society, vol. xii., N.S., p. 395.

migrate from their original seat in Central Asia towards the south, and to settle along the rivers Mekong, Menâm, Irâwadi, and Brahmaputra.

Opinion of Hodgson.

The near kinship of the Burmese people with the tribes designated Lohitic is deduced from the physical likeness which exists among them all. Their languages still show a common source. The tribes now dwelling in the mountains of Arakan, chiefly the Kamî and the Khyeng, are included in the same family. The progenitors of all those tribes, descending at a remote period of the past from their original home in the land of Bhote, through, as Hodgson expresses it, "the hundred gates of the Himâlaya," after having dwelt for a time in the country of the middle Brahmaputra, now known as Asâm, reached the basin of the Irâwadi.

Tradition as to the first kings in Burmese national history.

The Mahâ Râjâweng, or history of the Burmese kings, knows not this kinship. It opens with an account of the first formation of the earth according to Buddhist cosmogony, and the appearance thereon of the progenitors of the human race. It then describes the small states of the Sâkya Râjâs in Northern India. Prince Siddhârtha, destined to become Buddha, was the son of the Râjâ of one of those states. Long before his birth, in consequence of wars among the Sâkya clans and between them and their neighbours, a chief to whom tradition gives the name of Abhî Râjâ, left Kâpilavâstu and came with an army to the country of the Middle Irâwadi. There he established himself and built the city of Tagaung, the ruins of which still exist. At his death he left two sons, the elder named Kân Râjâgyî, and the younger Kân Râjângê. They disputed the succession to the throne. It was agreed that the difference should be settled in favour of him who should first complete a religious building. By an artifice the younger brother made it appear that he had finished his in one night, and he was declared the winner. He therefore succeeded to his father's kingdom. The elder brother collected his followers and went down the Irâwadi. He reached the mouth of the Khyengdweng river, which he ascended, and then established himself in the southern portion of the country now known as the Kubo valley, at or near a hill called Kalê. The tribes Pyû, Kânrân, and Sâk are described as then in the land, and Kân Râjâgyî made his son Muddusitta king over them. He with his followers went towards the south-west, until he reached a mountain in the northern part of Arakan, now called Kyaukpândaung. There he established the capital of his kingdom. Following this legend, the Arakanese chroniclers derive their whole race from this king and his followers, and claim to be the elder branch of the Mrâmmâ family. The date they fix for the commencement of the reign of Kân Râjâgyî answers to B.C. 825. The Burmese chronicle is silent upon this point. Leaving for the present the elder though less distinguished branch of the race, the fortune of the younger in the country of the Irâwadi has to be followed.

First Arakanese king.

Early Burmese monarchy destroyed by invaders from the east.

Kân Râjângê reigned in Tagaung, the city of his father. The Burmese chronicle records that he had thirty-one descendants, who reigned successively in that city. The last king of the dynasty, named Bhinnakâ, was overthrown by an invasion of tribes coming from a country to the east called Gandalarît, in the land of Tsin or Sin, which corresponds generally with Yunnân.[1] These invaders are termed "Taruk" and "Taret," the names given in after times to the Chinese

[1] Tsin, it will be remembered, was the name of a Chinese dynasty reigning B.C. 249, which lasted only for three years. A second Tsin dynasty was established A.D. 265, which lasted until A.D. 317. The kings of this dynasty reigned in the western and southern part of the empire. After the Mongol invasion of Burma in the thirteenth century, the name Taruk is applied to the Chinese in the Burmese chronicles. It is probably the same as Turk. The word Taret is applied to the Mongol and the Manchu. Gandalarît is a name transferred by Burmese chroniclers in modern times from the Buddhist geography of India, in which Gandhara was placed west of the Indus and mainly north of the lower course of the

and Manchu, and may be considered as designations incorrectly applied by later copyists of the chronicles to the earlier conquerors. King Bhinnakâ fled to Malê, now a town on the west bank of the Irâwadi below Tagaung. There he died, leaving a queen who is called Nâgahsin. His followers separated into three bodies. One remained with the queen; another moved to Kalé, where the descendants of Muddusitta still reigned; the third went eastward into the Shân country.

Second monarchy established and overthrown.

About this time, Goadama Buddha being still alive, a second band of immigrant Kshatriyas from Gangetic India arrived, led by Daza Râjâ. They settled at Mauriya, east of the Irâwadi, near a village now called Mwêyen. The Râjâ afterwards moved to Malê, married Queen Nâgahsin, and they then went north and built a city close to the ancient capital Tagaung, now known as Old Pugân. In the Burmese chronicle no mention is made of the invaders from the east interfering to prevent this settlement, and the ancient capital not long after was again occupied. Sixteen kings succeeded this founder of the second dynasty. The last of them, Thado Mahâ Râjâ, having no son, the queen's brother was appointed Ainshêmeng, and declared to be heir to the throne.[1] The king was dethroned by invaders, but whether by

Kabul river. See The Middle Kingdom, by Wells Williams, vol. ii. p. 211, New York, 1861; Cunningham's Ancient Geography of India, p. 47; and Yule in Journal of Royal Asiatic Society.

[1] Ainshêmeng is the modern title in Burma of the heir-apparent to the throne, and means literally "Lord of the eastern house." The office is similar to and is derived from that of the Yuva Râjâ in the ancient Hindu kingdoms. In Burma, the heir-apparent to the throne, like Râma in the kingdom of his father, Dasaratha, is in some degree associated with the king in the government, and is *ex officio* commander-in-chief. The son or younger brother of the king generally fills this post, according to the pleasure of the sovereign. A somewhat similar position is held by the second or junior king in Liam, and also in Cambodia; and there are traces of the same arrangement in some of the Shân states. It is possible that the office of Shiogoon or Tycoon, in Japan, may have originated from the same influence. The government of Butân under a Dhurmarâja, the spiritual head, and a Debrâja, the temporal head, may have been derived from the same model, but considerably altered by time and circumstances from the original.

the descendants of the former conquerors, or by others from the eastward, is not stated. He hid himself from the invaders, and his queen gave birth to twin sons, who were born blind. The legend runs that the Ain-shêmeng, when out hunting, followed a wild boar so eagerly that he lost his way in the forest. Wandering on, he became wearied with the world, and determined to become a hermit. Down the course of the river, far from his country, he lighted on a hill where was a cave close to the present town of Prome, and there he dwelt. The three tribes before mentioned were in this land. In Tagaung, the twin sons of the dethroned king, being blind, were according to custom to be put to death as being unfit to rule. But the queen concealed them until they had become young men. They were then put into a boat and set afloat on the Irâwadi. While borne along by the stream they received their sight, and at length reached Prome.[1] There they met a daughter of the hermit, whom they saw drawing water from the river, and found that her father was their uncle. The elder of the princes, Mahâ Thambawâ, was then married to his cousin. He was the first of the dynasty established at or near Prome, about 483 years before Christ, according to the Mahâ Râjâweng. From this ruler the kings of Burma claim descent, though several breaks in the succession appear in the course of time. The national chronicle makes no further reference to the country of Tagaung for several centuries.

Legend of the preservation of the royal race.

Monarchy established at Prome.

Mahâ Thambawâ reigned only six years, and was succeeded by his brother, Sulathambawâ, who reigned for thirty-five years. The son of the elder brother then came to the throne. He is called Dwuttabaung. The capital city of this dynasty had hitherto been Prome. A new city was now founded on an extensive plain about

[1] The town called Prome by Europeans is Pyî or Prî in Burmese. The name may possibly be connected with the tribal name, Pyû or Prû.

five miles to the eastward, and called Tharêkhettarâ.[1] The ruins still exist, and are known as Rathêmyû or "city of the hermit." The name Dwuttabaung, whether representing a mythical or a real personage, is held in deep veneration by the Burmese people. A well near Prome is still shown to travellers as having been dug by the good king, and the water of it is presented to those whom the people desire to honour. Nevertheless it is related that he committed an act of injustice by forcibly taking possession of land dedicated to a monastery; that misfortunes then overtook him, and that having gone to sea, his ship was wrecked at Nagarît, the whirlpool where the sea-dragon carries down vessels to the ocean depths.[2] The name Mahâ Thambawâ, it is observed by Lassen, cannot be personal, but is an expression of the matter of fact that the ruling race in Tharêkhettarâ descended from the old family in Tagaung, as the word signifies in Pali "the great origin." Most students of Burmese history will concur in the soundness of this opinion. New capital built.

In the Mahâ Râjâweng the destruction of the first monarchy established at Tagaung by Abhî Râjâ is attributed to an invasion by Taruk and Taret; but, as has already been stated, these are modern terms now applied to the Chinese and Manchu. But the story of the overthrow of the early kingdom probably rests on a historical event which has been referred to an earlier period than inquiry will support. From the indication of language, Professor Max Müller is of opinion that the ancestors of the Tai people were the first to migrate southwards from their original seat in Central Asia, Irruption of the Tai or Shân people from the east.

[1] Tharêkhettara is interpreted by Lassen as representing Srîkhetra, "the field of fortune." Khettarâ is also the Burmanised form of Kshatriya, and the name has been interpreted as referring to the race from which the kings of Burma claim to have descended.

[2] The bluff of land so called by the Burmese is known to European sailors as Cape Negrais, a corruption of the Burmese name. From the violence of opposing tides it is still the scene of frequent wrecks of native craft.

and that they settled along the rivers Mekong, Menâm, Iṛâwadi, and Brahmaputra. There does not appear to be now any trace of the Tai branch as having originally dwelt with other Mongoloid tribes in that part of the Irâwadi valley where the kingdom of Tagaung lay; but at the time when that kingdom was formed, people of the Tai race were no doubt in the country of the next river to the eastward, the Sâlwin; and there is evidence of an irruption of that people into the country of the Irâwadi during the first century of the Christian era, as mentioned in a Shân chronicle preserved in Manipûr.[1] From that it appears that early in the Christian era the Shân, coming from the eastward, entered the country now called Burma; first had their chief seat at Muanglong on the Shwêlê river; and that their first king is called Khûllyi, whose reign is said to have commenced A.D. 80. The Shân dominion was gradually extended in the country of the Irâwadi, and long after Murgnow was king. The kingdom is in the Shân
A.D. 767. chronicle called Pong.[2] The after history of that kingdom, which in later times was broken up into several independent states, will appear in a future chapter. It
A.D. 777. will be sufficient to state here that Murgnow died, leaving two sons, Sûkamphâ and Samlongphâ. The first ascended the throne of what at that time may properly be called the kingdom of Pong. The second was employed by his brother to subdue the surrounding countries. He conquered Kachâr, Tippera, Manipûr,

[1] Pemberton's Report on the Eastern Frontier of Bengal. Calcutta, 1835. See also Anderson's Report on the Expedition to Western Yunnan. Calcutta, 1871, pp. 1 to 7. Also British Burma Gazetteer, vol. i. pp. 173–176.

[2] The term "Pong" is not known to the Burmese. It appears to be the name by which the country of the Upper Irâwadi is still called in Manipûr. In Dalrymple's Oriental Repertory, vol. ii. p. 477, there is a narrative by an Indian fakîr who visited Manipûr about A.D. 1763. He calls that country Meckley, a corruption probably of Moitay, the race-name of the inhabitants. He speaks of the Upper Irâwadi as the country of Pong or Poong. From discussions as to the right to the Kubo valley in 1830, the name appears applicable to the state called by the Burmese Mogaung. See Historical Review by Bayfield. Calcutta, 1835.

and Asâm. From him the Ahom kings of the last-named country were said to have descended. Robinson, however, in his work on Asâm, places the arrival of the Ahoms in that province about the beginning of the thirteenth century of the Christian era, Chukaphâ being the first king of whom there is any authentic record. An incursion into Asâm by Samlongphâ may have occurred, but since the conversion of the Ahom kings to the Brahmanical faith, the princes of this dynasty have claimed descent from the god Indra, and the continuity of their history or traditions is lost. However uncertain the period of the first advance into Asâm, it may be accepted as historical that the Tai race became supreme in the country of the Upper Irâwadi early in the Christian era, and continued to be so under a consolidated monarchy for several centuries. When Sookamphâ died, it appears probable that the A.D. 808. Shân kingdom began to be broken up into states under separate independent chiefs, in which condition it continued until the Burmese monarchy acquired power under Anoarahtâ in the eleventh century.

Probable cause of migration of Tai people into Burma.

Some help to an explanation of the movement of the Shân people from the eastward into the valley of the Irâwadi is derived from the history of China.[1] In the time of the Han, the country now known as Yunnân, or a great part of it, was called Tëen. The inhabitants are described as barbarians. A Chinese general, Chwang Keaou, occupied a site on what is now a lake in the vicinity of the city Yunnân, and established himself as king of Tëen. Assuming the garb of the barbarians and adopting their customs, he was accepted as their chief. In the year B.C. 122, an expedition was fitted out by the emperor of the Han dynasty, to find the way through the south-western

[1] See History of the South-Western Barbarians, translated by A. Wylie, with introduction by W. H. Howorth, Jour. Anthropological Inst., vol. ix. p. 53.

barbarians to India; but the officers of the expedition
B.C. 109. were stopped by the king of Tëen. After this an army was sent against Tëen, when the king submitted. Imperial officers were then appointed, and the region was
B.C. 86. named Yĭhchow. But an extensive rebellion occurred among the tribes in Yĭhchow: many thousands of people were killed, and over ten thousand head of cattle were carried off. When Wang Mang usurped
A.D. 9. the imperial throne, the barbarians again rebelled, and killed the grand director of Yĭhchow. This caused further chastisement by the imperial armies, and great destruction of life. From these statements it may reasonably be inferred that the tribes of Tai or Shân race dwelling in the country of the Upper Mekong and Salwin rivers were driven westward, and that their first appearance in the basin of the Irâwadi began earlier than the date assigned for the establishment of their monarchy on the Shwêlê river. This movement gradually gathered strength; and when the numbers of the immigrants had become sufficient to assert their superiority, the result was what has been told in the Burmese history as the irruption of barbarians, who overthrew the monarchy founded by Kshatriya princes. The event, however, has in that history been antedated by several centuries. The descendants of those princes, being driven from their kingdom, are represented as establishing themselves near Prome; and for several centuries the national history is silent as to events in the upper country.

Remains at the ancient city of Tagaung support tradition.

The existing ruins of Tagaung, so far as they have been explored, give support to the general truth of the tradition as to the seat of the ancient Indo-Burmese monarchy. The Shân people make no claim to heritage in them. Buddhist images, and bricks bearing the effigy of Buddha stamped thereon, and Pali inscriptions in ancient devanâgari character, have been found among the ruins.[1] The letters are of the form referred to the time of the Guptas, used during the two first centuries of the Christian era. There appears no good reason for concluding that these bricks were made at a later period than that during which similar letters were in use in India. It has been suggested that the bricks may have been made at Gayâ, and brought from thence. If so, the fact would show an early communication between Upper Burma and Gangetic India. It is, however, more probable that workmen from India were brought to make the bricks or to carve the forms used to stamp them. At Lower or New Pugân bricks of a similar character, but of much later age, exist in thousands, having been used to construct the relic chambers of pagodas. They are so numerous as to preclude the probability of their having been imported. The traditions of the Burmese and the present remains and names of ancient cities, render it probable that early communication between Gangetic India and Tagaung existed, and was carried on through Eastern Bengal and Manipûr, rather than through Thahtûn or Pegu generally. In after times the revival of religion, and the reduction of the Burmese language to writing in the form now existing, were accomplished by teachers coming from the latter country; but this does not invalidate the strong presumptive evidence there is of the long anterior arrival among the Mongoloid tribes dwelling in the upper part of the Middle Irâwadi, of Indian settlers coming through Eastern Bengal, and the gradual consolidation of those tribes into a nation, through the instruction of a more advanced race.

[1] Journal of Asiatic Society of Bengal, vol. iv., and Anderson's Report on the Expedition to Western Yunnan, p. 206.

Note on the Identity of some Words in the Languages of the Bhotiya and Burmese Peoples.

In the following list the words in Tibetan are taken from Mr. Hodgson's Essays. In one or two instances words from the languages of the Gurung and Magar tribes have been given as illustrating the connection with Burmese more distinctly than Tibetan. The letters G and M are attached to such words. In some instances the Arakanese form of word is given instead of Burmese. To these the letter A is attached.

English.	Tibetan.	Burmese.
Arrow.	Myá (G and M).	Hmyá.
Day.	Nyí'mo.	Né.
Dog.	Khyí.	Khwé.
Ear.	Na.	Ná.
Eye.	Mík.	Mrák (A).
Fire.	Mé.	Mí.
Fish.	Gná.	Ngá.
Hair of the head.	Chham (M).	Tshán.
Hand.	Lagpa.	Lak (A).
Head.	Gó.	Gaung.
Hog.	Phag. Wak (M).	Wák (A).
Moon.	Láva.	La.
River.	Changpo.	Khyaung.
Road.	Lam.	Lán.
Salt.	Tshá.	Tshá.
Sun.	Nyima.	Né.
I.	Gnyá.	Ngá.
Thou.	Nang (M).	Nang (A).
One.	Chik.	Tit.
Two.	Nyi.	Nhít.
Three.	Súm.	Thun.
Four.	Plí (G).	Lé.
Five.	Gná.	Ngá.
Six.	Drúk.	Krauk.
Nine.	Gú.	Ko.
Ten.	Chuh.	Tshai.

CHAPTER II.

PROME AND PUGAN.

Kingdom of Prome or Tharêkhettarâ—Extent not known—Kingdom ended by civil war and invasion — Pugân founded — Burmese chronicle obscure as to the fall of the monarchy of Tharêkhettarâ —Connection claimed between the dynasties of Tagaung and Pugân—Establishment of the present Burmese era—Dragon-worship—Anoarahtâ, the hero-king of Burma.

THE founder of the city of Tharêkhettarâ having perished at sea, was succeeded by his son, Dwuttarân. Nothing is recorded regarding him or his successors, and the dynasty came to an end B.C. 110, according to the chronology of the Mahâ Râjâweng. The king then reigning adopted a son, who succeeded him, and the regular succession continued uninterrupted until the reign of Thupinyâ, who ascended the throne A.D. 84. In the Burmese chronicle twenty-seven kings of this dynasty are said to have reigned in Prome and Tharêkhettarâ during five hundred and seventy-eight years. Kingdom of Prome or Tharêkhettarâ.

Throughout that period, except occurrences at the beginning and end of the monarchy, no event of importance which can be accepted as historical is mentioned. The extent of country ruled by the kings is not indicated. It may be conjectured that the kingdom included the valley of the Irâwadi for a few miles north and south of Prome, and that petty chiefs of tribes near akin to those from which the Burmese people were formed, ruled in small tracts of land up to the border of the country occupied by the Tai race. To the south was the kingdom known later as Pegu, Extent of the kingdom not known.

which, about the time when Tharêkhettarâ came to an end, had become consolidated under foreign kings from Telingâna with the capital at Thahtun, had been enriched by commerce with India, and civilised by religious teaching. How far similar benefits had been extended to the kingdom of Tharêkhettarâ is not known. It is probable that the people were in a much ruder condition than those in the delta, and that the rudimentary Buddhism originally introduced under the Kshatriya kings had become hidden beneath wild superstitions.

Kingdom ended by civil war and invasion. City of Pugân founded.

In the Burmese chronicle a strange story is told of the event which led to the ending of the kingdom. The tribes then existing under the monarchy were the Pyû, Kânrân, and Mrâmmâ. A civil war arose; the two former tribes fighting for pre-eminence. The last king, Thupinyâ, died during the struggle, after a reign of eleven years. The quarrel of the tribes was at last settled by a method already known in the legends of the Burmese monarchy—the building of a pagoda or other religious fabric. In this peaceful contest the Pyû were victorious, and the Kânrân retired westward. A section of this tribe was already settled in the hilly country of southern Arakan. The Pyû now fought among themselves and separated into two parties. One division having occupied the hilly district to the south-east of Prome, was attacked by the Talaings, and then crossed the great river into the country west of Padaung. There they were attacked by the Kânrân as intruders into land already occupied, and were driven north to Mendun. They retired farther north, and then crossing the Irâwadi under their leader Thamuddarît, said to be nephew to Thupinyâ, arrived at a place on the river-bank called Yunhlwutguen. Near to this the city of Pugân, called New Pugân, was founded. Thirteen years had been occupied in the wandering of the tribe. After this period the separate tribes are seldom mentioned, except in ancient ballads, and the name Mrâmmâ appears as the national designation for all.

Burmese chronicles obscure as to fall of the monarchy of Tharêkhettar

No distinct explanation is found in the chronicles as to the events which led to the destruction of the kingdom of Tharêkhettarâ. The general inference from the narrative in the Mahâ Râjâweng is that civil war among the tribes led to their dispersion. But the mention of the Talaing having attacked the Pyû after the first contest, and the flight of the latter from Tharêkhettarâ, makes it probable that the kingdom was conquered by the people from the delta. At the time—the first century of the Christian era—when the fall of the monarchy is placed, and for some centuries later, the kingdom, of which Thahtun was the capital, was existing in prosperity. Though the chief city was outside the basin of the Irâwadi, the territory included the whole of the delta of that river. The kings were of Indian race from Telingâna, and their country was known as Suvârna Bhûmi, of Buddhist fame. But as the country, known better from the later capital as Pegu, was conquered in the eleventh century by the king of Pugân, and all records were destroyed or carried away, no account remains of the early history and the extension northward of the Talaing kingdom. That can only be now gathered from tradition and a few fragmentary notices.

Connection between the dynasties of Tagaung and Pugân.

The Burmese Mahâ Râjâweng relates, in the manner that has been stated, the establishment of the Pugân monarchy by Thamuddarît, as chief of the Pyû tribe. He was not directly descended in the male line from the Kshatriya kings of Tagaung; and the chroniclers, probably in order to exalt the glory of later kings, have produced a hero of that race to connect the modern occupants of the throne of Burma with the ancient monarchy. It is told, that though the upper country was still in confusion, consequent on the ancient

Kshatriya dynasty having been overthrown by invaders from the eastward, that nevertheless the race of the former kings was not extinct. A younger son of Thado Mahâ Râjâ, the father of the twin sons set afloat, as has been told, on the Irâwadi, had remained in the kingdom, although hidden from observation, and survived the conquest. His descendant at the time of the destruction of Tharêkhettarâ was named Aditsa, the name of the sun-god. He lived concealed at Malê, a town on the Upper Irâwadi, where he had a son born to him called Soatî. The young prince came to the newly founded city of Pugân, and lived in the house of a Pyû peasant. The country was then infested by savage animals and flying monsters, which devoured the people. Soatî destroyed them, and King Thamuddarît gave him his daughter in marriage, and appointed him ainshêmeng, or heir-apparent. He did not, however, succeed to the throne on the death of his father-in-law. On that event, a hermit, styled Rathê Kyaung, was, with the consent of the heir-apparent, raised to the throne, and he reigned for fifteen years. Soatî, called also Pyû Mentí, because he had been brought up in the house of a Pyû, then became king. It is stated that he extended his dominions to the upper course of the Irâwadi, regaining much of the territory that had been lost by the fall of the old kingdom, and defeated the Chinese, who had invaded that part of the country situated east of the river, called Koathâmbî.[1] His reign, it is said, extended over seventy-
A.D. 243. five years, and he was 110 years old when he died. After his death nothing of importance is recorded until
A.D. 388. Kyaungdarît ascended the throne. It is stated that in his reign the Buddhist Scriptures having been brought to Thahtun by the great teacher Buddhaghoso, Pugân participated in the benefit derivable therefrom. There

[1] A district so called after the Gangetic India, Kosâmbi in the famous Buddhist kingdom in Dúab.

are, however, inconsistent statements on this subject; or, if the books of the Pitika were brought to Pugân in the time of Buddhaghoso, they were afterwards lost; for the Mahâ Râjâweng relates how, about six hundred and fifty years later, King Anoarahtâ, in order to reform religion, undertook a war to gain possession of these sacred writings. Kyaungdarît reigned twenty-five years, or until about A.D. 413. The mission of Buddhaghoso to Thahtun probably occurred several years later.[1] Although these books probably were not known in Pugân until long after, still the simple precepts and practices of religion were no doubt taught and observed before the time of Buddhaghoso, but among the bulk of the people were mixed up with numerous superstitious rites inconsistent with pure Buddhism.[2]

No prominent event is mentioned after this until the reign of Thenga Râjâ. He had been a monk, but "became a man"—as the Burmese phrase is—married the queen of his predecessor, introduced many improvements in the administration, and arranged for the reformation of the calendar. The common era which he established commenced in A.D. 639, on the day when the sun is supposed to enter the first sign of the zodiac. *Establishment of the present Burmese era.*

This era is now observed in Burma. The reformation of the calendar was probably brought about by the assistance of Indian astronomers. The Burmese system of astronomy and method of computing time are essentially those of the Hindus.[3] Nearly two centuries later, A.D. 924. it is related that in the reign of an usurper, Soa Rahân, a corrupt worship, called Nagâ or dragon-worship, was intro- *Dragon-worship.*

[1] About A.D. 450, according to Rhys Davids, Buddhism, p. 231.

[2] I have seen in a remote part of Burma an idol placed in a small hollow temple in the midst of a secluded jangal, to which buffaloes and other animals were sacrificed by the surrounding Buddhist population.

[3] It may be remarked that Bentley, in an article in the "Asiatic Researches," has from internal evidence calculated the period when the Brahma Siddanta was written or revised as A.D. 538, just one century before the existing Burmese era was adopted.

duced. It is however probable that this worship had long existed but now became more prominent. Soa Rahân caused the image of a dragon to be set up in a beautiful garden, and there it was worshipped. The priests of this worship, called Ari, were now supreme, and temples were built in which images of dragons were placed. To these offerings of food and spirituous liquors were made. The Ari priests lived in monasteries, but are represented as leading immoral lives. The Mahâ Râjâweng states that the whole country was devoted to this wicked superstition. The king, Soa Rahân, was at length deposed by Kwunhsoa Kyaung Phyû, the son of a former king, Tannet, but he, after a reign of twenty-two years, was deposed and retired to a monastery. Two sons of Soa Rahân then reigned successively, and the second of them was put to death by the son of Kwunhsoa Kyaung Phyû, who was consecrated king with the title

A.D. 1010.

Anoarahtâ Soa.[1] This king is regarded as the great hero of the Burmese in historical times, and during his reign events become more clearly defined than before.

Anoarahtâ, the hero-king of Burma.

The Mahâ Râjâweng represents Anoarahtâ Tsâu as the restorer of the ancient power of the monarchy and the recoverer of much of the territory in the Upper Irâwadi which had been conquered by the Shân from the Tagaung kings. He is also glorified as the great reformer of religion, who established Buddhism in the form in which it exists at the present time. He sent an envoy to India to a king who is called the Râjâ of Wethâli,[2] to demand his daughter in marriage. The princess was escorted to Burma through Arakan, and after some hesitation consequent on scandalous reports, was received into the palace as one of the queens. Her

[1] This date is approximately correct, but some copies of the Mahâ Râjâweng place the accession of Anoarahtâ thirteen years earlier.

[2] Vâisâla, the modern Besarh, twenty miles to the north of Patna.

son afterwards succeeded to the throne under the name of Kyântsitthâ. King Anoarahtâ conquered what remained of the ancient kingdom of Thahtun. From this time the country of the delta and the adjoining districts to the east became subject to Burma, and continued to be so, with intervals of partial independence, for several centuries.

It will therefore be suitable to interrupt here the narrative of Burmese history, and relate what is known of the early events of the kingdoms of Thahtun and Pegu.

CHAPTER III.

PEGU.

Colonists from Southern India in the delta of the Irâwadi—Country known as Suvarna Bhumi—Vincent on the commerce of the ancients—Suvarna Bhumi in Buddhist story—Buddhist missionaries deputed to the country of the Irâwadi—Traditions regarding the aborigines—First settlement from India by two hermits—City called Thahtun built—People called Mun or Talaing—Mongoloid tribes civilised by Dravidians—City of Pegu built by colonists from Thahtûn—Two brothers the founders—List of the kings of Pegu imperfect—Struggle between Brahmanists and Buddhists.

Colonists from Southern India in the delta of the Irâwadi.

ACCORDING to traditions current among the people of Pegu, Indian colonists from the country of the lower courses of the rivers Kistna and Godaveri, had at a remote time crossed the sea, and formed settlements in the delta of the Irâwadi and on the adjoining coast.

Country known as Suvarna Bhumi.

In Buddhist legends the country they occupied became known as Suvarna Bhumi or "golden land."[1] A name resembling the Pali form of this designation, Sobana, occurs in Ptolemy, and is applied by Colonel Yule, in his remarks on the ancient map of India, to a promontory or place on the coast of the Gulf of Martaban. Lassen considers that the country named by that geographer, Chryse, means approximately the present Pegu. Thahtun, the native name for the ancient capital, or more correctly Htawtun, has in the Mun language the same signification as the Sanscrit name. It is not

[1] Manual of Buddhism, by Hardy, pp. 182, 183; Life or Legend of Gautama, by Bishop Bigandet. Rangoon, p. 101.

necessary to conclude that this name was given to the country from gold being found in the soil. It is probable that that metal was from early times brought from South-Western China down the river Irâwadi and exported to India. The name, therefore, may have been given from that fact. It is only within the last twenty years that the import of gold bullion from Yunnân to the country of the Upper Irâwadi has diminished; but gold-leaf, which is in great demand in Burma, is an article still largely imported from the same country.

Vincent on the commerce of the ancients.

This view receives support from the researches of Dr. Vincent,[1] though that learned author does not appear to have recognised that Pegu was referred to in the authorities he quotes under the name Khrusé. He considered that the word was applied to the peninsula of Malacca. From his work, however, and from the geography of Indo-China, and later information derived from Indian sources, it appears most probable that the fleets which went to Khrusé, or the golden Chersonese, in the time of Ptolemy, came from Ceylon or the coast of Southern India to a port in Pegu, to which port there was a trade with China by inland navigation and overland journey. In Vincent's translation of the sequel to the Periplus of the Erythrean Sea, occur the following passages:—"Immediately after leaving the Ganges there is an island in the ocean called Khrusé or the golden isle, which lies directly under the rising sun, and at the extremity of the world towards the east. But still beyond this, immediately under the north, at a certain point where the exterior sea terminates, lies a city called Thina, not on the coast but inland, from which both the raw material and manufactured silk are brought by land." These words exactly suit the application of Khrusé to the port now named, and no other place fulfils the conditions so completely. Raw

[1] Vincent's Commerce and Navigation of the Ancients. See vol. ii. pp. 460, 507, &c.

silk constitutes to this day one of the principal articles imported from Yunnân by the Bamoa route into Upper Burma, and thence down the Irâwadi. Nor is there any other route by which overland traffic between south-western China and any point on the coast of the bay of Bengal could so readily be carried on. The city or country called Thina in the above passage may be accepted as representing Tsin or Sin, which was the name by which China was known in Burma during the early centuries of the Christian era. The identity of the Khrysé of Ptolemy, of the Suvarna Bhumi of the Buddhist legends, and of the city of Thahtun in Pegu, all having the same signification, appears nearly certain.

Suvarna Bhumi in Buddhist story.

The earliest notice of Suvarna Bhumi in Buddhist story is found in the jâtakas preserved in Ceylon.[1] Therein it is related that when Goadama, after he had attained perfection, remained in contemplation in the Kiripalu forest or grove, two brothers, named Tapusa and Palikat, arrived with five hundred carts of merchandise. They had come from Ukkalaba, a port in their native country, Suvarna Bhumi.[2] They made an offering of honey to Buddha, and they entreated that he would bestow upon them something that they might honour as a relic. He therefore gave them eight hairs of his head, which they brought to their own country. These were enshrined in a pagoda, since known as the Shwé Dagun, near the modern town of Rangoon.

Buddhist missionaries deputed to the country of the Irâwadi.

At the time of the third great Buddhist synod at Pataliputra, about B.C. 241, when missions were sent to foreign countries to propagate religion and extirpate heresy, Sono and Uttaro were deputed to the golden land.[3] According to the Talaing chronicles, they were

[1] Hardy's Man. of Bud., p. 182.

[2] Ukkalaba was the name of a town to the west of the present town of Rangoon, and near a village now called Twantây.

[3] Cunningham's Bilsa Topes, p. 116; Rhys David's Buddhism, p. 227; Bishop Bigandet's Legend of the Burmese Buddha, p. 386.

at first violently opposed; but gradually they acquired influence; their preaching converted the people, and religion was revived. This reference in authentic Buddhist records to the religious condition of the people of Suvarna Bhumi in the third century B.C. shows the deep interest taken in India at that time in the affairs of the country. It supports the local traditions as to the previous establishment of Indian colonists on the coast, and as to the existence of one or more important commercial ports at an early period.

Traditions regarding the aborigines.

In native traditions the early inhabitants of the coast, especially near the mouth of the Salwin river, are represented as savages, called in Burmese Bîlu, the equivalent of Râkshasa. They rejected all intercourse with civilised men; and even Goadama himself, who, it is fabled, came to the country, was stoned and driven away by those whose descendants were afterwards distinguished by their religious zeal. It may be concluded that the original inhabitants dwelling in the delta of the Irâwadi, belonged to the same race or family as the Mongoloid tribes in the upper course of the river, but that their ancestors had left the great hive on the north of the Himâlaya mountains, from which both swarmed, at an earlier period than the progenitors of those upper tribes. The first settlement from India among these savage tribes is, in Talaing tradition, said to have been made by the two sons of King Titha or Tissa, who reigned in the country of Karanaka and the city of Thubinna. The name Tissa, as here applied, cannot be historical, and no doubt has been taken from the lists of kings of Ceylon in the Mahawanso, or has been suggested by that of the brother of Asoka. These sons of the king come to dwell as hermits in the savage land; and, according to a wild legend, as if to connect the aborigines with the later ruling race, bring up a child born of a dragon on the sea-shore, who, when grown up, builds the city of Thahtun, and reigns as

First settlement from India by two hermits.

City called Thahtun built.

Siha Râjâ. Even this name has probably been taken from Sihala, the fabled father of Vijaya, first king of Ceylon. Nevertheless tradition which appears trustworthy points to ancient Telingâna as the original home of the colonists.[1] The principal city or port of these colonists was Thahtun, situated on a tidal creek opening into the gulf of Martaban. Extensive remains of the ancient city still exist. But so altered are the present conditions of the sea and land, consequent on the gradual rise of the coast and bed of the gulf of Martaban in the long lapse of ages, that the creek is no longer approachable from the sea except in small boats and at great risk, by reason of the force of the tide.

People called Mun or Talaing.

The people of Pegu have long been known to the Burmese and to all foreigners by the name Talaing, which is obviously connected with the word Telingâna; but the name by which they call themselves is Mun or Mwun. The word Talaing was no doubt originally applied only to the colonists from India, but is now, and long has been, used by foreigners to designate all those supposed to be descended from the original inhabitants, and those whose descent cannot be traced to races who have come to the country within the memory of man. The Mun language is now spoken only by a small number of people in Pegu, though it survives among many thousands who fled in the last century into Siam.

Mongoloid tribes civilised by Dravidians.

It is interesting to compare the difference of method, and to some extent of result, in the two instances of Mongoloid tribes in the north and south of the basin of the Irâwadi who received their civilisation from Indians of different races. In the north the tribes were civilised by Aryans; in the south by Dravidians. In the former case a ruler came with followers to

[1] Telingâna, Cunningham considers, corresponds with the Trikalinga, which includes Karnáta. Ancient Geography of India, pp. 516, 517, and 519.

establish a dominion; the aborigines were subjected, and a name for the united tribes was adopted, which included the conquerors, and in time became permanent and national. In the south the original settlers were traders. Though they probably came to the coast with no other object, yet gradually they converted and civilised the savage tribes around them. They became rulers, but there was an absence of original purpose of consolidation, and the native name of the race they found, or some designation other than their own, has been continued in the language of the people. The term Talaing is not acknowledged in the Mun language, and the Dravidian settlers have become entirely absorbed in the indigenous and, except in ancient chronicles, obscured race. In the north, though the Aryans have left permanent marks of their early influence, the physical difficulty of the intervening country prevented continuous communication with the fatherland, and the fall of Buddhism in Gangetic India severed religious communion between the two regions. With southern India and Pegu constant intercourse was maintained by sea. By this route the Buddhist scriptures were brought to Pegu, and thence reached Burma; and the alphabet now used by the Burmese people shows the same influence.

City of Pegu built by colonists from Thahtun.

Of the early history of Thahtun only vague tradition remains, though a list of fifty-nine kings, for the most part fabulous, who are said to have reigned there, is found in the Talaing chronicles. The first building of the city of Hansâwadi, called also Pegu, is attributed, and probably correctly, to a company of people proceeding from Thahtun. In the sixth century of the Christian era two sons of the reigning king, named Thamala and Wimala, who, on account of a prejudice against their mother, had been excluded from succession to the throne, collected people from the surrounding country, and going towards the north-west,

A.D. 573. selected a site whereon to build a city. The sacred or classic name given to the city was Hansâwadi, from a legend of sacred geese, or, indeed, of the great teacher himself in that birth-form, having lived on the spot when it was a sandbank just appearing above the sea. The common name of the city was Bago or Pegu, which was never changed; but at a later period the country of the delta was called Ramanya, from an inclination to Hinduism which appeared in after times. In the Rajawanso of Ceylon the name is rendered Arramana.

Two brothers the founders.

As in other instances in Indo-Chinese history, two brothers are represented as sharing in the foundation of the city. The original city was probably a short distance to the east of that included within the present rampart, which was only constructed in the sixteenth century. Thamala, the elder brother, reigned first. After twelve years he was killed by the younger, Wimala, who then became king. After his death the son of Thamala succeeded to the throne, with the title of Kâtha Kummâ. This monarchy gradually established its power over the whole delta and eastward to the Salwin river.[1] The Burmese kingdom of Tharêkhettarâ (Prome) was probably overthrown by the Talaings of Thahtun long before Pegu was founded. There is no distinct record of this in Burmese history; it may have been mentioned in the ancient Talaing chronicles, but they were carefully destroyed by the conquerors of Pegu. After the building of the new city the descendants of the ancient kings appear to have remained unmolested in Thahtun, but no mention is made of the extent of country over which they ruled. Probably their territory was little more than the boundary of the city wall. But from the destruction of the

[1] The names Wimala and Thamala may be traced in the lists of Chalukya kings and the kings of Vijayanaga. There is an obvious resemblance in this story to that of the two brothers who first reigned at Prome.

ancient books, and from the loss of independence having crushed the spirit of the people, it appears now impossible to trace events in Talaing history during several centuries. This difficulty has been felt by every inquirer into the history of Pegu.[1]

List of the kings of Pegu imperfect.

In the appendix to this volume will be found a list of the first dynasty of the kings of Pegu as entered in the Talaing chronicles. But that dynasty extends only to the year A.D. 781, when the reign of king Titha or Tissa came to a close. From that time until the conquest of Pegu by Anoarahtâ, that is, for about two hundred and sixty-nine years, no events are recorded in the Talaing annals. The conquest by the king of Pugân is not to be found therein. From indications in the Talaing annals as to the reigns of King Tissa and his predecessor, it appears probable that for a long period the country was disturbed by religious struggles, Brahmanical and Buddhist votaries contending for the mastery. Later chronicles have been unwilling to refer to the troubles and degradation of their country caused by heretical disturbance and foreign rule, so that the course of events can only be conjectured. Coins or medals bearing Hindu symbols which have been found, and which no doubt were struck in Pegu, probably belong to this period, and lend support to the conclusion as to events which the native chroniclers have obscured or suppressed.[2] Excepting a few vague sentences, no notice is taken in the Talaing chronicles of the conquest by Anoarahtâ. Thus the native annals of Pegu, from the period when pure Buddhism was for a time restored under King Tissa,

Struggle between Brahmanists and Buddhists.

[1] See Essay on the Pegu Pagoda, by Captain H. A. Browne, Journal Asiatic Soc. of Bengal, No. 2, for 1867.

[2] Indications of similar alternations in the prevalence of religious systems having happened in Arakan may be traced in the chronicles of that country. The hints given in the chronicles are also supported by coins.

until the fall of the Pugân monarchy, near the close of the thirteenth century, a period of about 500 years, are almost a blank.

Note on supposed reference to Pegu by Hiouen Thsang.

The Chinese pilgrim of the seventh century, when at Samatata, which is identified with the delta of the Ganges, or more especially Eastern Bengal, mentions the names of countries to the east of that region. The first country is said to be to the north-east, and the name has, from the Chinese characters or syllables, been transliterated into Çrichatra, and applied to Silhet. If, however, we might be allowed to conjecture, that for north-east from Samatata south-east was intended, then Çrichatra, the exact name of Srikhetra, or the ancient city of Burmese history, near Prome, will fulfil the conditions of the text. And the road to it by land from Eastern Bengal, first along the sea-coast and then over mountains into the valley of the Irâwadi, exactly corresponds with the travelling directions given by the Chinese pilgrim.

The next place mentioned beyond to the south-east is the kingdom of Kamalanka. If it were possible here to suppose that *k* has been written or misprinted in Europe for an *r*, in that case Ramalanka would apply to the delta of the Irâwadi, which was known as Râmanya at the time the pilgrim was in India. In fact, the name of Râma has been applied to several places on the Burmese coast, —the island of Râmree, for instance, and Râmāpura, the classic name for Moulmein. There was also Râmanagar, not far from Rangoon. Further east, the pilgrim states, is the kingdom of Tolopoti. This is rendered Dwarawati by M. Julien. Dwarawati is the classic name of the town and district of Sandoway in Southern Arakan ; but in Burmese history it is applied to more than one country, and, among others, to Siam. In the instance now in question, Siam would agree with the direction indicated by the Chinese pilgrim, from Samatata to Srikhetra, thence to Ramalanka or Pegu, and thence east to Dwarawati or Siam. Beyond that, still east, Tsanapura is not recognisable ; but still farther east, Mahâchampa, mentioned by the pilgrim, represents, beyond doubt, the ancient kingdom of Cambodia. See paper by Mr. James Fergusson in "Journal of the Royal Asiatic Sociaty" vol. vi., N.S., 1873.

CHAPTER IV.

PUGAN MONARCHY—(Continued).

Religious reform by Anoarahtâ—Invades Pegu and captures Thahtun—Capture of Hansawadi not mentioned—Anoarahtâ marches to China—Search for a relic at Tharêkhettarâ—Extension of Burmese dominion on west and north—Son of Anoarahtâ succeeds—An Indian prince comes to Pugân—Buddhist temple—Anânda built—Reign of Alaungsithû—King murdered.

Religious reforms by Anoarahtâ.

ANOARAHTÂ had a deep dislike to the Nâga or dragon-worship which prevailed in his country. The priests of this religion, who were called Arî, lived in monasteries like Buddhist monks, but their practices resembled those attributed to the votaries of the sect of Vâmâchâris in Bengal. There is no information in the Burmese chronicles regarding the introduction of this worship, which led to the wicked deeds of which the Arî priests are accused. Nâga-worship had in earlier times prevailed in Northern India. The Chinese pilgrim Fa Hian found that offerings were made to a dragon at Samkassa, in recognition of his supposed beneficence in causing gentle showers to fall upon the fields.[1] In after times, in the sixth century, as pure doctrine died away, the Tantra system—a mixture of magic and witchcraft and Siva-worship—was in the Punjab incorporated into the corrupted Buddhism.[2] From some external influence which has not been explained, a similar change happened in Burma. The system excited the indignation and the horror of Anoarahtâ. He

[1] Fa Hian, chap. xvii.
[2] Buddhism, by T. W. Rhys Davids, p. 208.

yearned for a full revelation of the true doctrine, which he knew only by imperfect report. At length a great teacher, called in the Mahâ Râjâweng, Arahân, who had attained the blessed state of a Rahânda or Arahât, arrived at the Burmese capital. He had come from Thahtun. Having heard of the absence of all true religion in Pugân, he came there with the sincere zeal of a missionary. He was invited to appear before the king, to whom he preached the law of Buddha. Anoarahtâ was at once converted. The false Arîs were expelled from their monasteries and stripped of their robes; ordained orthodox Rahâns were invited from Thahtun, and true religion was established.

The king invades Pegu and captures the city of Thahtun.

The king now desired to possess the Buddhist Scriptures, the Tripitaka. He knew that those precious volumes existed at Thahtun. He sent an ambassador of high rank to Manuha, the king of that city, to ask for a copy of the holy books. The king answered haughtily that he would give nothing. Anoarahtâ, with a sudden fierceness altogether opposed to the spirit of the religion which he had embraced, determined to punish what he deemed an affront. He collected a large army and went down the Irâwadi. The king of Thahtun had no means of meeting the invader in the field, but the city was well defended by a wall. After a long siege the citizens were reduced by famine and the city was surrendered. King Manuha, his wives and children, were carried away captive to Pugân. The city was utterly destroyed. Nobles and artificers, holy relics and sacred books, golden images and treasures of all kinds were carried off; and from that time the country of Pegu became for more than two centuries subject to Burma. As a fit sequence to such a war, the unhappy Manuha, his whole family, and the high-born captives were thrust down to the lowest depth of woe by being made pagoda slaves.

Although in the Burmese chronicles the conquest of

Thahtun and of the country of Pegu are fully described, nothing is said of the occupation of the city of Hansâwadi, the later capital. It has already been mentioned that this event is not directly narrated in the fragmentary Talaing chronicle now existing. All that is said of the conquest is contained in a few brief sentences of lamentation for the fall of the kingdom to hateful foreigners. There appears only one probable explanation of the omission in the Burmese history of the capture of the city of Pegu. The high destinies of the city had, according to legends which were believed to be divinely inspired truths, been foretold by Goadama himself; and miraculous events at the first building of the city were believed to have foreshadowed its permanent immunity from conquest and the rule of foreigners. The authors of the Burmese chronicle appear to have shrunk from deliberately setting forth events, which falsified a prediction, the authenticity of which they were not prepared to deny; and while silent as to the fate of the city of Pegu, they apparently settled down to the belief that, having been founded by a colony from Thahtun, its fortunes were to be counted as being included in those of the mother city, and that no special mention of its fall was required.

Capture of Hansâwadi not mentioned in Burmese history.

Anoarahtâ, prompted no less by ambition than by religious zeal, not satisfied with the relics which he had obtained in Thahtûn, desired to possess the holy tooth said to be preserved in China.[1] He marched with an army, as an escort of honour, to that country, or to a province of it called Gandalarît. That name, which in Indian Buddhist works is given to the district round the modern Peshawar, is in the Burmese chronicle applied to a part of Yunnân. The Emperor of China

Anoarahtâ marches to China.

[1] A tooth of Buddha, it is stated in Chinese annals, was brought to China in A.D. 530 by a Persian ambassador. A supposed tooth of Buddha is now shown in a monastery at Fuchau. See note in Yule's Marco Polo, vol. ii. p. 266.

at first took no notice of the king. At length they had a friendly meeting. Anoarahtâ failed to obtain the relic he sought, but brought away a golden image which had been sanctified by direct contact with the holy tooth. About this time the state of affairs in Yunnân admitted of a visit being made by the Burmese king to the local ruler. In A.D. 861, the prince of Nanchao or Yunnân cast off his allegiance to the Emperor of China. The Tang dynasty was too weak to subdue the rebel, and it was only under the Sung dynasty that the empire was reunited. But the Emperor Jintsong, who died A.D. 1063, had not apparently even then established effective authority in Yunnân, and it was in his reign that Anoarahtâ went to Yunnân.[1] On his return to his own kingdom, while passing through the Shân state of Moa, he married the daughter of the chief; and the romantic events which led to the marriage, together with the trials through which the bride passed, and her final triumph over the plots of jealous rivals, are represented in a drama which is one of the most popular on the Burmese stage. But one incident of this progress brought trouble to Anoarahtâ's successor in long after years. Some presents of golden vessels which he made to the Emperor were received as tribute offerings to his superior, and were made the ground of demand for similar gifts by the Mongolian conqueror Kublaikhan.

Search for a relic at Tharêkhettarâ.

Disappointed in his search for a relic in China, Anoarahtâ sought for one elsewhere. There was at this time a general belief that a forehead bone relic of Buddha was enshrined in a pagoda built at Tharêkhettarâ by King Dwuttabaung. Anoarahtâ caused the pagoda to be pulled down, and intended that the relic should be deposited in the Shwézîgun pagoda which was building at Pugân. It is however stated that, either in consequence of the sin he had committed in

[1] Boulger's China, vol. i. pp. 329, 397.

destroying the original pagoda, or from some other hidden cause, the holy relic disappeared. He then sent to Ceylon to endeavour to obtain the famous tooth-relic enshrined there; but he was forced to be contented with what is represented as a miraculous emanation or mysterious growth of homogeneous substance from the holy tooth. This representative of the original was brought with great ceremony to Pugân, and was deposited in a suitable building at the gate of the palace.[1]

Extension of Burmese dominion west and north.

Anoarahtâ is said to have made a progress through the western portion of his dominions as far as Bengal. The Arakanese chronicle relates that he invaded that country, and he no doubt exacted from the king a promise of tribute. But it does not appear that payment was long made. Nearer home his power was more firmly established. The Shân dominion in the north, which had endured for several centuries, and which is called in the chronicle preserved in Manipûr, the kingdom of Pong, was broken by the conquests of Anoarahtâ. Individual states of Shân chiefs in the Upper Irâwadi, still retained independent power; but from this time those to the south of Bamoa, were more or less subordinate to the Burmese monarchy. In the country north of Bamoa there were several Shân chiefs, among whom there was a frequent change of relative rank and power, according to their own development, and the strength or weakness of each sovereign of Burma.

The reign of Anoarahtâ came to an end about the middle of the eleventh century. Different copies of Burmese chronicles are not in accord as to the date when he ascended the throne. The difference may have arisen from his becoming king during the lifetime of his father, a solitary instance of such supersession in Burmese history. He is the great hero of the Burmese people. A.D. 1052.

Son of Anoarahtâ succeeds.

Anoarahtâ was succeeded by his son Soalú. He appointed his foster-brother, Nga Ramân Khân, gover-

[1] A somewhat similar mission to Ceylon, with a like result, occurred about twenty years ago.

nor of Pegu. The governor not only ungratefully rebelled against his king and benefactor, but marched with an army against Pugân. Soalú was killed in battle, but his brother Kyansitthâ, who succeeded to the throne, defeated and killed the rebel.

An Indian prince comes to Pugân.

The mother of Kyansitthâ was said to have been a daughter of the king of Vaisali in Tirhût. Not long after Kyansitthâ came to the throne, there appeared at Pugân an Indian prince, who is styled in the Mahâ Râjâweng the son of the king of Palikkarâ.[1] The prince desired to marry the daughter of Kyansitthâ, but by the advice of the nobles this alliance was publicly disallowed, lest the country should become *kulâ* or foreign. But a strange story is told as the sequel of this adventure. The Indian prince from chagrin committed suicide. The daughter of Kyansitthâ, whom he had desired to marry, gave birth to a son, and notwithstanding the refusal to celebrate the proposed marriage, the king caused the child to be consecrated by the ceremony of *bithêka,* as if he were to be forthwith acknowledged as king. It is related in the history of Ceylon,[2] that Buddhism had entirely decayed in that island during the Malabar domination, and that when the kingdom was recovered by Wijayo Bahu, in A.D. 1071, there were not to be found in the whole island five of the superior order of Rahâns called "tirunansis." An embassy was therefore sent to Arramana, as Pegu is called in the Mahâwanso. This was in the reign of Kyansitthâ, but no mention is made of this embassy in the Burmese chronicle. There is, however, architec-

[1] This word as used in the Burmese history may represent the title of a king or the name of a country. In either case it refers to a part of Bengal where Buddha was worshipped. Whether the word has any connection with the Balharâ of the Arab voyagers, or with the Pâla kings who still reigned in Bengal in the eleventh century, is uncertain. See Dr. Râjendra Lâla Mitra on Pâla Râjâs, Journal A.S. of Bengal, vol. xlvii., N.S., p. 384.

[2] See Emerson Tennent's Ceylon, vol. i. p. 406. Burma has preserved books which were lost in Ceylon. Rhys Davids, in his paper on Ceylon coins, observes: "All the Ceylon MSS. of the Dipavansa are derived, mediately or immediately, from Burma."

tural and sculptural evidence at Pugân, of communication with Southern India, if not with Ceylon. The magnificent temple Anânda was built by this king. Though the earliest of the great temples which still exist amidst the ruined city, it is, as observed by Colonel Yule, in some respects the most remarkable.[1] They all suggest, but this perhaps above them all suggests, strange memories of the churches of southern Catholic Europe. The ground-plan is a perfect Greek cross. Along the massive walls of the dim and lofty vaulted corridors, disposed in niches, are sculptured groups of figures on stone slabs, illustrating events in the life of Goadama Buddha. These figures tell of a sculptor from Southern India, especially by the arrangement and ornaments of the hair in the female figures. Of the four great temples at Pugân, Colonel Yule remarks that there is in them an actual sublimity of architectural effect which excites wonder, almost awe. There is no trace as to the source from whence the designs for these temples were derived. Much of their ornamental detail has been found in buildings on the continent of India and in Ceylon. No timber is used in any part of them. Mr. James Fergusson remarks on the almost universal use in them of the pointed arch, not only in the openings, but in the vaulted coverings of the passages, and finds that in no other country of Asia, from the Euphrates to the Ganges, is the existence of such form, in buildings of the period to which they belong, to be met with.

Buddhist temple Anânda built.

Kyansitthâ was succeeded by his grandson, who took the title of Alaungsîthu. Early in his reign he built the Shwèku temple at Pugân. He visited the western province of his dominions, travelling through Arakan to the adjoining part of Bengal. He made many improvements in the administration of the law, and he regulated weights and measures. During the reign of his grand-

Reign of Alaungsîthu, A.D. 1085

[1] See Yule's Embassy to Ava, pp. 36, 39, for a detailed description of this temple.

father, the heir to Meng Bilû, the king of Arakan, named Mengré Báya, whose father had been killed by a rebel, came to Pugân as a refugee. He lived there for many years, and dying, left a son, who is called in the chronicles Letyâmengnân. Alaungsîthu, yielding to the entreaties of this prince, determined to establish him in the kingdom of his ancestors. The prince marched with a large army, which, in the boastful words of an old Burmese ballad, numbered one hundred thousand Pyûs and one hundred thousand Talaings. The expedition met with no opposition, and the prince was placed on the throne, according to the Arakanese chronicle, in A.D. 1103.[1] Alaungsîthu caused the Buddhist temple at Gayâ to be repaired. He maintained communication with the Palikkarâ king whose daughter he married. When he became old he was much troubled by the disobedience of his sons. His eldest son, Maung Sheng Soa, was sent to govern the country of the Upper Irâwadi. He settled near the spot where the city of Amarapúra was afterwards built, and first commenced the excavation and embankment of the great lake now called Aungpenglè. The king's second son remained at the capital. Impatient to gain the throne, he hesitated not to accomplish his object by parricide. The aged king was carried to the temple he had built, and there was smothered under a heap of cloth. He reigned for seventy-five years.

King murdered, A.D. 1160.

At this period, when Arakan had been brought into close connection with the Pugân monarchy, the early history of that country as told by its own chroniclers will be related.

[1] A stone inscription in the Burmese language exists at Buddha Gayâ, of which a facsimile is given in vol. xx. of the "Asiatic Researches." It records frequent reparations of the temple at that place, and also that by Letyâmengnân, who is called therein Pyútathinmeng. The figures which form the date assigned to that reparation are rather uncertain, but in all probability represent 467 = A.D. 1105. The inscription itself was carved in 668 = A.D. 1306, and recapitulates the several reparations to the temple in former years.

CHAPTER V.

ARAKAN.

Native name Rakhaing—Arakanese tradition of the early kings—Arrival of Kân Râjâgyî from the country of the Irâwadi—Buddhism predominant until the eighth century—Chandra dynasty—Invasion by the Shân—Arakan tributary to the king of Pugân—Burmese inscription at Gayâ.

Native name Rakhaing.

THE country known in Europe as Arakan extends for 350 miles along the eastern shore of the bay of Bengal. It is called by the natives Rakhaingpyî, or land of the Rakhaing. The same word in the Pali form, Yakkho, and also Raksha, is applied to beings, some good and some bad, who have their abode on Mount Meru, and are guards round the mansion of Sekra or Indra. It was given to the aborigines of Ceylon by their Buddhist conquerors.[1] The term appears to be applied by Indian Aryans to people of Dravidian and Mongolian race before conversion to Buddhism. Among the Arakanese of the present time, the word means a monster of the ogre sort, in the vernacular Bîlu, which, it has already been seen, is applied in the history of Pegu to the wild inhabitants of the country while still unconverted. The people of Arakan have not been ashamed to retain the name for themselves as dwellers in Rakhaing-land, but they claim to be by descent Mrâmmâ, and the elder branch of that family. They no doubt are descendants from

1 Emerson Tennent's Ceylon, vol. i. p. 331; Hardy's Manual of Buddhism, pp. 44, 47, 56.

ancestors belonging to Mongoloid tribes, closely akin to those from whom sprung the Burmese of the Upper Irâwadi. Their language is the same, with a few dialectical differences, though the pronunciation as spoken frequently renders it unintelligible to a modern Burmese.

In an interesting paper on the oldest records of the sea-route to China from Western Asia by Colonel Yule,[1] that author identifies the country named Argyrê in Ptolemy with Arakan, the name being supposed to be derived from silver mines existing there. This name may be a corruption of the native name Rakhaing, from which the modern European form, Arakan, is derived. The word Rakhaing for the country is undoubtedly ancient, and would have been heard by the voyagers from whom Ptolemy derived his information. There is no tradition or record of silver having ever been found in Arakan. In the neighbourhood of Martaban and Maulmein argentiferous galena ore is plentiful. In some spots the yield of silver has been nineteen ounces of silver per ton of lead.[2]

Arakanese tradition of the early kings.

The chronicles of Arakan open with describing the emergence of the world from the water of a deluge, and the appearance thereon of the beings who were the progenitors of the human race. The first kings reigned in Banâras, and to a son of one of these kings Arakan was allotted. He reigned in a city called Râmawati, supposed to be near the present town of Sandoway, though that was afterwards the classic name of the island now known as Rambyi, corrupted by Indians and Europeans to Ramrî. This position assigned to the first capital supports the native tradition of the Kânrân tribe having migrated from the country of the Irâwadi to the southern part of Arakan,[3] though

[1] Proceedings of the Royal Geographical Society for November 1882.

[2] See Theobald's geological report, quoted in Gazetteer of British Burmah, vol. i. p. 64.

[3] See chapter i.

the story of a king coming from Banâras is a fiction invented to connect the rulers of Arakan with the kings of that famous city. In after ages Sandoway fell to ten brothers, who because of their tyranny were expelled by the people and killed. Their sister survived, and went north to the country of Arakan proper with a Brahman, to whom she was married. The Brahman became king of Arakan; but it was not from this pair that the Arakanese chroniclers chose to derive the royal race which they still reverence as their ancient kings. A strange legend tells how a wild doe in the forest brought forth a human child in the country of the upper Kuladân, the principal river of northern Arakan. A chief of the Mro or Mrú tribe, a remnant of which still exists, was out hunting; he found the new-born boy, and carried him home. The boy was brought up among the Mrú tribe, and is called Mârayo, a name which has probably been formed by the chroniclers from Mâramâ, the Arakanese form of Mrâmmâ, and *yo* or *aro*—race. When grown up he married a daughter of the Mrú chief, and eventually became king of Arakan. He then married a female descendant of the Brahman king, and built the capital city called Dhinyawâti, which became the classic name of the country. The whole legend may be accepted as the expression of the traditions of kinship between the Arakanese and the Mongoloid tribes who still dwell in the hills on the borders; and as a rude expression of connection with the princes of the Indian dynasty who settled in the Upper Irâwadi, though there is a confusion in the chronology of one legend with the other.

Arrival of Kan Râjâgyî from the country of the Irâwadi.

The time when Mârayo became king is by the Arakanese chroniclers placed at an extravagantly remote era—2666 B.C. The dynasty he founded is represented as having lasted for eighteen hundred and thirty-three years. A rebellion then broke out, and the queen of the last king retired to a mountain with her two daughters. About this time Kân Râjâgyî, a Kshatriya, who had been obliged to relinquish the kingdom of Tagaung to his younger brother,[1] arrived in Northern Arakan, and established himself with his followers on the high mountain called Kyaukpândaung. The queen of the last king of the Mârayo dynasty joined him there, and he married her two daughters. The summit of Kyaukpândaung is a gently undulating plateau several miles in extent. Though in the midst of a mountain region inhabited by rude tribes, recent exploration has discovered traces that it was once occupied by a civilised race. Palm and other trees, which are not natural products of the surrounding jangal, are found there. The remains of pagodas also exist, and these, though comparatively modern, with the other evidences of former habitation in this secluded spot, give support to the belief of its having been the resting-place of the race which at a remote period gave kings to Arakan. After some years Kân Râjâgyî left the mountain and occupied the capital city in the lowlands, supposed to be on the site of the city now known as "Rakhaingmyu." The Arakanese chroniclers relate that sixty-two kings of the race of Kân Râjâgyî reigned in succession throughout seventeen hundred and eighty-two years. It is impossible, during this long period, to discern in the chronicles any event which may be accepted as historical. In the year A.D. 146 a king called Chanda-Surya succeeded to the throne. In his reign a metal image of Buddha was cast, and so famous did it become, that miraculous powers were attributed to it for ages afterwards. This image was carried away by the Burmese when they conquered Arakan in A.D. 1784. It is now in a temple to the north of Amarapura, and is an object of fervent devotion. It is probable that in the

[1] See chapter i. for the story as told in the Mahâ Râjâweng of Burma.

reign of Chanda-Surya, Buddhism was more distinctly established than heretofore, and images of Buddha may then have been introduced for the first time.

As far as can be gathered from the Arakanese chronicles, the Buddhist religion remained predominant in the country until the eighth century of the Christian era. A revolution then occurred during the reign of the fifty-third king in lineal descent from Kân Râjâgyî. The tumult which arose is explained as resulting from the mysterious decay of the fortune, or good influence, of the ancient capital. The astrologers declared that a change of site was necessary. The king, Mahâ Taing Chândra, therefore left his palace, the whole of the people following, and settled at a place where a new capital, called Wethâli, after the city of Vaisali in Tirhût, was built. At that city nine kings reigned in succession bearing the surname of Chândra. Their reigns lasted for one hundred and sixty-nine years. From coins still existing, and which are attributed to the kings of this dynasty, coupled with obscure references to their acts in the chronicles of Arakan, it appears probable that they held Brahmanical doctrines. No clue is given in the chronicles as to where these kings came from. They appear to have been foreigners, and it is possible that they were connected with the dynasty which reigned in Eastern Bengal known as the Sena Rajâs, and that the period of their rule in Arakan has been antedated.[1]

Buddhism predominant until the eighth century.

Chândra dynasty.

A.D. 788 to A.D. 957.

This dynasty was succeeded, or rather temporarily displaced, by a chief of the Mro tribe, whose reign, with that of his nephew, lasted for thirty-six years. A descendant of the Chândra dynasty then came to the throne, and a new site was occupied for the capital; but from the troubles which soon after arose it was abandoned.

[1] See paper by Dr. Rajendra Lâla Mitra in the Journal of the Asiatic Society of Bengal, vol. xlvii. p. 384.

Invasion by the Shâns.

The Shans from the Upper Irâwadi now invaded Arakan, and occupied it for eighteen years. They behaved like cruel conquerors, robbed the people, and plundered the temples of the valuable offerings therein. When they retired, Anoarahtâ, the great king of Pugân, invaded the country, desiring to obtain the famous image of Buddha. By divine interposition, the Arakanese chronicle remarks, he was persuaded to retire without carrying away what was regarded as the protector of the kingdom.[1] A few years later a descendant of the Chândra dynasty was, with the assistance of Anoarahtâ, placed on the throne. The capital was established at Pingtsâ, and Arakan became tributary to the king of Pugân. It remained so for sixty years, when the reigning king, Meng Bilu, was killed by a noble who usurped the throne. The heir-apparent, Mengrêbaya, fled with his wife to Pugân, where he was received by King Kyansitthâ. For twenty-five years the royal family remained in exile. Mengrêbaya had a son born to him, known in history as Letyamengnân. The father having died, the reigning king of Pugân, Alaungsîthu, determined to place the son on the throne of Arakan. According to popular tradition handed down in song, an army of 100,000 Pyûs and 100,000 Talaing was sent by sea and land to Arakan at the close of the rainy season. The usurper offered a stout resistance, and it was not until the following year that the restoration was effected. An inscription in the Burmese language on a stone slab exists at Buddha Gayá, in which is recorded the repairment of the temple there by Letyâmengnân (who is styled "The lord of one hundred thousand Pyûs"), in fulfilment of his engagement to the king of Pugân.[2] This engagement

Arakan tributary to king of Pugân.

A.D. 1102.

Burmese inscription at Gayá.

[1] In the Arakanese history this invasion is placed in the year A.D. 995. In some copies of the Burmese Mahâ Râjâweng, the year of Anoarahtâ's accession to the throne is placed fifteen years later than that date.

[2] See Asiatic Researches, vol. xx. Also Buddha Gaya, by Rajendra Lâla Mitra, LL.D., p. 208.

is not recorded in the chronicles either of Burma or of Arakan, and is only known from the inscription; but the facts related in the chronicles are evidently implied in the terms of the inscription.

Coin with Hindu symbols, struck in Arakan about the eighth century A.D.

Note on the name Mag or Maga applied to the Arakanese by the people of Bengal.

The Rakhaing people of Mongoloid race do not know this term. It is given to them by the people of Bengal, and also to a class of people now found mostly in the district of Chittagong, who call themselves Râjbansi. The latter claim to be of the same race as one dynasty of the kings of Arakan, and hence the name they have themselves assumed. They are Buddhists in religion; their language now is Bengali of the Chittagong dialect; and they have a distinctive physiognomy, but it is not Mongolian. Their number in the Chittagong district, by the census of 1870–71, was 10,852 (Hunter's "Bengal," vol. vi. p. 250). A few are found in the district of Akyab. I was formerly of opinion that these people were a mixed race, the descendants of Arakanese, who, when their kings held Chittagong during the seventeenth century, had married Bengali wives. Further inquiry and consideration have led me to a different conclusion. I now think it most probable that the self-styled Râjbansi descend from immigrants into Arakan from Mâgada, and that the name given to them by the people of Bengal correctly designates their race or the country from which they came. It is very probable that one of the foreign dynasties of Arakan came from Southern Bihar, though, from modern jealousy of foreigners, the fact has been concealed by Arakanese chroniclers. The former existence in Southern Bihar of princes having the race name of Maga is an undoubted fact. The researches of Dr. Francis Buchanan, and later inquiries instituted by Dr. W. W. Hunter, show that the kings of Magada reigned at Râjâgriha in the modern district of Patna. They were Buddhists, and that a dynasty of this race reigned in Arakan may be considered to be true. The name Râjbansi has no doubt been adopted by the remnant of the tribe in later times, from a desire to assert their importance as belonging to the same race as the kings of Arakan. This term has been adopted in the district of Rangpur by the Chandalâs and other low castes, who had not the reasonable claim to it possessed by the class now under consideration. The name Maga having been extended to the whole of the Arakanese people, who are Mongoloid in race, is an ethnological error which has caused confusion among European writers upon this subject. But this error does not extinguish the fact of people descended from an Aryan race called Maga, who migrated from Bihar, being still in existence in Arakan and the adjoining district of Chittagaon. (See "Eastern India," by Montgomery Martin, from the papers of Francis Buchanan, vol. i. pp. 22 to 29; vol. ii. pp. 18, 114, &c. Also Hunter's "Statistical Account of Bengal," vol. xi. pp. 41, 79.)

CHAPTER VI.

PUGAN MONARCHY—(to its end).

Narathu succeeds to the throne—His cruelty—Builds a great temple —Killed by foreigners—King Narabadisîthu—Builds temples—King of Ceylon invades Pegu—Boadi temple built—Tarûkpyé-meng builds a costly pagoda—Rebellion in Martaban—Mongol armies in China—Mongol emperor demands tribute from Burma —Burmese army defeated—Mongol army occupies Pugân—Kyo-aswâ, last king of the Pugân dynasty.

ON the death of Alaungsîthu, his younger son, Narathu, at once took possession of the palace. The elder son, Meng Shengsoa, came down the river from the seat of his government to assert his right to the throne. Unsuspicious of treachery, he reached Pugân with only one boat and a few attendants. He was met at the landing-place by his brother, who behaved with due deference and escorted him to the palace with great ceremony. At once he was consecrated king, but that night was poisoned. Narathu then became king without opposition. He put to death many of his father's old servants and favourites. He commenced a magnificent temple known as Damayangyî, but from the difficulty of procuring labourers caused by the severity with which the work was pushed on, the building proceeded slowly. The most notorious of this king's crimes was the murder of his father's widow, the daughter of the king of Palikkarâ, whom he slew with his own hand. This led to a strange event. The father of the princess, on hearing of the murder of his daughter, disguised eight soldiers as brahmans, who

Narathu succeeds to the throne.

His cruelty.

Builds a great temple.

were sworn to revenge the crime. They arrived at Pugân, and were introduced into the palace under pretence of blessing the king. They killed him with a sword; after which they either killed each other or Killed by foreigners. committed suicide, so that all died in the palace. This king is known to this day as "Kulâ Kyâ Meng," or the king killed by foreigners.

He was succeeded by his son, who after three years was put to death by his brother. The latter then King Narabadisîthu; builds temples. became king with the title of Narabadisîthu. He built the temples called Goadoapaleng and Tsulamani. There was constant communication with Ceylon, from whence came four great Rahân, who introduced some new philosophical or religious doctrines, but no change in worship was made. This king's reign lasted thirty-A.D. 1204. seven years.

King of Ceylon invades Pegu. It is probable that during his reign events occurred which are recorded in the Mahâwansa of Ceylon, but of which no mention is made in the annals of Burma.[1] It is there stated that Parakrâma, the king of Ceylon, was at peace with the king of Râmânya or Pegu, which country was then subject to the king of Burma or Pugân. At that time it was the custom for the king of Ceylon to maintain an agent or so-called ambassador in Pegu, whose expenses were provided by the king of that country. Such indeed is the Burmese practice at the present day as regards the representatives of foreign powers. The king of Burma however discontinued the usual payments and stopped some Sinhalese messengers who were going to Kamboja, seized their ships, and committed other offensive acts towards subjects of the king of Ceylon. Parakrâma, a great warrior, determined to avenge these insults. He sent an army, which landed at one of the ports called Ukkâka, probably Ukkalaba, an

1 See paper on the conquests in the twelfth century by Parakrâma Bâhu, king of Ceylon, by Mr. T. W. Rhys Davids, Journal of Asiatic Society of Bengal, vol. xli., N.S., p. 197.

ancient city near the present town of Twantè, and took prisoner the governor of Pegu. Submission was now made, and tribute of elephants was promised. The importance of this affair has probably been exaggerated in the Sinhalese history, but it cannot be altogether an invention, and the silence of the Burmese history suggests that the incident was one not creditable to the Burmese king.

Boadi temple built.

Narabadisîthu was succeeded by his son Zeyathinhka, of whom nothing is recorded worthy of remark except that he built the temple at Pugân called Boadi, which was intended to be a copy of that at Buddha Gayâ. This was the last of the great temples built at Pugân. All the great religious buildings, which amidst a deserted city attract the traveller, were erected between the years A.D. 1057 and 1227. The reign of Zeyathinhka came to an end in the latter year.

Tarukpyèmeng builds a costly pagoda. A.D. 1248.

The time had now come when danger began to gather round the Pugân monarchy. The king, who, from the disaster that befell him, is called Tarukpyèmeng—the king who fled from the Taruk—lived in greater luxury than any of his predecessors. He commenced building a pagoda, costly in barbaric splendour, but wanting in the architectural grandeur of the temples built by his ancestors. After a time the work was stopped, as a saying went abroad among the people, "The pagoda is finished and the country ruined." But again the labour proceeded, and the building was completed. The relic-chamber, into which pious Buddhists delight to pour their choicest treasures, was filled with golden vessels. There were models in pure gold of the seven holy stations first occupied by Goadama after he had attained the position of Buddha; golden images of the previous Buddhas and holy personages; of all the kings of Pugân; and of the builder himself, his wives and children.[1] But according to the

A.D. 1274.

[1] In Marco Polo there is mention of a "tower" of gold at the city of Mien (undoubtedly Pugân), which probably refers to this pa-

Burmese history, these good works could not avert his fate. Evil deeds, whether in this life or in previous existence, determined his doom. Early in his reign an insurrection had occurred in the province of Martaban. A more serious revolt broke out later, when the Burmese governor, Alimmâ, was killed, and Wareru, a Shân by race, proclaimed himself king. The details of the events in Pegu will be told in a separate chapter. Amidst these disasters a still graver danger came from the north, and the great Mongol emperor of China sent an army against a kingdom already weakened by internal disorder.

Rebellion in Martaban, A.D. 1281.

Mongol armies in China.

Following out the plan of Jenghiz Khan, the Mongol armies had for thirty years been fighting to subdue the Chinese empire, then held by the Sung dynasty.[1] Kublai, the lieutenant of his brother Mangu, who reigned at Karakoram as great khan, had command of the Mongol armies in China. He determined, for reasons the advantages of which are not now apparent, first to conquer Yunnân, and in pursuance of that plan had to make a march from the province of Shensi, of more than a thousand miles across unsubdued country. He took most of the fortified towns in Yunnân, and then returned to Shensi, leaving Uriang Kadai in command. That general, according to Chinese history, turned his arms against Burma, and compelled recognition by the king of that country of the Mongol power. There is no mention in Burmese history of any collision on the Yunnân frontier at that time, and the character of the king, Tarûkpyêmeng, was not such as to render it probable that he would be the aggressor against a country more powerful than his own. It was not until

A.D. 1253-54.

A.D. 1255-56.

goda. Notwithstanding the statement of Marco as to the respect paid to such a building by the great Khan, it is probable that it was plundered during the invasion by the Mongols. See Yule's Marco Polo, vol. ii. chap. liv.

[1] See Boulger's History of China, vol. i., chaps. xxii., xxiii., and xxiv.; also Colonel Yule's Marco Polo, chaps. li. to liv., and notes.

more than twenty years later that the conquest of China was completed by Kublai Khan, who had then been proclaimed emperor; and it was three years after, according to Burmese history, that a demand was made, in the name of the Mongol emperor of China, for gold and silver vessels to be sent as tribute, on the ground that King Anoarahtâ had presented such tokens of homage. The ambassadors who made this demand were, according to Burmese history, insolent in their conduct, and the king, against the remonstrance of his ministers, had them put to death. The emperor of China assembled an army to punish this outrage. A Burmese army advanced towards the threatened frontier, and built as a support a stockade at a town called Ngatshaungyân, a position apparently to the south of Bamoa. The army then marched into the hill country by the course of the Tapeng river, where defence against attack from the eastward could be made with advantage. During three months the Burmese army resisted the invaders, in the hill country through which the Tapeng flows, but, overpowered by numbers, was forced to retreat. The Burmese then took up a position nearly a hundred miles to the south, opposite to the town of Malê, on the east bank of the Irâwadi. The Mongol army, having taken the stockade at Ngatshaungyân, pushed on in pursuit. A fierce battle was fought near Malê, when the Burmese were defeated, one of their generals was killed, and the army fled in disorder towards the capital.[1]

A.D. 1278.

Mongol emperor demands tribute from Burma.

Burmese army defeated.

At Pugân the inhabitants were in confusion and terror. The king abandoned the city, having made no adequate preparation for defence, and hurried with his whole court down the river to Bassein. There he had vessels ready to convey him to Ceylon. The Mongol army reached the city, and detachments were

Mongol army occupies Pugân, A.D. 1284.

[1] For the events of this campaign, as told by Chinese historians, see remarks in note at the end of this chapter.

sent about one hundred miles farther south, to a point on the east bank of the river known as Tarukmoa, or Turk point. The Mongol army, after plundering the capital, retired, as there was a difficulty in procuring supplies, and the immediate object of the expedition—to inflict punishment on the king for the murder of the ambassadors—had been attained. Some arrangement appears to have been made with a Burmese officer as to the future subordination of Burma to the Mongol emperor, but no details are recorded. The wretched king, after remaining five months at Bassein, set out on his return. The Burmese historian remarks with severity on the excessive luxury in which he lived amidst the desolation of his country. He reached Prome, where his son Thihathu was governor. The
A.D. 1285. prince forced his father to swallow poison.

Kyoaswâ, last king of the Pugân dynasty.

Tarukpyèmeng had several sons. Three of them, Uzanâ, Thihathu, and Kyoaswâ, disputed the succession. The last named, who was governor of Dâla in
A.D. 1286. Pegu, succeeded, and became king at Pugân. But the empire had fallen to pieces. The numerous Eastern Shân states which had been tributary, all Pegu except Bassein, and Arakan, became independent. Monyin and Mogaung, powerful Shân principalities to the north, were not claimed as being at this time part of the empire. Kyoaswâ, though only acknowledged as king in the territory around Pugân, maintained himself there for twelve years. During the reign of Tarukpyèmeng, men of Shân race had gradually risen to high distinction in the kingdom, and chiefs of that people were about to seize the supreme power.

Note on the Wars between Burma and China in the Reign of Kublai Khan.

In the account of the invasion of Burma by the Mongols I have followed the Burmese narrative respecting the field of the great battle, as being more consistent with the general events, in which both sides agree, and the topographical features of the country where the campaign occurred, than the statement on that point in Chinese history. According to the histories of both countries, there was only one great pitched battle, and both agree that victory therein lay with the Mongols. There is a discrepancy, amounting to about seven years, as to the date of the battle. The Burmese history may be in error to that extent.

The Chinese histories and Marco Polo place the scene of the great battle at Yung Chang, four days' march east of Momien, or Têng Yüeh Ting, which appears then to have been the frontier post of Burma. The battle and the preliminary movements are described in chapters li. and lii., book ii., of Marco Polo. It is there represented that the king of Burma, "a very puissant prince," hearing that the army of the great Khan was at Vochan (Yung Chang), determined in his ignorant truculence to read him a lesson.[1] He therefore advanced with an army of sixty thousand men, with numerous elephants and horses, but it was defeated with great slaughter by the Tartars under Nasruddîn on the "plain of Vochan." Marco Polo states that this battle occurred in A.D. 1272, but Colonel Yule considers that 1277 was more probably the date. The Burmese history represents the collision between the two sovereigns as happening some years later. It may be admitted that this battle cannot be directly connected with the operations mentioned as having occurred on the same frontier in 1255–56; and it must be considered as very improbable that the Burmese more than twenty years later would with reckless temerity have advanced so far from their own resources (which lay in the valley of the Irâwadi), across two large unbridged rivers, very difficult to cross, and through a continuous mountainous country, one range being more than eight thousand feet high, to attack an enemy whose power they had already been compelled to recognise.[2] Moreover, in 1277 Kublai Khan had nearly completed the conquest of China. He had assumed the title of emperor, and had given his dynasty the name of the Yuen in 1271. The Burmese could not at this time have been ignorant of the great power of the Mongol emperor, and were not likely to advance to a position of great danger and brave his wrath. Had they, however, marched on to

[1] In Boulger's History of China, vol. i. p. 567, it is stated that "the Burmese possessed an artillery force of sixteen guns. This is not mentioned in any Burmese history, and I am not aware on what authority the statement is made.

[2] See Boulger's History of China, vol. i. p. 505.

Yung Chang, there was no reason why the fact should have been omitted in their national history. That history states that the quarrel arose from a demand for tribute made by the Mongol emperor. Nothing is more likely to have occurred. Then the king, provoked by the insolence in his presence of the Mongol ambassadors—or messengers, as they are termed in Burma—put them to death. This is probable, as he considered himself secure by distance and difficult country. He would not have felt this had he been able to march to Yung Chang. The invasion followed as a matter of course, and the Burmese prudently remained on the defensive, but acknowledge they sustained an overwhelming defeat.

On the whole, I am of opinion that only one great battle was fought between the armies of the two peoples throughout the whole period of the operations by the Mongols on the Yunnân frontier against Burma, extending from A.D. 1255 until about 1284, and that the battle took place on a plain adjoining the Irâwadi. It is probable that in the account by Marco Polo and the Chinese historians there has been an error as to the locality of the engagement, arising from the fighting in the hill country of the Tapeng river, the upper course of one branch of which was close to the border of the *district* of Yung Chang.

It is worthy of remark that the Burmese history describes the Mongol army as consisting of two races: Tarūk (written Tarūp) and Taret. The first is probably Tūrk; the final letter, though written *p*, is pronounced as *k*. There were numbers of that race in the Mongol armies. Nusruddîn was probably a Tūrk. The word Tarūk is now applied by the Burmese to the Chinese generally. The Manchu are called Taret.

CHAPTER VII.

SHAN KINGS IN DIVIDED BURMA.

Three Shân brothers rise to power—King Kyoaswâ deposed—Mongolian army arrives to restore the king—Thihathu, the youngest of the Shân brothers, becomes king, and reigns at Pânyâ—Separate kingdom at Sagaing established—Pânyâ taken by the Shâns of Mogaung—A Mongol army takes Mogaung—Events in the Shân kingdom of Sagaing—Sagaing and Pânyâ both fall to Thadomengbyâ.

Three Shân brothers rise to power.

THE fall of the Pugân monarchy inevitably followed the Mongol invasion and the flight of the king from his capital. The weakness of the dynasty had long been manifest. Men of Shân race, who abounded in the country, had acquired great influence, and became powerful through royal favour. Early in the reign of Narathihapatè, the chief of the small Shân state of Binnahkâ died, leaving two sons. They quarrelled regarding their inheritance, and the younger, named Thinghkabo, fled to Burma. He settled at Myinsaing, a few miles to the south of Ava, where there was already a Shân population. Thinghkabo had three sons, Athenhkarâ, Râjâthengyân, and Thihathu, also a daughter, who was married to Prince Thihathu, the second son of the king. The three Shân brothers became wealthy and powerful. They were appointed governors of districts: the eldest to Myinsaing, the second to Mekhkarâ, and the youngest to Penglê. After the capture of Pugân by the Mongol army, although no mention of any convention between the two powers is mentioned, it is probable than the Shân brothers agreed with the general of the invading army as to the future subordination of Burma to the Chinese empire. Their position would enable them to make this arrangement.

King Kyoaswâ deposed.

Kyoaswâ, who reigned nominally at Pugân, had no power beyond the small district around the city. The three Shân brothers exercised sovereignty within their own original governments, and gradually extended their authority over the adjoining country. One of the wives of the late king, known as Queen Soa, an active and ambitious woman, longing for direct power, determined to get rid of Kyoaswâ. By her persuasion he went to the consecration of a monastery which the three Shân brothers had built at Myinsaing. He was there seized

A.D. 1298.

and forced to become a Buddhist monk. The queen-dowager then returned to Pugân, where she became supreme, though Soanhît, son of the deposed king, was still alive. He was content to live in the palace, and assumed a royal title, without interfering in government; but his younger brother, Meng Sheng Soa, was made governor of Tharetmyu, with the consent of the Shân brothers. He more closely connected himself with them by marrying their sister's daughter by her marriage with his brother Prince Thihathu, who had been accidentally killed while hunting elephants in Pegu.

Mongolian army arrives to restore the king.

The deposed king, Kyoaswâ, or his son, the titular king, made complaint to the emperor of China that he, his tributary, had been deposed. A Mongol army was sent to restore the rightful king. This army, the Bur-

A.D. 1300.

mese history states, arrived at Myinsaing to restore the king. The three Shân brothers, following the advice contained in the words of a song sung at a public entertainment, determined to end all disputes by putting the rightful king to death. They did so, and showing his head to the Mongolian general, said that no claimant to the throne remained. They then made him valuable presents. In return for the presents, the general allowed his army to dig a canal for irrigation, which was finished in one night, and then withdrew from the country. This curious story probably represents an historical fact as regards the appearance of a Mongolian force to restore the rightful king, and its retirement without effecting that object. But the date assigned in the Burmese history is no doubt much later than that of the event itself. Kublai Khan died in A.D. 1294, and the second expedition to Burma apparently occurred earlier, as Marco Polo, who left China two years before the emperor's death, probably alludes to this second dispatch of a Mongol army into Burma in his fifty-fourth chapter as the march of "gleemen and jugglers," with "a captain and a body of men-at-arms to help them." There was no fighting, and the affair was settled with the Mongolian general at an entertainment. The descendant of the ancient kings was not placed on the throne. The three Shân brothers ruled in the country of the Irâwadi over only a portion of the ancient monarchy. The whole of the Shân states to the north were independent. To the south their influence did not extend beyond Prome. The territory of Taungu was separated from the kingdom. The three brothers governed justly, and for several years the country had rest. The second brother having died, the two others quarrelled, and the younger, Thihathu, having poisoned the elder, succeeded to the sole power. He searched for a suitable site to build a city, and a few miles to the north of Myinsaing, in digging the foundation of a pagoda, a golden flower was found, and there the city was built and called Pânyâ.

Thihathu, the youngest of the Shân brothers, becomes king, and reigns at Pânyâ.

A.D. 1312.

Thihathu now adopted the style and title of the ancient kings of Pugân. He married a daughter of Tarûkpyêmeng's, who had been married to her half-brother, Kyoaswâ, and had a son named Usanâ. That son was declared to be Ainshemeng, or heir-apparent. But Thihathu had a son named Athenghkarâ by his first wife of Shân race, and the inevitable hatred be-

Separate kingdom at Sagaing established.

tween the adopted and the own son, soon broke forth. Both received provinces, in which they maintained large bodies of armed men, and king Thihathu exer-
A.D. 1315. cised no control over them. Athenghkarâ at length declared himself independent at Sagaing, and ruled over a large tract of country to the north, up to the border of Manipûr. The king, his father, did not interfere, and thus commenced the line of kings of Shân race, who reigned at Sagaing for forty-nine years.
A.D. 1322. King Thihathu died, and was succeeded at Pânyâ by his adopted son, Usanâ.

Pânyâ taken by the Shâns of Mogaung.

Thihathu had a son by his marriage with the daughter of Tarukpyèmeng. The child received the name of Kyoaswâ, and as he grew up, his descent, which made him representative of the old and the new dynasty, gave him great influence, which seemed likely to secure stability to the kingdom. Usanâ was little more than a nominal king, though he reigned for twenty years. He then abdicated and became a hermit. Kyoaswâ
A.D. 1342. ascended the throne, and assumed the title of Ngâsîsheng, as the supposed lord of five white elephants. This was an announcement of his superior title and claim by descent, to the ancient monarchy. But he failed in the attempt to reduce to his authority the kingdom established at Sagaing. He reigned only eight years, and then was succeeded by his son, who also was named Kyoaswâ. After a reign of nine years his brother Narathu came to the throne, in whose time the Mau Shâns from Muangkung, called by the Burmese
A.D. 1364. Mogaung, attacked and took Pânyâ, and carried away the king. A prince, called in the Burmese history Usanâ Byaung, was placed in the palace, but after three months the city was taken by a prince of uncertain lineage, styled Thadomengbyâ, who founded the city of Ava. The kingdom established at Pânyâ and Myinsaing thus came to an end, after having lasted sixty-six years.

During this period the dynasty established by Athenghkarâ at Sagaing had maintained itself with varying fortune; but before describing events in that state, mention must be made of an occurrence which shows the relation at this period borne by the Chinese empire to the governments existing in the country of the Irâwadi, but which is not noticed in the Burmese history. It appears from the Shân chronicle, discovered in Manipûr,[1] that about A.D. 1332 a dispute arose between the king of Pong—so the chief of Mogaung is termed—and the governor of Yunnân. A Chinese or Mongol army invaded the country, and after a struggle of two years, the capital of Mogaung, to the west of the Irâwadi and north of Bamoa, was taken. The king, Sugnamphâ, fled to Sagaing, where Tarabyâgyî then reigned, and, on demand, he was surrendered to the emperor of China. The sons of Sugnamphâ succeeded to their father's kingdom, which, after the break-up of the Burmese monarchy, from a state of occasional subordination had become independent. A Mongol army takes Mogaung.

The founder of the kingdom of Sagaing died after a reign of seven years. He left three sons and a daughter, but was succeeded by his half-brother Tarabyâgyî, who reigned for fourteen years, and then was dethroned by his son, Shwèdaungtet. A party was formed against the usurper, who was slain after three years, and his father was put to death at the same time. The children of the founder of the kingdom, Athenghkarâ, now succeeded; the eldest son, Kyoaswâ, being raised to the throne. He reigned ten years, and after his death his two brothers successively succeeded, but died after short reigns. The daughter of the first king still remained. She had been married to a young man of unknown descent, called Thadohsenghtin, said to be of Events in the Shân kingdom of Sagaing, A.D. 1322. A.D. 1339.

[1] Report on the Eastern Frontier of Bengal, by Pemberton. Calcutta, 1835.

the race of the ancient kings of Tagaung. He died, leaving a son named Rahula and two daughters. Their mother now married a Shân chief named Mengbyauk, who, in right of his wife, was raised to the throne, and assumed the title of Thihapatè. His stepson, Rahula, supposed to be of the royal race of Tagaung, was sent to govern that province, where he assumed the title of Thadomengbyâ. After a few years he was attacked there by Thohkyinbwâ, the king or chief of Mogaung, at the instigation of Narathu, king of Pânyâ. Tagaung was taken, and the governor with difficulty escaped and fled to Sagaing. There his stepfather, enraged at his defeat, put him in irons. The chief of Mogaung followed up his success, and appeared before Sagaing with a large army. Mengbyauk was obliged to abandon the city, and fled to the south. The Mogaung
A.D. 1364. chief, on the ground that King Narathu had given him no assistance in the war, now attacked and took the city of Pânyâ. The city was plundered and the king taken prisoner. The Shân chief then retired to his own territory, leaving the people of the conquered cities to settle their own affairs.

Sagaing and Pânyâ both fall to Thadomengbyâ.

When Mengbyauk abandoned Sagaing, the people were deeply discontented at his want of courage. They rallied round Thadomengbyâ, who put his stepfather to death. He then determined to seize Pânyâ,
A.D. 1364. where he attacked Usanâ Byaung, and put him to death.

Thadomengbyâ had now no rival. He was believed to be descended from the ancient kings of Tagaung, and through his mother he was the grandson of the Shân king of Sagaing, Athenghkarâ. His ambition prompted him to restore the Burmese kingdom, which had been broken up into many fragments, and he began the work without delay.

CHAPTER VIII.

BURMA WITH CAPITAL AT AVA—SHÂN KINGS IN PEGU.

City of Ava founded—Mengkyiswâ Soakai recovers the Burmese kingdom as far as Prome, and resolves to conquer Pegu—Affairs of Pegu at the close of the Pugân monarchy—Tarabyâ becomes king—Warêru becomes king in Martaban—Conquers Pegu—Succeeded by Khunloa—Zoazip makes Hansâwadi, the city of Pegu, his capital—Binyâu driven from Martaban—Makes Hansâwadi his capital—Râjâdirit becomes king of Pegu—War between Burma and Pegu—King of Burma invades Pegu a second time—Râjâdirit takes Martaban—Defeated at Bassein—Restores the ancient capital—Death of Mengkyiswâ Soakai—Mengkhaung, king of Burma—Râjâdirit invades Burma—Retreats from Ava—Besieges Prome—Peace made—War renewed—King of Burma invades Pegu and fails—The Prince of Burma leads an army of invasion—War with Thinsâ—Râjâdirît besieges Prome—Retreats to his own country—Burmese prince killed—Chinese army before Ava—Deaths of Mengkhaung and Râjâdirît.

City of Ava founded.

THADOMENGBYÂ determined to found a new capital, and selected the site near the mouth of the Myitngè, an affluent of the Irâwadi. The city was called Awâ or Ava, the Pali or classical name being Ratanapura, or city of gems. The work was carried on with great energy,—swamps were drained, pagodas were built, and the city wall marked out. The palace was in the centre and was the citadel of the defences. A.D. 1364.

While this labour was in progress, the king marched to subdue the country to the south, which had not submitted to him. The city of Sagu, under a local chief, offered a stubborn resistance, and while engaged before it Thadomengbyâ caught the smallpox. He set out to return to Ava, but feeling that he must die, sent on a confidential follower with orders to put his queen to death, so that she might not fall to his successor. He died soon after, having reigned less than four years. He left no children. He is denounced in Burmese history as a man of cruel disposition, who altogether disregarded religion.

Mengkyiswâ Soakai recovers the kingdom as far as Prome, and resolves to conquer Pegu.

The nobles now elected to the throne Tarabyâ Soakai, governor of the district of Amyin. He was the son of Meng Sheng Soa, who was the son of the deposed king Kyoaswâ, and his mother was niece to the three Shân brothers, so that he united the claims of both races. He took the title of Mengkyiswâ Soakai. His sympathies appear to have leaned more to the Shân race than to the Burmese. He gradually recovered the territory to the south which anciently belonged to the Pugân monarchy, and entered into apparently friendly communication with Binyâu, the king of Pegu. That kingdom had been re-established under a new dynasty, and the king of Burma, who had gained possession of Prome, only waited for an opportunity to recover it as pertaining to the Burmese monarchy.

Affairs of Pegu at the close of the Pugân monarchy. Tarabyâ becomes king.

Before the fall of the Pugân monarchy the people of Pegu had become restive under foreign rule, and the weak government of Tarukpyèmeng made the Burmese officers in that province, many of whom had formed connections among the Talaings, desirous of establishing an independent government. The first open act of rebellion was committed by a Burmese officer named

A.D. 1273.

Ahkâmwun. He had married into a Talaing family, and gained influence among the people. He took possession of the ancient capital, Hansâwadi; defeated an army that was sent against him; and proclaimed himself king of Pegu. He soon became hated for his tyranny, and after two years was put to death by his brother-in-law, Lenggyâ; who himself was killed by another relation, who then was consecrated king under the title of Tarabyâ.

About the same time the country of Martaban (properly Muttamâ) was disturbed by a movement made to establish independence. Many Shâns had settled here from Zimmè and other adjoining states, and a merchant of that race named Mâgadu had acquired wealth and authority. He went to Thuhkatè, then the seat of the ruling Siamese chief on the upper course of the Menâm, and probably gained approval of his plans. On his return he raised a rebellion against Alimma, the Burmese governor, and put him to death. He now became king of Martaban under the name of Warêru.

Warêru becomes king in Martaban.

A.D. 1231.

The king of Pugân sent an army to recover Pegu. The Burmese were stockaded at Dâla, and Tarabyâ not feeling strong enough to attack the post, applied to Warêru to assist him. The king of Martaban came with an army, and the allies advanced by land and water against Dâla. They forced the Burmese to retire within their own frontier. The two kings with their armies then came down the river and encamped to the south of the city of Pegu. Here a quarrel arose which was provoked by Warêru; a battle was fought, and Tarabyâ was defeated and fled. Warêru at once took possession of the capital. Tarabyâ was caught by some villagers and delivered up to his rival. The conqueror proclaimed himself king, but did not choose to fix the seat of his government at Hansâwadi. After having settled the affairs of the country, he returned to Martaban, taking Tarabyâ with him. The deposed king was soon after put to death for entering into a conspiracy.

Warêru conquers Pegu.

Warêru possessed a white elephant which the three Shân brothers who ruled at Pânyâ endeavoured by war to obtain. They were defeated, and Warêru for the rest of his reign was free from foreign attack. He was assassinated in his palace by two sons of Tarabyâ, whose lives he had spared. They took refuge in a monastery, but were dragged forth and put to death.

Assassinated.

A.D. 1306.

Succeeded by Khunloa.

He was succeeded by his brother Khunloa, whose first care was to solicit recognition of his title from the king of Siam. This was granted, and the regalia were forwarded to him. An attack was made by the chief of Zimmè on a town to the east of the Sittaung river, and as the king made no effort to defend his territory, he was put to death by his brother-in-law, Meng Bâla, who placed his own son Zoaoa, nephew to the late king, on the throne. The young king was married to a daughter of the king of Siam; but, notwithstanding this, he took possession of Tavoy and Tenasserim, which for a time had been possessed by Siam. The reign of this king was prosperous. Pegu was held safely, having nothing to fear from Burma. But the king's desire to be independent of Siam led to future wars between the two countries.

Zoazip makes the city of Pegu his capital. A.D. 1323.

The successor of Zoaoa was his brother Zoazip, who took the title of Binyarânda. He removed the seat of government to Hansâwadi, leaving Martaban under a governor, with a strong garrison. But though he was supreme in the country of the delta, the southern provinces, Tavoy and Tenasserim, were retaken by the king of Siam.[1] He hoped to compensate himself for this loss by taking possession of Prome. That city, important from its position on the Irâwadi, appears at this time to have been held by an independent chief, whose name is not stated. Binyarânda besieged the place with a large army and flotilla, but was defeated and

A.D. 1330.

slain. Amidst the confusion which ensued, an officer of the palace at Martaban, styled Dibbân Meng, proclaimed himself king, but was put to death after a few days. A similar fate befell another competitor for the the throne, Egânkân; and a son of Khunloa, who at

[1] It is stated in the history of Siam that King Phra Ramathibodi founded the capital Ayuthia, A.D. 1350, and that Tenasserim, Tavoy, Martabân, and Maulmein were then subject to him. The two first-named towns may have been, but not the two last at that time. See Bowring's Siam, vol. i. p. 43.

the time was governor of Hansâwadi, was at length consecrated king with the title Binyaêloa. The king of Siam, angered at the death of Egânkân, who was his daughter's son, sent an army to punish his murderer. The Siamese force was defeated, and from this time the subordination of the dynasty of Warêru to Siam, ceased.

Binyaêloa reigned for eighteen years at Hansâwadi. He had freed his kingdom from foreign supremacy, but the country was disturbed by a quarrel between his son and the next nearest heir, Binyâu. The son having died, Binyâu succeeded, and assumed the title of Hsengphyusheng, as possessor of a white elephant. He made Martabân his capital.

Binyâu, driven from Martaban, makes Hansâwadi his capital

Three years after he came to the throne the Shâns of Zimmè attacked the fortified town of Dunwun, which was to the north of Thahtun. This attack was probably instigated by the king of Siam. After some fighting the Shâns were driven out. Binyâu sent an ambassador to Ceylon and obtained a holy relic, for which a pagoda was built near to the scene of the last victory over the Shâns. But misfortunes gathered round the king. The governor of Pegu rebelled, and though he was easily subdued, the white elephant died, a portentous event to a Buddhist sovereign. While Binyâu was in the forest endeavouring to capture another white elephant, his relation Byâttabâ rebelled, and took possession of Martaban. The king was forced to take refuge in Dunwun, and Byâttabâ for several years remained supreme in Martaban. In Pegu, however, the king consolidated his power, and restored the ancient capital, Hansâwadi; but, under the influence of his favourite queen, he endeavoured to set aside the claims of his eldest son, Binyânwè, in favour of her children. Binyânwè, in self-defence, took possession of Dagun, now Rangoon, and engaged the services of some Western foreigners, probably Muhammadan adventurers from India or the shores of the Persian Gulf, who had more seaworthy boats than those used by the Talaings. The king was too ill to exert himself to uphold his authority, and by order of the queen an army was sent against the rebellious son. This he defeated, and during the struggle the king, his father, died.

Râjâdirît becomes king of Pegu, A.D. 1385.

Binyânwè now became king without opposition. He assumed the title of Râjâdirît. He forgave most of those who had opposed him during the lifetime of his father, and even treated with respect the queen, who had endeavoured to exclude him from the throne. But there was one powerful noble, Laukbyâ, the governor of Myaungmyâ, a member of the royal family, who hated him, and determined not to submit to his authority. The state of affairs in the neighbouring kingdom made this opposition dangerous to the king of Pegu. The kingdom of Burma had become consolidated under Meng Kyiswâ Soakai, and he determined to recover the territory which had belonged to the kings of Pugân. The chief of Myaungmyâ entered into communication with him, and suggested that he should invade Pegu, engaging, if placed on the throne, to hold the kingdom as a tributary. The king of Burma made preparations to carry out the plan.

War between Burma and Pegu.

An army composed of two columns was sent against Pegu. One, under the king's elder son, advanced by the valley of the Paunglaung river to Taungu, and on to Pangyoa, north of Hansâwadi. The other, under the second son, and accompanied by a flotilla, marched down the left bank of the Irâwadi, and took possession of the town of Hlaing. Both columns were thus within striking distance of the capital, but they did not act in concert. Laukbyâ rendered no efficient support, and Râjâdirît severely defeated the Burmese force at Hlaing. The rainy season, which in Pegu renders movement of troops by land very difficult, if not impossible, was at hand, and the two princes made a rapid retreat.

But the king of Pegu, though successful, dreaded another invasion, and sent an envoy with a letter and presents to the king of Burma, hoping to avert further attack. Meng Kyiswâ Soakai answered sternly that the Talaing country belonged to his ancestors, and must be recovered. The presents were scornfully rejected.

After the rainy season, the king of Burma himself headed an army, which, as in the previous campaign, took possession of Hlaing. Laukbyâ gave active assistance to the invader. Râjâdirît established himself in a strong stockade at Maubî. The Burmese were detained before this work so long that the dreaded rainy season drew nigh, and Meng Kyiswâ Soakai retreated. The Talaing army followed in pursuit as far as Prome, but did not venture to attack that city.

King of Burma invades Pegu a second time. A.D. 1387.

The king of Pegu being rid of the formidable invader, determined to conquer those who still defied his authority within the ancient Talaing kingdom. He sent an army against Martaban, where Byâttabâ still ruled. He, however, abandoned the city and fled to a foreign country, leaving two Muhammadan officers in command. They were defeated in a battle outside the city, and Râjâdirît took possession. A.D. 1388.

Râjâdirît takes Martaban.

The king next proceeded against Laukbyâ in his town of Myaungmyâ. He went with a large force, but the place, which at this period appears to have been the principal port for this part of Pegu, was so strongly fortified that he did not dare to attack it. He sent his army against Bassein, where Laukbyâ's three sons commanded. This town was defended by foreign decked boats armed with guns.[1] The king's army suffered a defeat. The general was killed, and the attacking force retreated. But in subsequent operations Laukbyâ, who

Defeated at Bassein.

[1] Probably of the kind known as "jingal," a metal tube about three feet long, mounted on a wooden stand, and throwing a ball generally less than one pound weight.

appears to have become too venturesome after success, was taken prisoner, and Myaungmyâ surrendered. His
A.D. 1390. son fled to Sandoway in Arakan, but was delivered up on demand, and he was made a pagoda slave to the Shwêdagun.

Râjâdirit restores the capital of Pegu.

Râjâdirît now beautified his capital, Hansâwadi, and improved the defences. On the northern frontier he drove the Burmese from a town they had occupied within his territory. He entered into friendly communication with the king of Siam, who claimed him to be of the same race as himself, and feeling now secure in his kingdom, he settled the internal affairs of the country. But he suspected his eldest son of conspiring against him, and put him to death.

Death of Meng Kyiswâ.

The warlike king of Burma, Meng Kyiswâ Soakai, died, and was succeeded by his son, Hshengphyusheng;
A.D. 1400. but he soon after was murdered, and his brother Meng Khaung was placed on the throne.

Meng Khaung, king of Burma.

Meng Khaung became involved in a quarrel with the king of Arakan, who had made an incursion into the province of Ava. This led to an invasion of Arakan by the king of Burma; but though it was successful, the occasion seemed to Râjâdirît to afford a suitable opportunity to take revenge for the invasions by Meng Kyiswâ Soakai. He assembled an army and a great flotilla,

Râjâdirît invades Burma, A.D. 1404.

with which he advanced up the Irâwadi at the close of the rainy season. The army reached Prome, but the king of Pegu did not dare to attack the place, as guns were mounted on the rampart. The Burmese history states that some of the garrison were armed with muskets, which is no doubt an error. They probably had firearms which were held in the hand when discharged, and the name of the more modern weapon has been given to them by later copyists of the chronicles. The governor of Prome at this time was one of the sons of Laukbyâ, late governor of Myaungmyâ, from whence the firearms had probably been brought. Râjâdirît pushed on past Prome and reached Sagaing. Meng Khaung had no flotilla to oppose to him, but he remained secure within the walls of Ava, and the king of Pegu, though he had command of the surrounding country, could not carry the place by storm, and was not prepared to reduce it by blockade. He was glad of the pretence of being persuaded to retire by the eloquence of a famous Buddhist monk, who preached to him of the wickedness of war, which brought suffering and death to thousands. Before leaving, he broke up the magnificent floating palace in which he had ascended the Irâwadi, and with the timber built a monastery at Shwêkyet near Ava. Retreats from Ava.

Though foiled in his attempt on the Burmese capital, Râjâdirît considered the possession of Prome essential to the safety of his kingdom. After the rainy season, therefore, he advanced up the river with a large army, and established his camp on the right bank, nearly opposite to the town. He placed a strong detachment on the east bank to the north of the town, and with the help of his large flotilla, hoped by famine to force the garrison to surrender. The king of Burma, however, marched down and overwhelmed the isolated detachment, though it was strongly intrenched. The Talaing flotilla kept command of the river, and ravaged the country even beyond Myêdai. The two kings, finding that for the present they were too equally matched for either to become superior, came to an understanding and swore friendship at the Prome pagoda. The king of Pegu married the sister of the king of Burma, and the boundary between the two kingdoms was drawn south of the town. Besieges Prome. Peace made. A.D. 1406.

This reconciliation, even if sincere at the moment, was of short duration. The king of Burma took offence at a Talaing garrison being posted near the frontier. He desired also to punish the king of Arakan; and, to prevent Râjâdirît from interfering, sent a letter to the War renewed.

chief of Zimmè, desiring him to threaten the Peguan frontier near Sittaung. This letter was intercepted and the messengers were killed. The king of Pegu assembled an army at Bassein to watch affairs in Arakan, and to be prepared to interfere if advisable. The Burmese army marched into Arakan across the mountain pass of Nâtyêgân, and the king of that country fled to Bengal.[1] His son went south to the town of Sandoway, and thence to Bassein. The king of Pegu promised the prince support against the Burmese, and at once sent his army to occupy Sandoway. Kâmaru, the son-in-law of Meng Khaung, had been made governor of Arakan, with the title of Anoarahtâ. He was at the capital in the northern part of the kingdom. The Talaing army marched there. Kâmaru was taken prisoner, with his wife and children. They were carried to Bassein, where he was cruelly put to death, and his wife was taken into Râjâdirît's palace as one of the queens. The Talaing army left Arakan, having placed the son of the exiled king as regent at the capital. During these events a brother of the king of Burma, offended that he had not been appointed Ainshêmeng, or heir-apparent, rebelled, but was defeated and made prisoner. The king pardoned and released him, but he fled and took refuge with the king of Pegu. He was welcomed by Râjâdirît as an adherent who might be useful, and he gave him his sister in marriage.

King of Burma invades Pegu, and fails.

The cruel murder of his son-in-law and the treatment of his daughter, determined the king of Burma to invade Pegu. In vain his ministers besought him to wait, and represented the difficulty of operating in Pegu at the season of the year when the rain falls. He would brook no delay. It was late in the month of April when he marched from Ava by the Taungû route. The king of Pegu led his army northward from his capital

A.D. 1407.

[1] In the history of Arakan this event is stated to have occurred A.D. 1406. By Burmese history it was a year or more later.

to meet the invader, and his advanced guard being repulsed, he took up a position at Pângyoa. The Burmese plundered and burnt the towns and villages of the country they occupied; but the rainy season having set in, their movements were impeded, and provisions began to fail. Meng Khaung attempted to negotiate, but at last was forced to retreat, and his army was soon in disastrous flight. The Burmese suffered great loss; yet the king two years later again invaded Pegu with no better success.

The Prince of Burma leads an army of invasion.

Meng Khaung, depressed by defeat, no longer felt capable of leading an army; but his son, Mengrai Kyoaswâ, though only seventeen years of age, was put in command to retrieve the past disasters. His mother had been taken prisoner during the war of 1406 near Prome, and his sister was the wife of the governor of Arakan, who had been put to death. Both were still detained by Râjâdirît, and the young prince burned to avenge the insults his family had suffered. The point for attack selected was the western side of the delta; and the prince, leading an army of twenty thousand men, took possession of a post in the district of Bassein. Râjâdirît was at this time detained at Martaban, which was threatened by an attack from Zimmê, probably prompted by the king of Burma. The prince was unsuccessful in Bassein, and, after several months' operations, marched across the hills into Arakan, and proceeded to the capital of that country. He chased away the regent who had been appointed by Râjâdirît, and placed in authority an officer of his own. But a Talaing force occupied Sandoway; and though the prince endeavoured to drive it out, he was unsuccessful, and the Talaings once more drove out the Burmese regent at the capital of Arakan.

A.D. 1410.

War with Thinnî.

The king of Burma was now occupied with the Shân state of Thinnî. The origin of the quarrel is not stated, but Mengrai Kyoaswâ was sent against the chief

A.D. 1412. of that state, who was defeated and slain. His sons shut themselves up in their fortified city, and called in the Chinese to help them. The prince attacked the Chinese army while on the march, and defeated it. He then returned and reinvested the city, which surrendered. But at this time Râjâdirît determined once more to strike at Prome. He arrived there, and on account of the guns was forced to keep at a distance from the walls, but he hoped to starve out the garrison. The alarm of a Siamese army marching on Martaban recalled him to Pegu. His son was left in command to continue the siege. He after a time was compelled to stockade himself on the western bank of the river. The king returned to his support, but the valiant Burmese prince had arrived from Thinnî, and the Talaing army, worsted in many skirmishes, was forced to retire. The Burmese prince, not satisfied at having repelled the attack, followed the Talaing army into the delta. He even gained possession of Dâla, Syriam, and other places of importance; and his father, Meng Khaung, deeming that a final triumph would be obtained, himself came down to Pegu; but the king of Pegu stirred up a Shân chief in the north to attack some towns in the Burmese territory. At the same time the prince met with a defeat, and the king of Burma deemed it prudent to retire to his own country.

Râjâdirît besieges Prome.

Retreats to his own country.

Burmese prince killed.

The warlike prince of Burma thought he had only been prevented by accident from accomplishing all he aimed at. He once more occupied the Bassein district with an army, but was killed in battle, and the Burmese army retired. Another expedition to Pegu was made by his brother, Thihathû, but it was unsuccessful.

A.D. 1416.

Chinese army before Ava.

During this war a serious danger threatened the Burmese king. Two Shân chiefs had attacked Myêdu, which was subject to Ava. The king sent a force against them, and they fled to the Chinese territory, while their wives and children were made prisoners.

A Chinese army marched down to Ava, and required that the wives and children of the two chiefs should be released. According to the Burmese chronicle, the point whether they should be surrendered or not was left to be decided by the result of a battle between two champions. A Talaing chief, who was prisoner at Ava, was allowed to represent the Burmese side. He killed the Chinese champion, who was clad in armour, and the Chinese army then withdrew without the demand for the prisoners being enforced.

Deaths of Meng Khaung and Râjâdirit.

A.D. 1422.

After this incident Meng Khaung undertook no more wars. He sought to gather merit by the performance of good works. He died after a reign of twenty-one years. His great enemy, Râjâdirît, also devoted his later years to religion. The two nations were exhausted after their long struggle. The Talaing king maintained his bodily activity to the last, and died from the effect of a wound received in hunting a wild elephant, only one year after the death of Meng Khaung. He reigned thirty-eight years.

CHAPTER IX.

ARAKAN.

Arakan subordinate to Burma—King of Arakan takes refuge in Bengal—Arakan the battlefield of the kings of Burma and Pegu—Arakan tributary to Bengal—Arakanese kings annex Chittagaon—Invasion of Arakan by the Burmese king—Invasion from Tippera repulsed.

Arakan subordinate to Burma, A.D. 1102-3.

ARAKAN became subordinate to the Pugân monarchy from the time when Letyâmengnân was placed on the throne of his ancestors. He fixed his capital at Parin. The country enjoyed rest for a long period, and there is nothing in the annals worthy of remark until after the capture of Pugân by the Mongols. In the early part of the fourteenth century mention is made of invasion by the Shâns, which apparently refers to attacks by the kings of Myinsaing and Pânyâ. In the last quarter of that century the king of Arakan became involved in the quarrel between Burma and Pegu by the son of the rebel governor of Myaungmyâ having taken refuge in Sandoway, from whence he was surrendered to the king of Pegu. About the same time communication was made by the king of Arakan to the king of Bengal. The latter country is called Suratân, which may be a corruption of Sunargaon, which had for a time been the capital; or may refer to the title sultân. Presents were interchanged by the two sovereigns, the ruler of Arakan probably hoping to find an ally against attack from Burma. According to the Burmese history, the king

A.D. 1373.

of Arakan having died without leaving an heir, the nobles of that country offered the throne to Meng

Kyiswâ, king of Burma, who appointed his uncle, Soamwungyî, tributary king. The Arakanese annals at this time narrate how the country was for many years in great confusion, and that usurpers, one after another, became the rulers. At length, the native king, Meng Soamwun, was driven from his kingdom by an army sent by Pyinsing Mengswâ, called also Meng Khamaung, king of Burma, which took possession of the capital, then Laungkyet. A.D. 1406.

King of Arakan takes refuge in Bengal.

Meng Soamwun fled to Bengal, an event that led to a close connection between the two countries, and which lasted for more than two centuries. At this time the Mussulmân kings of Bengal were independent of the emperors of Dehli, and their capital was at or near Gour. The events narrated in the annals of Arakan as having occurred during this interval are generally consistent with the history of that country, and there is a coincidence of dates which supports the chronology of the Arakanese statements.[1] According to the latter, the dethroned king was for twenty-four years residing in Bengal. During that time the king of Bengal was attacked by the king of Dehli, and the exile rendered good service to his protector. Now, though the king of Bengal was not attacked by the king of Dehli at this period, his kingdom was invaded by Ibrahim, the king of Jounpoor, who carried off many prisoners. A.D. 1430.

Arakan the battlefield of the kings of Burma and Pegu.

During the exile of Meng Soamwun, the kings of Burma and of Pegu made Arakan one of their battlefields. The former placed his son-in-law on the throne, with the title of Anoarahtâ. The king of Pegu attacked him, took him prisoner, and put him to death. This led to an invasion of Pegu from Burma. Arakan suffered in the contest between the two stronger countries; and after a severe struggle, with varying fortune, Râjâdirit succeeded in occupying the capital of Arakan;

[1] See Marshman's History of Bengal, 4th edition. Serampore, pp. 16, 17.

and the tributary king or governor he placed there, appears to have remained in power until A.D. 1423.

A.D. 1426. Ahmed Shah, the king of Bengal, died, and as he left no son, the nobles placed Nazir Shah on the throne. He undertook to restore Meng Soamwun. At first a general styled in the Arakanese history Wali Khan was charged with this duty; but he betrayed his trust, and joining with a discontented Arakanese chief, imprisoned Meng Soamwun. The king escaped, and a second army was sent, which overcame all opposition, and placed the exiled king on the throne of his ancestors. He founded the city of Myauku, now known as Arakan city, which continued to be the capital for four hundred years.

Meng Soamwun restored, A.D. 1430.

Arakan tributary to Bengal.

The restored king agreed to be tributary to the king of Bengàl. This subordinate relationship did not last long; but from this time the strange anomaly occurs of Buddhist kings using, in addition to their own names, Muhammadan designations and titles, and even issuing coins bearing the Kalima. This practice probably was first introduced in fulfilment of the promise made by Meng Soamwun, but was continued in later times as a token of sovereignty in Chittagaon, which was recognised as lying geographically beyond the country of the Burma race.

Arakanese kings annex Chittagaon.

Meng Soamwun was succeeded by his brother, Meng Khari, who also bore the name of Ali Khan. He did not long submit to the authority of the king of Bengal. He took possession of the country as far as Râmu, and during a reign of twenty-five years kept his country free from attack by his dangerous eastern neighbours.

A.D. 1459. His son, Basoahpyu, who succeeded him, took possession of the town of Chittagaon. The king of Bengal at this time was Barbek Shah, who allowed the affairs of his kingdom to fall into confusion. Basoahpyu issued a coin bearing the Kalima, and in Arakanese history is known by that designation. Though highly praised by his countrymen, he lost his life in a rebellion by his son Doalyâ, who succeeded him. For the next half-century the kings of Arakan, though by A.D. 1482. reason of the weakness of the kings of Bengal they retained Chittagaon, yet were troubled with rebellions at home, and several of them were assassinated. At length a young king of great ability, named Meng Beng, came to the throne. In his time European ships A.D. 1531. first arrived, and in one or two instances attacked and plundered villages on the coast without provocation, as it is stated in the native annals. It is supposed that these were Portuguese ships. Meng Beng hearing of the conquests of Tabeng Shwêhtî in Pegu, had the sagacity to foresee that his country might be invaded. He at once commenced extensive earthworks to defend his capital, and dug a deep moat which could be filled by tidal water. The work was pushed on with great energy, and the event which Meng Beng had prepared for, came to pass. An army from the eastward took posses- A.D. 1544. sion of Sandoway, but the Arakanese opposed a stiff resistance when the enemy attempted to march northward. The invaders held Sandoway for two years, when Tabeng Shwêhtî himself appeared with a force which the Arakanese were unable to withstand. The Burmese king marched northward with an army of Burmese, **Invasion of Arakan by the Burmese king.** Talaing, and Shân. He came before the capital, but found it too strongly fortified to admit of capture by assault, and shrank from the delay of attempting to force surrender by blockade. He was glad to come to terms in order to secure an unmolested retreat, and Meng Beng was willing to be rid of so formidable an enemy without driving him to desperation.

While Meng Beng was thus engaged, an enemy had **Invasion from Tippera repulsed.** appeared from the north called in the Arakanese history the Thek or Sâk king, by which term the Râjâ of Tippera appears to be meant. He had penetrated to Ramu, but was now driven back, and Meng Beng again occupied Chittagaon. Coins which bear his name and the title of sultân were struck at that city. He reigned until A.D. 1553.

Kalima coin,
Struck by a king of Arakan.

Coin of Meng Beng,
Struck in Chittagaon.

CHAPTER X.

SHAN KINGS OF BURMA AND THE KINGS OF PEGU, UNTIL THE RISE OF THE TAUNGU MONARCHY.

Burmese invasion of Pegu—King of Burma deposed—Chief of Monyin becomes king of Burma—Rising power of Taungu—Binyâ Rânkit, king of Pegu—The king of Pegu allies himself with the king of Burma—Sheng Soabu, queen of Pegu—Constant wars between Burma and the Northern Shân chiefs—Chinese invasion of Burma—Long and peaceful reign of Dhammâzedi in Pegu—Kingdom of Burma reduced in power—The chief of Monyin puts his son on the throne of Burma—Burmese nobles fly to Taungu—Pegu enjoys a long peace under Binya Rân.

Burmese invasion of Pegu.

IN Ava, Meng Khaung was succeeded by his son Thihathu, and in Pegu Binyâ Dhammâ Râjâ succeeded his father Râjâdirît. The quarrel between the two countries was renewed, being excited by the king of Pegu's brothers, Binya Rân and Binya Keng. Believing that their lives were in danger from enemies in the palace, they gathered followers and came to open war with the king. But the elder of the two ceased his opposition and was declared heir-apparent. Binya Keng had written to the king of Burma for support and tendered his allegiance. He occupied the town of Dâla, which was strongly blockaded; and a Burmese army came down and was received by the prince. But the Burmese commander allowed his troops to plunder the town, and Binya Keng, disgusted with his allies, abandoned them and submitted to the king his brother. The Burmese force now retired to Prome. Binya Keng for a short time returned to his former government at

Dâla, but soon moved to Martaban; while Binya Rân, who still maintained secret designs to establish his own power, received the governorship of Bassein, including all the western part of the delta. The king of Pegu was entirely in the hands of a court faction, and this explains the restless, and apparently ungrateful conduct towards their brother of the two princes. Binya Rân again entered into communication with King Thihathu and occupied Dagun, now Rangoon. A Burmese force again came down and took possession of Dâla, while the prince, as a pledge of his good faith, gave his sister in marriage to the king of Burma. The princess, who had already been married once, was by an unusual proceeding consecrated as a queen, and then went to Ava, where the highest rank in the palace was accorded to her. She afterwards became famous in Peguan history as Sheng Soabu. This marriage, however, was the immediate cause of the deposition of Thihathu. His chief queen, Soahpomè, jealous of the high distinction granted to a stranger, called in a Shân chief, Unbaunglè, who advanced with an army to Ava. The king had been induced to go outside the city to direct the excavation of a canal. He was suddenly attacked by a band of armed men and wounded by an arrow. He escaped and fled to Monyin, where he died soon after. Queen Soabu then married a nobleman named Tarabyâ.

King of Burma deposed.

Chief of Monyin becomes king of Burma.

The citizens of Ava joined together against the Shân army of Unbaunglè, which retired from the city. An infant son of Thihathu was put on the throne; but Queen Soahpomè called in the chief of Kalè, who came with an army, seized the palace, and killed the infant king. The usurper's reign was short. The chief of Monyin, named Mengnânsî, was a man of great influence. He was of Shân race, but claimed to be descended from the ancient kings of Pugân through a daughter of Ngâtsîsheng Kyoaswâ, who reigned at

Pânyâ. He determined to assert his claim to the throne of Burma. He marched at the head of a large army and invested Ava. There was a general combination against the chief of Kalè. He fled, accompanied by Queen Soahpomè. Mengnânsî took possession of the palace as king. The Kalè chief died in the jangal, and the queen, the companion of his flight, was received back into the palace with her former rank. The Shân chief found some trouble in reducing the provinces to obedience to his rule. Taungu was governed by Soalu, who was too powerful to be regarded otherwise than with respect. He came to Ava, and was treated almost as an equal. Before long he strengthened his position by forming an alliance with the king of Pegu, and his younger brother was made governor of the province of Tharâwadi. Many Burmese families of high rank, unwilling to remain under the Shân king, settled in Taungu, and made it the nucleus of a power, destined in the next century to reunite the scattered territories, into which the ancient monarchy of Pugân had become divided.

A.D. 1426.

Rising power of Taungu.

In Pegu, Binyâ Dhammâ Râjâ had been got rid of by poison, and his brother, who had been acknowledged as heir-apparent, succeeded to the throne, and is known as Binyâ Rânkît. He allowed Binyâ Keng to remain as viceroy at Martaban, where he exercised almost independent authority; and the province was governed by his successors for many years, with nominal subordination to the king of Pegu.

Binyâ Rânkit, king of Pegu.

The ruler of Taungu, who desired to strengthen himself against Ava, induced Binyâ Rânkît to join in an attack on that country. He claimed to be the rightful king of Burma, and promised that, if successful in establishing his claim, he would present gold and silver flowers annually to the king of Pegu. The attack was made; but the king of Pegu deserted his ally, and married a niece of the king of Burma. Sheng Soabu,

King of Pegu allies himself with the king o Burma.

being dissatisfied with her position in Ava, fled secretly to Pegu, and was received by her brother with great
A.D. 1446. distinction. Binyâ Rânkît died after a reign of twenty years. He was succeeded by his nephew and adopted son, Binyâ Waru, who was the son of Sheng Soabu by her first marriage. He reigned only four years, and two other members of the family successively came to the throne. The last, Mhoadoa, was a cruel tyrant, and he was put to death. All the male descendants of Râjâdirît having been murdered, the whole people im-
Sheng Soabu, queen of Pegu. plored Sheng Soabu to take the sovereign power. She consented, and was consecrated. A Buddhist monk, who had accompanied her on her return from Ava, threw off his monastic frock and became a layman, married the queen's daughter, and was declared heir-apparent, with the title of Dhammâzedi. The queen
A.D. 1460. reigned for seven years, and Dhammâzedi then succeeded.

Constant wars between Burma and the Northern Shân chiefs. For several years war between Burma and Pegu had ceased. In the former kingdom, the Monyin chief who reigned with the title of Mengnânsî was succeeded
A.D. 1439. by his son Mengrê Kyoaswâ, who reigned for three years. On his death his brother, who had been governor of Prome, ascended the throne, and took the title of Bureng Nârâbadî. These kings were constantly engaged in war with the Northern Shân chiefs, and particularly with the Soabwâ of Mogaung. Taungu had long successfully resisted their authority, but a Shân chief—Tarabyâ—was for a short time placed in that state as governor or tributary king. Suddenly an unlooked-for danger threatened the king of Burma. A
Chinese invasion of Burma. Chinese army appeared on the frontier. The commander, halting at Muangmo (Burmese Maingmo), on the Shwèlê river, sent to Ava three hundred horsemen, with a message requiring payment of tribute, as had been rendered by the kings of Pugân. Nârâbadî refused, on the ground that since the foundation of Ava no such

demand had been made. The Chinese then came down to Bamoa, and the king advanced with his army. The Chinese now ordered that the Soabwâ of Mogaung, named Thongânbwâ, should be surrendered to them. This was refused, and a battle was fought, in which the invaders were defeated. In the following year the Chinese returned in great force and marched down to Ava.[1] They renewed their demand that the chief should be surrendered. The king, in evident imitation of a supposed service having been rendered in a previous reign, before a former similar requisition had been complied with, suggested to the Chinese general that he should subdue the chief of Ramêthen, who was in rebellion. This service having been performed, the Mogaung chief would have been surrendered, but he took poison and died. His body was then delivered to the Chinese, who carried it off. A few years later the Chinese again marched to attack both Monyin and Mogaung, but were defeated. The reason of these attacks is not satisfactorily explained, but they probably arose from the determination of the Ming dynasty of China, which had succeeded the Mongolian, A.D. 1368, to assert a right of sovereignty over the Shân chiefs in the country of the northern Irâwadi. King Nârâbadi was frequently involved in wars with the Shân states, and also with Taungu, where he failed, notwithstanding great efforts, to establish his authority. His son raised a rebellion, in which the king was wounded. He fled to Prome, where his second son was governor, and there died.

A.D. 1444.

A.D. 1468.

Long and peaceful reign of Dhammâzedi in Pegu.

In Pegu Dhammâzedi reigned in peace for the long period of thirty-one years. Though brought up from early youth in the seclusion of a Buddhist monastery until he was more than forty years of age, he reigned

[1] The circumstances here recorded have some resemblance to the events of A.D. 1332–33, when the chief of Mogaung, Sugnâmpha (apparently the same name as Thongânbwâ), fled to Sagaing, and was on demand given up to the Mongolian general. See chap. vii.

with dignity and wisdom; his moderation reconciled to his rule the diverse interests of the grandees of the land. Embassies were sent to him from the neighbouring countries and from Ceylon. Though he made no wars, yet he extended the boundaries of the kingdom eastward, and after death he received the funeral honours of a Chakrawartti or universal monarch. The strict observances of Buddhism were in his case disregarded, and a pagoda was built over his bones, which was crowned and gilded as for an object of worship. He was succeeded by his son, who took the title of Binya Rân, and enjoyed among his subjects the respect and love which belonged to a grandson of Sheng Soabu.

Kingdom of Burma reduced in power

During this period, when Pegu had rest from war and internal strife, the kingdom of Burma was involved in constant struggles with the Shân states to the north, and dwindled in territory and power until it equalled only one of the inferior of those states. After the death of King Nârâbadî, his son, Mahâ Thihathura, succeeded him. His brother governed at Prome, and scarcely acknowledged his superiority. After a reign of twelve years, his son came to the throne with the title of Thîrithudhammâ Râjâ. The troubles of the monarchy now increased. The king's brothers, who governed at Saleng and at Ramêthen, rebelled, and his uncle proclaimed himself king of Prome with the title of Thadomengsoa. The Shân Soabwâ of Myêdu declared himself independent, and this brought an unfriendly territory nearer to the gates of Ava than the dynasty had yet known. The king, apparently to secure the loyalty of his eldest son, made him joint-king, with the title of Mahâ Thihathura. He lived in the same palace with his father, and displayed a white umbrella as the symbol of sovereignty. He died before his father, after having been associated in the kingdom with him for fifteen years; and the reign of King Thîrithudhammâ Râjâ came to an end after twenty-one years. He was succeeded by his second son, who assumed the title of Mahâ Râjâ Dibati. A.D. 1501.

The chief of Monyin puts his son on the throne of Burma.

The state of the kingdom was now desperate. The chief of Monyin took possession of Myêdu. The kings of Prome and Taungu combined to attack the city of Salê. The king called in the chief of Unbaung to his assistance, and the allies were defeated. In the north Salun,' the chief of Monyin, pursuing his aggressive movements, occupied the important province of Tabayîn, the ancient seat of the race from which the royal family of Burma sprung. He next attacked the chief of Unbaung at Bamoa. While so employed the king invested Myêdu, but his force was driven away by Shân allies of Salun. After several years of desultory warfare, the Monyin chief marched down and took possession of Sagaing. Then pursuing his course along the right bank of the Irâwadi, and plundering the towns, he reached Thayetmyu. While there, Thadomengsoa, king of Prome, sent messengers to him, offering, if placed on the throne of Ava, to be friendly, and even subordinate. The agreement was made. The Shân army crossed to the left bank of the river at Myêdè, and marched northwards, while the king of Prome proceeded by water. Mahâ Râjâ Dibati had no army to defend his capital, but the chief of Unbaung came to his assistance. Some fighting occurred near the city. The chief of Monyin was victorious, and, according to his promise, placed Thadomengsoa in the palace at Ava. He then retired to his own country. The king of Prome could not retain his position, and was obliged to fly. King Dibati returned to his capital with the chief of Unbaung. For two years this unfortunate king endured his degraded position, when the chief of Monyin, determined to crush him, marched to Sagaing, and, crossing the river, laid siege to Ava. The city was taken by storm after eight days, and the king was killed while attempting to escape on an elephant. The Mon-

A.D. 1523.

yin chief had no wish to reign himself. He placed his son, Thohanbwâ, on the throne, and returned to his own country. Most of the Burmese nobles and men of rank fled, some to Prome and most to Taungu, which had become a refuge for those who were determined not to submit to Shân domination. Thohanbwâ, though he showed a deep hatred to the Burmese race, induced Rânaung, a Burmese noble, though with Shân blood, a man of ability, to become chief minister. Against the advice of his minister the king determined to attack both Prome and Taungu. He saw plainly that the latter state, though hitherto insignificant, was becoming a centre of power which would be dangerous to himself. It was easier first to attack Prome. There Thadomengsoa had been succeeded by his son, Bureng Htwe. Thohanbwâ, with his father, Salun, who brought a large army, marched down, besieged and took that town, and carried the king off towards Monyin. But by a sudden burst of treason Salun himself, while on the march, fell a victim to a conspiracy of his subordinate chiefs, and Bureng Htwe escaped. He returned to Prome, where his son had become king, with the title of Nârâbadî. The son basely shut the gates against his father, and Bureng Htwe died in the adjoining forests.

Burmese nobles fly to Taungu.

A.D. 1533.

Pegu enjoys a long peace under Binya Rân.

During the conflicts which agitated the ancient Burmese country under Shân kings, Pegu enjoyed comparative rest. Binya Rân was on the throne, and his reign extended throughout thirty-five years. During that long period only two instances are mentioned in the native chronicles in which he appeared as aggressive to his neighbours. In one, he made an expedition at the head of an army up the Irâwadi. In the Peguan history it is stated that the movement was intended as a pilgrimage to the Shwèzîgun pagoda at Pugân; that no collision with any other power occurred; and that though the king passed Prome with a considerable escort, the peaceful nature of his journey was acknowledged by the king of that state. The other instance is not mentioned in the history of Pegu, but is recorded in the Mahâ Râjâweng of Burma. It is there represented that the king of Pegu was jealous of the rising power of Taungu, and attacked with a large army the fort of Dwârawadi, which the ruler of the latter state had built to protect his capital. The Talaing army was defeated, and though no immediate retaliatory move was made, the rulers of Taungu from this time treasured up a feeling of hatred against their southern neighbour, and only waited for an opportunity to take revenge. The character of this king is favourably described by European observers. The narratives of two Italian travellers who visited Pegu at this period have been preserved; and one of them mentions the king as a prince "of great magnificence and generosity," and "of such humanity and affability, that a child may come to his presence and speak with him." Binya Rân died A.D. 1526.

The dynasty which ruled the small territory of Taungu was destined before long to become supreme in the land of the Irâwadi, and the remarkable events which led to this revolution will now be traced.

CHAPTER XI.

TAUNGU.

Position and extent of Taungu—Governor appointed by the king of Pugân—Governors after the fall of Pugân—Sîthu Kyoahteng becomes king—Meng Kyînyo seizes the throne—His son, Tabeng Shwèhtî, succeeds—Invades Pegu—Takes the capital—Marches to attack Prome—Takârwutbi dies, and Tabeng Shwèhtî becomes king of Pegu.

Position and extent of Taungu.

TAUNGU is the name of a province situated in the middle course of the river Paunglaung or Sitang, the basin of which lies between the rivers Irâwadi and Salwin. The extent of this province, when it is first mentioned as having a distinct government, was about eighty miles from north to south, with a breadth, including the dependent mountain tracts, of about a third of that extent. The greater portion of the original province is now British territory. On the east of the valley, watered by the Paunlaung, are high mountains, where the Karen tribes, only lately reclaimed from wildness, are still numerous. From a remote time they were practically independent. The hills on the west seldom exceed a thousand feet elevation, and few Karens are now to be found there. Burmese colonists from the north and Talaings from the south, at a time beyond the memory of man, occupied the valley, leaving the hills to the Karens. There is no tradition of any race having inhabited the hill country before the Karens. Until the twelfth century of the Christian era, no mention can be found in local annals of any event in the province of

Taungu which can be accepted as historical.[1] The sovereignty of the land from that time, for about four centuries, generally followed the fortune of one or other of the two neighbouring dominant states. Narabadi, the king of Pugân, is said to have visited the country in the twelfth century, and to have appointed a governor. But the isolated position of the territory rendered it difficult of control from a distance, except to a settled and energetic power. In two generations, the successors of this governor had become independent. Warêru, the Shân king of Martaban, is said to have entered the province towards the end of the thirteenth century, and to have carried away the chief then ruling. But that chief's two sons afterwards established themselves in the hills to the west of the river, in a stronghold on a projecting point of a hill, called in the Burmese language, from its formation, Taungu. When, in after times, the capital city was built in the valley on a wide plain near the river, the old name was still retained among the people.

Governor appointed by the king of Pugân.

After the fall of the Pugân monarchy, the Shân king, Thihathu, who reigned at Pânyâ, sent his adopted son, Uzanâ, who was son to the last king of Pugân, to govern Taungu. The rulers continued to be for some years dependent on Ava; but as the power of that kingdom declined, that of Taungu increased. When Mengnâusî succeeded to the throne of Burma, the ruler of Taungu was Soalu. He came to Ava when invited, and was received with high distinction. This friendly treatment did not conciliate him, and not long after he entered into an alliance with the king of Pegu. They made a joint attack on Prome, then nominally subject to Burma. On his death the king of Pegu, Binya Rânkit, interfered to place his son Mengsoau on the throne of Taungu. After five years he was deposed by the king

Governors after the fall of Pugân.

A.D. 1313.

A.D. 1426.

A.D. 1437.

[1] See sketch of Taungu history by the Rev. Dr. F. Mason, Jour. Asiatic Society of Bengal, vol. xxviii., 1859, p. 9.

of Burma, who appointed as governor Tarabyâ, a Shân A.D. 1445. chief. This chief was succeeded by his son, Meng Kaungngè. The kings of Burma in vain tried to retain the small state in subjection. An army was sent by king Mahâ Thihathura to place a new governor, Zâlathengyân, in authority. Being the king's foster-brother, it was hoped he would be faithful to his sovereign. But he soon ceased to remit tribute, and even invited the king of Pegu to support him in his rebellion. The king of Burma next dispatched an army under a general styled Sîthu Kyoahteng, who was accompanied by two of the king's sons. The governor resisted, but though supported by the king of Pegu, he was defeated. The princes spared his life, and carried him off to Ava, A.D. 1470. leaving Sîthu Kyoahteng as head of this troublesome province.

Sîthu Kyoahteng becomes king.

Sîthu Kyoahteng soon threw off his allegiance to Ava. In the Mahâ Râjâweng he is described as a man of excessive ferocity; as delighting in the slaughter of men, whence he was called "Bilu," or ogre. He assumed the title of king, and for eleven years ruled after such fashion as a drunken savage might. He was succeeded by his son, known as Meng Sîthu or Sîthungè, who, expecting to be attacked from Ava, sent his wife and children to Pegu, where they were received by King Dhammâzedi. His reign lasted only four years, and he was then assassinated by his A.D. 1485–6. sister's son, Meng Kyînyo.

Meng Kyînyo seizes the throne.

This prince at once took possession of the palace, and assumed the title of Mahâ Thiri Zèrathura. The king of Burma, Dutiya Meng Khaung, sent him a white umbrella and other ensigns of royalty, thus formally acknowledging the independence of Taungu. The descent of Meng Kyînyo through his father, Mahâ Thenghkayâ, and through his mother, both from the last king of Pugân, and from the first Shân king of Pânyâ, is set forth in the Burmese history. Whether

this descent from the ancient kings of Burma was capable of proof may admit of doubt; but when the time came for the claim to be put forth by his son, beyond the limit of the small kingdom of Taungu, it was acknowledged by the general consent of the Burmese people. Meng Kyînyo soon became powerful, and his alliance was sought by the kings of Pegu and Siam, though from border disputes he was occasionally involved in hostilities with the former kingdom. Burmese men of rank, dissatisfied with the Shân kings A.D. 1526.
who reigned in Ava, came and settled in Taungu; and after the Monyin chief had taken Ava by storm, and his son Thohanbwâ with strange cruelty persecuted the Buddhist monks, there was an extensive emigration, and the king of Taungu was looked to as the refuge and hope of the Burmese race. He made a league with the king of Prome against Ava, in support of a rebellion by two brothers of the king, which, however, accomplished nothing of importance. He built the new city of Taungu, the rampart and ditch of which existed up to a recent period. His long reign of forty-five years A.D. 1530.
enabled him to consolidate his power; and dying, he left his kingdom to his son Mengtara, or Tabeng Shwèhtî, then only sixteen years of age.

The young king, though of an impetuous temper, His son Tabeng Shwèhtî succeeds.
had great ability. He was proud of his position as representing the ancient kings of Burma, and as the recognised champion of the Burmese people. The distracted state of what remained of the kingdom of Burma under Shân kings, and the weakened condition of Pegu after the death of Binya Rân, prompted him to assert his claims to the ancient monarchy which had been destroyed by the Mongolian invasion. He made careful preparations, collected arms and embodied men, and excited the enthusiasm of the Burmese for the restoration of the dominance of their race in its ancient seat. Four years were occupied in preparations, and it was deemed advisable first to attack Pegu.

Invades Pegu.

In that kingdom Binya Rân had been succeeded by his son, Takârwutbi, a youth of fifteen, who passed his time in frivolous amusements with bad companions. Tabeng Shwèhtî appeared before the capital of Pegu, which was defended by two Shân nobles. They held it so obstinately that the invader was obliged to retreat. In the following year he again advanced, and the city was now defended by many Indian Muhammadans with firearms, so that the besiegers were repulsed. It was not until a year later that Tabeng Shwèhtî took the city, and he was largely indebted for his success to the desertion of their master by the leading officers of the king of Pegu. For the first time Europeans now took part in the wars of Burma. The Portuguese viceroy had sent from Goa a galliot commanded by Ferdinand de Morales to trade in Pegu. A battle was fought between the Burmese and Talaing flotillas, in which the former were victorious, and the Portuguese commander, who had fought with the Talaings, was slain.[1] The capital then surrendered. Takârwutbi retired up the Irâwadi, intending to take refuge with his brother-in-law, the king of Prome. The question for the conqueror now was, whether it would be better to go on and attack Prome, or first to subdue Martaban, the second city of the kingdom, which had become a great seaport.

Takes the capital, A.D. 1538–39.

Tabeng Shwèhtî's principal general was his brother-in-law and kinsman, Kyoahteng Noarahtâ, who at once followed up the fugitive king and drove him beyond the Peguan frontier. He was received by Nârâbadî, the king of Prome. The general received the title of Bureng Naung, as designating him heir to the throne, though not appointed Ainshêmeng. It is the title by which he is best known. Throughout the reign of the young king he was all-powerful in the direction of

[1] The Portuguese in India, by Manuel de Faria of Sousa. Translated into English by Stevens. London, 1695.

affairs, and, with rare fidelity in that age and nation, loyally did his duty.

Marches to attack Prome, A.D. 153

It was determined to follow up the king of Pegu to Prome. The ambitious designs of Tabeng Shwèhtî had excited the alarm of the king of Burma and of the northern Shân chiefs. Thohanbwâ led a Shân army to repel the attack on Prome. Tabeng Shwèhtî arrived there with a strong flotilla, and an army on land, commanded by Bureng Naung. The flotilla captured such boats as the king of Ava had brought down, but a decisive action between the armies was avoided. Tabeng Shwèhtî either did not feel himself strong enough to take Prome, or affairs in the south called for his presence there. He suddenly retired down the river with his whole force.

Takârwultbi dies and Tabeng Shwèhtî becomes king of Pegu.

The king of Pegu now called upon his allies to follow the retreating army and restore him to his throne. This they refused, and the unfortunate king in his despair entered the delta with a small armed band, and either was killed in a skirmish, or died of sickness in the jangal. He was the last king of the dynasty established by Warêru. From this time Tabeng Shwèhtî is recognised as king of Pegu. His hereditary kingdom, Taungu, was ruled by Thingathu, the father of Bureng Naung, as tributary king.

CHAPTER XII.

PEGU UNDER A BURMESE KING, AND BURMA UNDER SHAN KINGS.

Tabeng Shwèhtî settles the country of the delta—Siege and capture of Martaban—Tabeng Shwèhtî consecrated king—Prome besieged and taken—Revolution in Ava, where the chief of Umbaung becomes king—Tabeng Shwèhtî consecrated king of kings—Invades Arakan—Invasion of Siam—Retreat from Yuthia—Tabeng Shwèhtî murdered.

Tabeng Shwèhtî settles the country of the delta.

TABENG SHWÈHTÎ, on his return to Pegu, arranged for the administration of the country. He desired to conciliate the people, and he appointed Talaing nobles to govern the districts. He commenced to repair the capital and strengthen its defences. He then prepared to proceed against Martaban. The wide territory which belonged to that city was governed by an officer styled Soabinyâ, brother-in-law to the late king of Pegu. He lived as viceroy in great state, and had a large armed force at his command. Since the opening of trade with Europe by the Cape of Good Hope, Martaban had become a great port. The Portuguese, who had occupied Malacca under Albuquerque in the year A.D. 1511, extended their trade northwards, and Antony Correa
A.D. 1519. concluded a commercial treaty with the viceroy at Martaban. Under that sanction they established a depôt where the produce of the country was stored for export to Europe.

Siege and capture of Martaban.

Tabeng Shwèhtî summoned the viceroy to submit. He, distrusting all offers of favour, and relying on the support the Portuguese could give him with ships, guns, and small firearms, refused compliance. The king of Pegu had assembled an army of 130,000 men, with hundreds of boats and vessels, large and small. Bureng Naung was the commander-in-chief, but the king himself accompanied the army, which marched by land A.D. 1540. from Pegu; the flotilla conveying stores and provisions proceeded by sea. Martaban, at that time a populous city, but now reduced to the size of a village, is situated at the mouth of the river Salwin. On the sea face the defence was intrusted to seven ships of European build, heavily armed, and manned by Europeans and Indians, which were moored close inshore. On the land side the city was protected by substantial earthworks, and a broad and deep ditch which defied assault. Bureng Naung saw no means of taking the place, except by strict blockade to starve the inhabitants shut up therein. Lines of besiegement, therefore, were drawn round the city on the land side, while the numerous flotilla prevented the approach of relief by sea. On the opposite side of the river, where now stands the opulent town of Maulmein, was a stockade, the commandant of which deserted his master and served the invader. For seven weary months the siege went on. In the besieging camp were seven hundred Portuguese under Cayero, formerly a naval officer. The viceroy also had a band of Portuguese under one Seixas. When affairs became desperate they left the city. The Burmese besiegers were repulsed in several attempts to force their way across the ditch and rampart; but they succeeded in setting fire to the ships by means of huge blazing rafts of bamboo, set adrift when the tide was favourable for floating them to where the ships were moored. In the city, famine had reduced the whole population to despair. The unfortunate viceroy endeavoured to avert his fate by negotiating with the conqueror, and begging to be allowed to live in retirement. Under promise that his life would be spared, he came out of the city with his wife, children, and a numerous body of attendants, men and women; but all were without mercy put to an ignominious death. Immense booty was obtained by the victors, and the city was set on fire and utterly destroyed.

Tabeng Shwèhtî consecrated king.

Tabeng Shwèhtî took measures for occupying the country to the eastward of the Salwin. Military posts were established on the frontier of the Thaungyîn river, to watch Zimmè and Siam. He then returned to Pegu, and was solemnly consecrated king according to the ancient ceremonies, in the capital. He was careful to crown the two great national pagodas at Hansâwadi and Dagun with new Htîs; and while endeavouring to secure the attachment of the Talaing people, he always put prominently forward his claim to Burmese nationality and sovereignty.

Prome besieged and taken, A.D. 1541.

The king lost no time in pushing his enterprise to recover Ava from the Shâns. At the close of the rainy season he advanced up the Irâwadi to occupy Prome. In that city Meng Khaung had succeeded his brother Nârâbadî, and was tributary to Thohanbwâ, reigning at Ava, whose daughter he had married. The army, with Bureng Naung as commander-in-chief, marched up by the east bank of the river, moving in concert with the fleet of boats. Prome was strongly fortified and well defended with guns and wall pieces. The plan of the invader was, as at Martaban, to reduce the city by famine; and with this object the army was disposed round the walls on the land side, while the numerous flotilla watched the river face. The king of Burma, supported by several northern Shân chiefs, marched down to the relief of his son-in-law. The king of Arakan sent a force across the mountains to operate on the flank of the invader. Bureng Naung marched to meet the Shân army, and utterly defeated it a few miles to the north of Prome. The guns which he brought into the field, and which were worked by Portuguese, mainly contributed to this victory. The Shâns fled to the north, and made no farther attempt to save Prome. The investment of that city was now resumed. The Arakanese force was easily defeated, and only saved from destruction by the hilly country, which favoured its flight. All help from the outside being thus cut off, and the soldiers and citizens exhausted from hunger, the king of Prome was forced to surrender. The king, the queen, and the chief officers were massacred with revolting cruelty, and Tabeng Shwèhtî not being then prepared to march on Ava, appointed a kinsman of Bureng Naung tributary king of Prome, with the title of Thado Dhamma Râjâ, and returned to Pegu. There he sought to atone for the guilt of bloodshed by founding costly religious buildings.

June, A.D. 1542.

Revolution in Ava, where the chief of Unbaung becomes king.

The progress of Tabeng Shwèhtî in accomplishing his plan deeply agitated the Burmese people. The cruelty of Thohanbwâ and his sacrilegious plunder of pagodas, had made him hated by Shâns as well as Burmese. While he was at a temporary palace near the capital, a band of conspirators overpowered the guards, and, in the language of the Burmese chronicler, "the king was seen no more." Shân influence was still the strongest in Ava, and the chief of Unbaung, known as Khun Mhaingngè, was invited to fill the vacant throne. He arrived at the city in the same year that Prome surrendered. Feeling that the presence in that frontier town of a ruler, the representative of Burmese ascendancy, was a direct menace to himself, he moved down with a Shân army and appeared before the place during the last month of the year. Tabeng Shwèhtî without delay came to the rescue. The Shâns again were defeated near Prome, and were followed up with untiring energy by Bureng Naung. He chased them to the very gates of Ava, but retiring from thence, occupied the ancient capital, Pugân. Tabeng Shwèhtî once more returned to Pegu, being convinced

A.D. 1544.

that the confederation of the northern Shân chiefs was still too strong to be successfully attacked. But, as if again to proclaim his right of sovereignty to the whole empire, when his army had occupied the ancient Burmese capital, he was solemnly consecrated with the title of King of kings. The tributary kings of Prome, Taungu, and Martaban did homage; and Bureng Naung was formally appointed Ainshemeng or heir-apparent. The monarch now gave his attention to the internal affairs of the kingdom. The people longed for rest after the wars and tumults of so many years, but this was not to be while the great object was still unattained.

Tabeng Shwèhtî consecrated King of kings.

Invades Arakan.

Chance enabled the king to interfere in Arakan, to pursue his plan of subduing the whole territory formerly dependent on, or tributary to, the ancient monarchy; and also to take revenge for the assistance given to his enemies. The king of that country, Meng Beng, had the sagacity to foresee this danger and prepare for it.[1] His brother, discontented, had fled to Pegu, and, like other royal refugees in the countries of Indo-China, offered, if placed on the throne of Arakan, to hold it as a tributary. Tabeng Shwèhtî occupied

A.D. 1546.

Sandoway after the rainy season, and marched on the capital. But the defences were too strong to be forced, and as news arrived of an incursion on Tavoy by a Siamese force, the invader was glad to make an arrangement under which he retired without molestation.

Invasion of Siam.

Provoked by the attack from the king of Siam, Tabeng Shwèhtî determined to invade that country. His preparations were on a great scale, and occupied him during the greater part of the year. Near the

A.D. 1548.

close of the year, when the country is dry after the heavy rainy season, the whole army was assembled at

[1] See chapter ix.

Martaban.[1] The arrangements for the campaign were, as on all previous occasions, under the orders of Bureng Naung. A small body of Portuguese, probably employed only as gunners, formed a part of the army. They were commanded by James Soarez, who afterwards rose to high office. The army crossed the Salwin river, and marching in an easterly direction, reached the Menâm river in its upper course. From thence it marched down the river-banks in three columns. When nearing Yuthia or Yodayâ, the then capital, the invaders met with a spirited resistance, but after severe fighting forced their way to the vicinity of the city. The king of Pegu, as had happened to him in Arakan, found the defences so strong, and by reason of the channels of the river so difficult of approach by an army, that, on the advice of Bureng Naung, he determined to retreat. The difficulty of feeding his large army also contributed to this resolution. The Siamese incessantly attacked the retreating invaders, thousands of whom were slain or died of hunger and disease. Fortunately for the Burmese king, the son-in-law of the king of Siam was taken prisoner in a skirmish. This led to negotiations, and the Burmo-Talaing army was allowed to continue its retreat without further attack. The expedition occupied five months.

Retreat from Yuthia.

From this time the character of Tabeng Shwèhti entirely changed. He was still young, being only thirty-six years of age, and had reigned twenty. From being active, diligent, and sober, he gave himself up to debauchery, and became incapable of attending to public duties. He made a companion of a Portuguese youth, a nephew of James Soarez, who supplied him with liquor, and became a confirmed drunkard. Bureng

Tabeng Shwèhti murdered.

[1] In the history of Siam, this first invasion by the king of Pegu is stated to have occurred A.D. 1543. See Bowring's Siam, vol. i. p. 46.

Naung banished this young man from the country and assumed the office of regent, maintaining with rare fidelity the nominal authority of the king. But notwithstanding his moderation and ability, there was deep discontent in the country. The Talaings writhed under the oppressive rule which forced them to become soldiers and carried them on distant expeditions, in which more perished from fatigue and disease than from the sword. This hatred of forced service had sunk deep into the minds of the people, and the imbecility of the king inspired them with hopes of deliverance from a foreign yoke. Not long after the remnant of the army had returned from Siam, a son by an inferior wife of Binya Rân, king of Pegu, who had been a Buddhist monk, put off his religious habit, roused the people to rebel, and took the title of Thaminhtoa Râma. He was joined by many; but being driven from the vicinity of the capital, he retired to the western part of the delta, where the difficult nature of the country gave him security. Bureng Naung followed him up, and took post at a central point to direct operations. A Talaing noble, Thaminsoadwut, a scion of the expelled royal race of Pegu, who had been appointed governor of Sittaung, was so thoroughly trusted that he was put in charge of the palace, and of the person of Tabeng Shwèhtî. The king was persuaded by him to go to reside at a country place; and a report being brought of a white elephant having been seen, he was induced to go to a secluded spot in the jangal to see the capture of the animal. There he was assassinated by order of his treacherous guardian.

The conspirator shut himself up in the town of Sittaung, which was strongly stockaded, and around which the whole population of the country was Talaing. He at once proclaimed himself king. The city of Pegu was at this time held by a half-brother of Bureng Naung, who had the title of Thihathu. He found the garrison too weak to support his authority against the citizens; he therefore left and marched to Taungu, where the family was all-powerful. Thaminsoadwut forthwith came to the capital, where the whole of the people rallied to his cause, and he had high hopes of restoring the native kingdom. Thus the dynasty established in Pegu as representing the ancient Burmese monarchy appeared to be ruined.

CHAPTER XIII.

PEGU AND BURMA UNITED UNDER A BURMESE KING.

Bureng Naung retires to Taungu—The last Talaing king—Bureng Naung conquers Pegu—Takes the city of Ava—Conquers the Shân states of the Upper Irâwadi—Subdues Zimmè—Religious measures—Invasion of Siam and capture of the capital—Operations in Zimmè—Rebellion in Pegu—Expedition to Laos; the queen taken prisoner—Second invasion of Siam—Bureng Naung marches into Laos without success—European travellers' account of Pegu—Laos becomes tributary under a new king—Revolt of the Northern Shâns—A pseudo-relic received from Ceylon—Bureng Naung appoints his son to be tributary king of Zimmè—Preparations to invade Arakan—Death of Bureng Naung.

Bureng Naung retires to Taungu.

Bureng Naung, in spite of his great name and the power he wielded, was for the moment vanquished by the overwhelming events of a few weeks. But many influential officers, Burmese, Talaing, and Shân, still trusted the ability, the generosity, and the fortune, of the designated successor to the throne. Finding the bulk of the Talaing population hostile, he determined to retreat to Taungu, where he might gather strength to retrieve his position. He marched past the city with only a small force, his reputation protecting him from attack, and made direct for his native city. His father had died two years before, and his half-brother Thihathu shut the gates against him. He retired to a position on the skirt of the mountains, and, undismayed, watched his opportunity to strike a blow.

The last Talaing king.

In the capital Thaminsoadwut by his cruelty soon alienated the goodwill the Talaings had felt for a chief of their own race. The other claimant to the throne, Thaminhtoa, driven from the delta, had gone to Martaban, and there collected round him a large body of men, undisciplined, but devoted to him. He was secretly invited by the Talaing leaders to come to the capital. A battle was fought between the rival kings near the city, in which Thaminhtoa was victorious. The other, who had occupied the palace for about three months, though he escaped from the battlefield, was taken prisoner and beheaded. The conqueror was consecrated king according to the ancient ceremonies, and is recognised in the Talaing chronicle, under the title of Zaggalî Meng, as the last representative of a native dynasty.

In the meantime many chiefs with their followers had joined Bureng Naung at his camp. He forced the surrender of the city of Taungu; pardoned his brother; and was consecrated king of his native land as his father's successor. He next determined to occupy Prome, where another of his brothers, who had been tributary king under Tabeng Shwèhtî, had been driven out by a local insurrection. He marched across the hills, retook Prome, and reinstated his brother as tributary king. The country up the Irâwadi as far as Pugân also submitted to him. His design was, as the lawful representative of the ancient kings of Burma, to drive the Shân usurper from Ava; but he deemed it prudent in the first place to conquer Pegu. He returned to Taungu, from whence the capital, Hansâwadi, was more accessible, as he had no flotilla to hold the great river in an advance by that route.

Bureng Naung conquers Pegu A.D. 1551.

Bureng Naung marched south with an army, not numerous, but well appointed, towards the close of the year. Thaminhtoa disdained to shut himself up in the capital, and met the invader in the field a short distance to the north of the city. A fierce battle ensued, in which the native king was defeated and fled. Bureng

Naung entered the city on the following day. Unwearied in his determination to stamp out rebellion, he two days later started in pursuit of the fugitive. Driven from the delta, the last Talaing king reached Martaban by sea in an open canoe. After three months' hiding he was taken prisoner and put to death. Bureng Naung appointed one of his many half-brothers tributary king of Martaban. He himself assumed the title of king of kings, and was consecrated with great solemnity, while his eldest son was declared heir-apparent, with the ancient designation among Hindus and Buddhists of Yuva Râjâ. A new palace was commenced at the capital of Pegu, which, when completed, exceeded in extent and magnificence any building that had been raised in these countries, and which excited the wonder and admiration of European travellers.

While engaged in these works for his own glorification before his people, the king incessantly prepared for the invasion of Ava. The power of the Shân monarchy had fallen low. Thohanbwâ, by his cruelty, and still more by his impiety, had incurred the hatred of Shâns and Burmese. After his death his successor, Kunmhaingngè, had authority only in a small extent of territory round the capital. A son of the Shân chief of Monyin occupied Sagaing, and proclaimed himself king there. Kunmhaingngè reigned for three years, and was succeeded by his son, who, feeling his helplessness, fled to Bureng Naung. The Shân chief at Sagaing then occupied Ava, and assumed the title
A.D. 1551-52. of Nârâbadî.

There appeared no strength in Ava capable of resisting Bureng Naung. He sent an army of observation up the Irâwadi, under the command of the heir-
A.D. 1553. apparent, during the rainy season. But the prospect of a powerful king being established in Ava made the Shân chiefs for a time curb their mutual jealousies, and renew their league against the common foe. Large

bodies of men appeared at Tarukmyu and other towns on the river to oppose invasion, and the reconnoitering army did not advance beyond Pugân. The king, seeing the formidable resistance to be encountered, spared no exertion to ensure success. An immense army was raised, and a flotilla of war boats and transports for provisions numbering fourteen hundred. The army advanced in two columns—one by the line of the Irâwadi, accompanying the flotilla; the other, with which was the king himself, by the valley of the Sittaung river on Taungu. The heir-apparent was left at the capital as his father's deputy, and precautions were taken on the frontiers to guard against attack from Arakan and Siam.

Takes the city of Ava, A.D. 1554.

The army marched after the rainy season. The flotilla had been dispatched earlier. The king had a bodyguard of four hundred Portuguese, dressed in uniform and armed with arquebuses. The main body advanced to Ramèthen, and from thence—all except a corps under the king of Taungu—inclining to the left, debouched upon the great river at Pugân, where the flotilla soon after arrived. The king of Taungu, continuing to march north, met with little opposition, and entrenched himself in the neighbourhood of Pânyâ. Bureng Naung, for some reason not explained, crossed to the west bank of the river, and marched northward, crossed the Hkyendwin river at Amyin, and then appeared with his whole army and flotilla at Sagaing, opposite to Ava. There was no force capable of meeting him in the field, and he communicated with his brother near Pânyâ to make a combined attack on the city. The king of Taungu issued from his entrenchment, and was at once attacked, though feebly, by the Shân king of Burma. The Shâns were defeated and retired into the city. Bureng Naung now crossed the river and the city was invested. From his numerous army and great flotilla he held complete command of the river and the country; while, from the dejected temper of the garrison, and the hatred the citizens bore to the Shân king, a stubborn defence was not looked for. In a few days a general assault was made, and Ava fell to the conqueror. The Shân king was made prisoner and sent to Pegu. Bureng Naung determined to continue the city of Pegu as the capital of his empire, and made his brother tributary king of Ava, with the title of Thado Mengsoa. He himself remained at Ava for some months, watching the movements of the northern Shân chiefs; but the season being too advanced for operations in the field, he returned to Pegu. He built a new fort near his southern capital, and gilded his father's pagoda at Taungu. He also opened communication with the king of Ceylon, and sent rich offerings to the holy tooth relic in that island.

March, A.D. 1555.

Conquers the Shân states of the Upper Irâwadi.

An opportunity soon occurred for carrying out the plans of the king of kings against the northern Shân chiefs, and this was facilitated by the characteristic jealousies and dissensions of those rulers. The chief of Umbaung having died, a dispute arose in the family as to the succession. The chief of Monè interfered, and one claimant appealed to Ava for assistance. Bureng Naung without delay proceeded with his whole court to Ava. There a large army was assembled. In a few months he had overrun the whole of the country of the Upper Irâwadi, as far as the Patkoi range, which separates Burma from Asam. His soldiers, though born and nurtured in the tropics, urged on by his spirit and example, chased the fugitive Shâns into the mountains on the north-east, amidst the region of snow. The two most powerful chiefs, Mogaung and Monyin, swore fealty to the king of kings, and religious reforms were introduced to bring the worship of the Shân people into conformity with the Buddhism of Burma. The practice which existed of sacrificing an elephant, a horse, and even slaves, at

A.D. 1557.

the funeral of a chief, was strictly prohibited, and from this time appears to have ceased.

Bureng Naung returned to Pegu, but the following year had to punish the states of Thiboa and Monè. From the latter he marched on to Zimmè, the chief of which had assisted that state. The country presented grave difficulties, but the city was reached after forty-five days of arduous march. The king was compelled to surrender his capital and swore allegiance to the invader. He agreed to pay an annual tribute of elephants, horses, silk, and other products of his country. An army of occupation was placed at Zimmè to enforce the treaty and watch the frontiers of Siam and Lengzeng or Laos.[1] The conqueror then returned to Ava. He at once commenced to settle the taxation payable by the people of Burma, and received the homage of the chiefs of the country east of Bamoa up to the frontier of China. They were excused from paying tribute, probably from dread of offending the emperor of that country. While thus employed, news was brought that the king of Laos or Lengzeng was gathering a force to attack the Burmese army in Zimmè. The king of Ava was at once sent with reinforcements, and the attack having been repelled, he was recalled. Bureng Naung then proceeded to Pegu, where he arrived at the beginning of the rainy season.

Subdues Zimmè. *August, A.D. 1558.* *May, A.D. 1559.*

The king of kings, ambitious of being esteemed the greatest upholder of religion in the world of Buddhism, had already laid the foundation of a pagoda at his capital, and the work was now continued. Supposed holy relics were deposited in the interior chamber, with golden images of Buddha, of his disciples, and of the

Religious measures.

[1] Lengzeng is the Burmese name for what was the chief city of Laos, situated on or near to the Mekong river, a considerable distance below Kiang Kheng. The seat of government appears at different periods to have been Luang Phrabang, Viengchang, and Lantchiang. See Captain W. C. M'Leod's Journal, p. 39; Travels by Louis de Carne, p. 125 Travels by Mouhot, vol. ii. p. 141; and Bowring's Siam, vol. ii. p. 8, *note.*

royal family. Following up the measures of reform which he had carried out in Shânland, he prohibited the sacrifice of animals by the Muslim population of the city, and induced a number of those foreigners to profess, at least outwardly, the doctrine of the three treasures. The kings of Burma, though rigidly enforcing the observances of Buddhism by their own subjects, have generally been tolerant towards foreigners, and this is a solitary instance of an apparent departure from the rule of non-interference with the religion of strangers settled in the country.

The empire was at peace for three years. Afterwards, about the middle of the year, some of the small states east of Bamoa made attacks on Momit, which was tributary to Burma. Bureng Naung was convinced that they were instigated from China, and sent an army into the hill territory watered by the river Tapeng, to punish the aggression. Religious reforms were now introduced into this country, and measures were adopted for the entire subjection of the chiefs to Burma as the dominant power.

A.D. 1562.

Invasion of Siam and capture of the capital.

The king of kings, notwithstanding his power and glory, felt keenly the want of one distinctive mark in popular estimation of a great Buddhist sovereign in Indo-China—the possession of a white elephant. The king of Siam was known to have four of these venerated animals, and an opportunity was taken of some cause for dissatisfaction with that ruler, arising from events on the frontier, to send a demand that one of them should be given up. An ambiguous reply was returned, which the haughty monarch resented as a refusal, and determined to punish as an insult. An immense army of Burmese, Shâns, and Talaings was collected, and divided into four great corps, under the command of the heir-apparent and the three tributary kings. Instead of marching from Martaban, as in the invasion of 1548, the several corps assembled at Taungu

and other places on the Sittaung after the rainy season.[1] A.D. 1563.
The army marched on Zimmè, and from thence down the valley of the Menam to the capital, Yuthia. The city was invested. Three Portuguese ships, which were moored near shore and supported by batteries, were taken, and the king of Siam, disheartened at this loss, surrendered. The defeated king, his queens, and his younger son were carried away as captives, while the elder son, styled Brâmahin, was made tributary king. The conqueror then set out on his return, and determined to punish the king of Zimmè, who had failed to present himself on the arrival of the invading army. But hearing that a rebellion had broken out in Pegu, Bureng Naung hastened back, leaving his son in command. On reaching his capital, he found that many of the fine buildings he had erected had been burnt by the rebels. These were rebuilt, and a new palace, surpassing the former one in magificence, was commenced, but not finished until three years later. This palace is mentioned by European travellers as composed of an extensive group of grand pavilions "as big as an ordinary city," having the roofs of some apartments covered with plates of solid gold. No doubt the three white elephants brought from Siam were housed in some of these pavilions. March, A.D. 1564.

Operations in Zimmè.

In the meanwhile, the heir-apparent had not acted with vigour against the king of Zimmè, who had fled eastward, and was sheltered by the king of Lengzeng. Bureng Naung determined to proceed himself to direct operations. He left the capital, and proceeded to Labong, near Zimmè. A large force marched with him, which included many Indians and four hundred Portuguese as gunners. The petty chiefs of the Yun tribe were ready to continue the struggle for independence, but the king November, A.D. 1564.

[1] In the history of Siam this invasion is stated to have occurred in 1547. The Burmese army is said to have numbered 900,000 men. Bowring's Siam, vol. i. p. 49.

of Zimmè voluntarily submitted, saying he did not wish to reign longer. Detachments of troops were sent through the country to put down opposition.

Rebellion in Pegu.

While the king of kings was thus engaged, a rebellion broke out in Pegu, headed by a Shân captive named Binya Kyan, in which thousands of Talaings joined. They marched on the capital, where the officers in command became panic-stricken. The deposed king of Burma, Nârâbadî, who was in the city, pointed out that the rebels were a mere unarmed rabble. He was intrusted with a force, at the head of which he issued from the city and defeated the mob of peasants. Bureng Naung on hearing of this outbreak hastened back to his capital. On seeing that many of his fine buildings outside the city walls had been burnt, he was so enraged, that, without entering the city, he went on to Dâla to hunt down the remnant of the rebel body. Thousands were taken prisoners, and the king intended to enclose them all in a vast temporary building of bamboo, and burn them and their families alive according to Burmese law. On the intercession of the Buddhist monks he pardoned all except the leaders.

Expedition to Laos. The queen taken prisoner.

The Yuva Râjâ after the departure of his father continued operations against the Yun chiefs in the country east of Zimmè. He followed them in pursuit across the Mekong river, and at length the chiefs, or those who still held out, were driven to shut themselves up in the town of Maingzân, by which name the Burmese probably mean a fort near the Laos city Viengchang. The king of Lengzeng was in the stronghold with his family. The place was captured, but the king escaped in the confusion. Bureng Naung ordered the army to return, leaving a strong garrison in Zimmè, and the Yuva Râjâ reached the capital of Pegu in October. The

A.D. 1565.

queen of Lengzeng and many prisoners of high rank were brought in.

For three years there was a pause in the wars and

commotions which had so long disturbed and devastated the country. The king of Lengzeng still gave trouble to the Burmese officers in the territory of Zimmè, but his son-in-law came in and made his submission. Everything looked promising; the capital of Pegu was a scene of splendour exceeding all known in its past history; and trading ships from Europe, from India, and from Malacca, freely entered the seaports. With continued peace the country might soon have recovered the terrible loss of population, and decrease of agriculture, which the incessant wars in distant countries had caused; but those wars, and the hostile occupation of the conquered countries, rendered lasting peace impossible. An indulgence granted, it may be, from a generous feeling towards a fallen enemy, hastened the catastrophe, which probably it was hoped might, by showing confidence, be averted. The deposed king of Siam had become a Rahân, and was permitted to go to his own country to worship. His son, who had been his companion in captivity, died, and his widow was allowed to return home with her children. Brâmahin, the tributary king, when there were no hostages for his loyalty, soon began to take measures for asserting his independence. In this he was supported by his father, who abandoned his monk's habit, and secretly influenced events with authority, if he did not openly assume it. Bureng Naung at once made preparations for another invasion of Siam. The brother-in-law of the tributary king, who was governor of Pitsalauk, a stronghold on a branch of the Upper Menâm, refused to support the revolt, and held his post for the king of kings. Bureng Naung collected a vast army, which, including followers, may have numbered two hundred thousand men, and marching from Martaban, relieved the fort of Pitsalauk, which had been besieged by the Siamese. He then moved down to attack the capital, after having made arrangements to hold the country of the Upper Menâm. The

Second invasion of Siam, October, A.D. 1568.

Siamese were determined to make a desperate defence, and the invader could only hope to reduce the city by famine. After four months no effect had been produced, but the old king died. Brâmahin made offers of surrender, which, with unusual candour, were not accepted, though the Burmese army had suffered immense loss. The king of Lengzeng approached to relieve the city. Bureng Naung, leaving his most trusted officer, Binya Dâla, in command, proceeded himself with half his force to meet the king of Laos, who was defeated. The invader then returned to renew the siege. Affairs had become very serious, and he had recourse to stratagem. One of his Siamese adherents, a noble of high rank, pretending to desert, entered the city with irons on his legs. He was received with joy by Brâmahin, and appointed to a high command. Through his treacherous machinations one of the city gates was opened, and the besiegers entered in the night, after a siege of seven months.[1] The city was given up to plunder. The unfortunate Brâmahin was made prisoner, and either was put to death or committed suicide. The king of kings remained in Yuthia for two months, and appointed Thaungkyi, a member of the Zimmè royal family, tributary king.

August, A.D. 1569. Capital taken.

Bureng Naung marches into Laos without success.

Bureng Naung sent back by the nearest route to Pegu all sick and disabled men, with the plunder he had reserved and prisoners of importance; but with untiring energy he determined himself to follow up the king of Lengzeng. He proceeded with his hale and unwounded men to Pitsalauk, and from thence directed the march to the north-east of the several divisions of his army. In a few days he followed, and encamped

[1] In the history of Siam the prominent events of this invasion and siege coincide with the account given in the Burmese history; but the date assigned for the capture of the city is 1555. The Venetian traveller Cæsar Fredericke, who was in Pegu and the neighbouring countries apparently from 1567 to 1569, places the "coming home of the king" from this war in 1569. By the Burmese history he arrived home in 1570. See Bowring's Siam, vol. i. p. 51.

on the right bank of the Mekong opposite Maingzân. Some of the divisions passed the river higher up and moved down the left bank. As Bureng Naung was prepared to cross by a bridge of boats, the enemy evacuated the city. The place was made a depôt for stores and for the sick, the king of Taungu being placed in command, and Bureng Naung himself marched in pursuit of the enemy. The king of Laos was too wary to come to an engagement, and the invaders were soon wearied by long marches in a mountainous country, and by want of food. They returned to Maingzân thoroughly exhausted, and the whole army recrossing the Mekong, marched back to Pitsalauk. Bureng Naung, pushing on to his capital, arrived there a month later. Of the original army which marched against Siam, very few men survived to reach their own country. June, A.D. 1570.

European travellers' account of Pegu.

As if to atone for the demerit incurred by having caused the deaths of so many thousands of beings, Bureng Naung on his arrival made costly offerings to the pagodas. He also gave his attention to foreign trade, and built a ship of his own, which he sent to Ceylon and to ports of Southern India. At this period the Venetian traveller Cæsar Fredericke describes, as translated in Purchas' "Pilgrims," how "the king sitteth every day in person to hear the suits of his subjects, up aloft in a great hall on a tribunal seat, with his barons round about," while on the ground, "forty paces distant," are the petitioners, "with their supplications in their hands, which are made of long leaves of a tree, and a present or gift, according to the weightiness of their matter." And, adds the traveller, "the king of Pegu hath not any army or power by sea, but in the land, for people, dominions, gold and silver, he far exceeds the power of the Great Turk in treasure and strength." This is as strong testimony to the magnificence of the king of kings as is to be found in the pages of the Mahâ Râjâweng.

Laos becomes tributary under a new king.

In the year following the return of Bureng Naung there was a disturbance in the territories of Mogaung and Monyin, but it was suppressed without difficulty. Soon after, the king's great enemy, the king of Lengzeng, was killed in an attack he made on a town belonging to Cambodia. One of the prisoners who had been brought from Laos was Ubarît, brother to the deceased king. He consented, if placed on the throne of his native country, to be tributary to the Burmese monarch. An expedition was therefore sent under Binya Dâla. It was unsuccessful, and Bureng Naung, who never forgave a failure, either put to death the unfortunate general, hitherto a special favourite, or sent him into exile to a sickly place, where he soon died. The levy of another army to carry out this project was commenced, but the people, and even those in high office, murmured loudly, and the expedition was postponed. But the king of kings was not to be entirely
A.D. 1574. thwarted in his grand designs. After the rainy season he himself led an army, with Ubarît in his retinue, to Maingzân. From that post he issued a proclamation that he had come to place the rightful heir on the throne. He then departed, leaving some troops with the tributary king. The object of the expedition was attained. The nobleman who had usurped the throne of Laos had become hated, and was delivered up, together with his son, by his own officers. Ubarît was received by the people as king; and the Burmese commanders, rejoicing to quit a country where they gained neither fame nor riches, returned with their prisoners to Zimmè.

Revolt of the northern Shâns.

While affairs in Laos were prospering, another march to Monyin and Mogaung had become imperative. These restive states had refused to join the last expedition to Lengzeng, and were in open revolt. Bureng Naung proceeded from Maingzân to Ava, from whence he marched north against the rebellious chiefs. The prince of Monyin was killed, but the ruler of Mogaung fled; and though the royal troops followed in rapid pursuit to a tract of country where there was only snow for water, he was not captured. Bureng Naung, while still engaged in that northern region, had the usurper from Laos and his family forwarded to him as an exhibition to the northern Shâns of his success and power. But the desired effect was not attained, and the king of kings, recalling his son and the other officers from the pursuit, returned to his capital. The young chief of Mogaung was, however, afterwards surrendered by some of his own officers, and was ungenerously exhibited in fetters of gold at one of the gates of the city. Many of his officers were cruelly sold as slaves to foreign merchants, who carried them beyond sea.

July, A.D. 1576.

A pseudo-relic received from Ceylon.

At the very moment of his return to Pegu, Bureng Naung received intelligence which gratified his religious aspirations, and enhanced his glory as a Buddhist king throughout Indo-China. He had long been in communication with a Buddhist ruler in Ceylon, apparently Dharmapala, who reigned at Colombo, and professed to be a Christian, having the baptismal name of Don Juan.[1] Two years before, a Sinhalese princess had arrived, and had been received with high honour, though the Portuguese historian asserts, that the lady sent was only a daughter of the chamberlain. Now, at an auspicious moment, when the king of kings returned triumphant from war, a ship arrived from Ceylon at Bassein, with the holy tooth of Goadama Buddha. As the season was unfavourable for the ship to sail into the gulf of Martaban, a deputation of the highest nobles in the land was sent to receive the precious relic. They bore a golden vase, adorned with the

[1] His authority was confined to Colombo, his grand-uncles having possession of the rest of his dominions. He died A.D. 1581, and by will left the king of Portugal heir to his kingdom. Tennent's Ceylon, vol. ii. p. 13.

richest gems, the spoil of vanquished kings, in which it was deposited, and brought to the royal presence. A letter was also received from Dharmapala, in which he announced that he was the only orthodox king of four, who ruled in the island. It may be doubted whether Bureng Naung really believed in the genuineness of the relic, but the possession of a pseudo-tooth which his many millions of subjects believed in, was of the highest importance. Indeed, the first and immediate good result was the surrender of the young chief of Mogaung, which was attributed to the occult influence of the holy tooth, in favour of its royal custodian and worshipper. So munificently did he reward the king of Colombo, that, according to the Portuguese historian, the king of Kandy offered him a true daughter and tooth. The real tooth, which had been taken at Jaffna in 1560, had been destroyed by Don Constantine, the Viceroy of India, although Bureng Naung had then offered a sum equivalent to £41,000 sterling to ransom it. But, as stated by Faria y Sousa, two teeth were set up instead of that one, and the king of Pegu was now content with that he had secured.

Bureng Naung appoints his son to be tributary king of Zimmè, March, A.D. 1578.

In order to strengthen his position towards Lengzeng, Bureng Naung appointed his son, Tharâwadi Meng, who had shown great ability, tributary king of Zimmè. When he had left for his kingdom, the king his father, as if foreseeing future troubles, enjoined him to remember that he would owe allegiance to his elder brother, the Yuva Râjâ. He received the title of Noarahtâ Zoa. In the following year it was necessary once more to send aid to Ubarît in Lengzeng. The heir-apparent was sent to support the king of Zimmè, and the expedition was successful. From this time Laos as a tributary state is not mentioned in Burmese history.

Preparation to invade Arakan.

The great king of kings had now subdued all the countries which had occupied his attention during many years. Instead of resting and giving relief to his subjects, he turned his glance on Arakan. He determined that the king of that country should be reduced to the position his ancestors had held towards the ancient kings of Burma. A large fleet of vessels of various sizes was collected, in which an army amounting, with the crews, to eighty thousand men, was embarked. The fleet happened to be met by some Portuguese ships which were cruising near Cape Negrais. The Viceroy being then at war with Pegu, probably on account of the king's interference in the affairs of Ceylon, the ships attacked the Peguan or Burmese fleet, which they estimated at thirteen hundred sail. The Portuguese took some of the enemy, but were obliged to withdraw on account of the great number opposed to them. The Burmese fleet then continued its course, and the army disembarked at a point on the southern coast of Arakan, where the men were landed and marched to Sandoway. There the Burmese army remained inactive for twelve months. Probably Bureng Naung intended to lead the march on the capital, but found his health unequal to the exertion. To the last, he had not abandoned his design against Arakan, for reinforcements were sent on. The Burmese history states that he deputed ambassadors to the Emperor Akbar. This may possibly refer to messengers having been sent to the governor of Bengal after that province had been conquered by Akbar's general in 1576, and the object probably was to ascertain whether his occupation of Arakan would be viewed as an act of hostility to the Mogul emperor. But the plan of conquest of Arakan was suddenly frustrated by the death of Bureng Naung, after he had reigned for thirty years.

November, A.D. 1580.

October, A.D. 1581.

Death of Bureng Naung, November, A.D. 1581.

CHAPTER XIV.

PEGU AND BURMA AGAIN SEPARATED.

Successor of Bureng Naung—Establishes his authority in Burma proper—Failure of invasion of Siam—Desolation of Pegu—The tributary kings revolt—The city of Pegu besieged—The supreme king taken prisoner and put to death.

Successor of Bureng Naung. ON the death of Bureng Naung, his eldest son, the Yuva Râjâ, succeeded to the throne without dispute.[1] He at once recalled the army from Sandoway. His uncles, the kings of Prome and Taungu, came to Pegu and did homage, as also did the king of Siam. His uncle the king of Ava, Thadomengsoa, made excuses, and communicated with the kings of Prome and Taungu, endeavouring to draw them into a league for becoming independent of the supreme king. They disclosed the intrigue, and the supreme king suspecting that many of his officers had joined in a conspiracy against him, caused them, their wives, and children, to A.D. 1583. be burnt to death. This dreadful scene was witnessed by Gasparo Balbi, a Venetian merchant, who was in Pegu, and feelingly mentions his "great compassion and grief that little children, without any fault, should suffer such martyrdom."

Establishes his authority in Burma proper. The supreme king now marched on Ava, being joined with their forces by the kings of Prome and Taungu. Advancing up the valley of the Sittaung river, the army May, A.D. 1584. encamped near Pânwa. A battle was fought, in which

[1] In the Talaing chronicle this king is called Nanda Bureng. In the Mahâ Râjâweng he is styled Gnâ su Dâragâ, and is surnamed Taungu Yauk Meng, from having been carried as prisoner to Taungu.

the uncle and nephew, each on his elephant, with a small body of followers, engaged in fierce combat. Though the elephant which the supreme king rode fell exhausted, the rider instantly mounted another and gained the victory. The king of Ava fled from the field, and escaped over the Chinese border, where he died soon after. The supreme king at first appointed a governor to Ava, but before long his son, Mengrè Kyoa-swâ, was made tributary king.

During this war the conduct of Byanarît, king of Siam, was first suspicious, and then openly hostile. He had been summoned as a vassal to attend his superior with his army. He appeared on the frontier near Sit-taung, and the Yuva Râjâ, who was regent during his father's absence, directed him to march on Ava. Instead of obeying this order, he came near the capital of Pegu, and hovering about, menaced an attack. Hearing, however, of the victory of the supreme king, he retired to Martaban, and carried off from thence a number of the inhabitants into Siam.[1] A force under the Yuva Râjâ was sent to avenge this insult. The expedition was hastily planned and badly conducted. In marching down the banks of the Menâm the Yuva Râjâ was attacked by Byanarît, and forced to retreat with heavy loss. To retrieve this disaster the supreme king himself led an army, which invested Yuthia. But the son, though brave, lacked the great administrative qualities which had distinguished his father. The arrangements for the army were utterly defective. Thousands died from want and exposure. No hope of success remained, and a disastrous retreat was made. The king reached his capital with a small escort. With unreasoning obstinacy, he, three years later, sent an invading army into Siam under the Yuva Râjâ. This force was destroyed by incessant

Failure of invasion of Siam

A.D. 1587.

June, A.D. 1587.

[1] These events appear to be referred to in the history of Siam as having occurred A.D. 1564. Bowring's Siam, vol. i. p. 52.

attacks from the Siamese under the valiant Byanarît. The supreme king, with blind fury, once more dispatched an army under his son, with orders to take the Siamese capital. The Yuva Râjâ penetrated near to Yuthia, but was defeated and killed in battle. The supreme king put many of his most loyal officers to death, and trusted none. The tributary king of Ava was appointed Yuva Râjâ, but was unable to moderate the cruelty of his father, who even slew many Buddhist monks of Talaing race. Thousands of people abandoned their country and fled, and the delta—the richest part of the kingdom—became depopulated from war, famine, and migration. The king of Siam advanced with an army to Martaban. He was moving on the capital; but hearing that a force was on the way from Taungu to attack him, he retired to his own country. A number of Talaings went with him.

February, A.D. 1593.

Desolation of Pegu.

The tributary king's revolt.

The king of Prome now rebelled against his father, and marched to take possession of Taungu during the absence of his brother, who had gone to defend the capital. He failed to enter that city, but carried off many head of cattle. The supreme king was abandoned by all who might have supported him. He had alienated his whole family except his younger brother, Ngyoung Ram Meng, who had succeeded Mengrè Kyoaswâ as tributary king of Ava, and still remained faithful. But though he professed allegiance to the supreme monarch, he rendered no active support. The king of Zimmè no longer abided by the injunctions of his father. The king of Taungu leagued with the king of Arakan, who possessed a powerful fleet, and the son of the latter, Meng Khamaung, brought a large force and took possession of Syriam, near to Dagun, and then the principal seaport of the delta. The nominally supreme king had no means of resistance to this aggression. The king of Taungu sent an army down the valley of the Sittaung, under his son Nat Sheng-

A.D. 1596.

naung, and, with the Arakanese fleet, Hansâwadi, the capital of Pegu, was invested. The city was surrendered, and the supreme king, the son and successor of the great Bureng Naung, was ignominiously sent prisoner to Taungu, where, not long afterwards, he was secretly put to death. The king of Taungu returned to his own dominion with the principal part of the plunder. The prince of Arakan received a portion of the treasure, with a white elephant, and one of the princesses of the family of the supreme king. He returned to his own country, leaving a garrison to hold Syriam; and the capital of Pegu, on the buildings of which Bureng Naung had lavished the gold and silver reft from the conquered countries, was left a heap of ruins.

The city of Pegu besieged. Supreme king taken prisoner and put to death, December, A.D. 1599.

The warlike king of Siam again appeared in Pegu. He desired to gain possession of the person of the supreme king; but this being impossible, he retreated to Martaban. He made a Talaing chief king of that province, with the old title of Binya Dâla; and Byathabaik was made tributary king of Tavoy. Thus the great empire of united Pegu and Burma, which a generation before had excited the wonder of European travellers, was utterly broken up; and the wide delta of the Irâwadi, with a soil fertile as Egypt, and in a geographical position commanding the outlet of a great natural highway, was abandoned by those who might claim to represent the ancient rulers, and left to be parcelled out by petty local chiefs, and European adventurers.

CHAPTER XV.

PEGU AND BURMA AGAIN UNITED.

The king of Arakan occupies Syriam—Philip de Brito appointed agent to the king—Seizes the port—Is supported by the Portuguese Viceroy of India—The king of Arakan attacks Syriam and is defeated—De Brito offends the Talaings by his evil deeds—Ngyaung Ram Meng, king of Burma, son of Bureng Naung—His son, Mahâ Dhammâ Râjâ, destroys Syriam and reigns in Pegu.

The king of Arakan occupies Syriam.

THE fate of Pegu was for the moment decided by the presence of Portuguese adventurers, who swarmed in Arakan and the neighbouring countries.[1] The king of Arakan at this time was Meng Râjâgyî, who had taken the Muhammadan name of Salim Shah.[2] His son, Meng Khamaung, had commanded the fleet and army which co-operated with the king of Taungu in the siege of the capital of Pegu. The prince, when leaving to return home with the booty he had acquired, placed a garrison in the port of Thanhlyin, called by Europeans Syriam. It was at that time the principal seaport of the kingdom, and remained so until superseded by Rangoon. The king of Arakan determined to retain Syriam, but saw that as the Portuguese had command of the sea, he could not safely do so without their concurrence. Too proud openly to ask for their assistance, he sought to obtain it by means of one of their own countrymen who was in his service. For some years there had been in Arakan a young Portuguese, origi-

[1] See chapter xviii.

[2] That this king was known by this name to foreigners is evident from the Portuguese historian, who has written it Xilimixa.

nally a shipboy, who had served as a menial in the palace, and was trusted by the king as a faithful servant. His name was Philip de Brito and Nicote.[1] He was sent by the king of Arakan to have charge of the custom-house at Syriam, and to represent the king with his own countrymen. The commandant of the garrison was an Arakanese. He had no authority over the Portuguese inhabitants, who were guaranteed the enjoyment of their own laws. De Brito appears gradually to have formed the plan of becoming master of the town and port. He got permission to build a custom-house of brick; a fort was afterwards constructed as a protection to the custom-house; and by the boldness of a Portuguese officer, Salvador Ribeyro, the Arakanese commander was expelled from the settlement. De Brito was now supreme as governor. He went to Goa to seek from the viceroy authority to hold the town under him. During his absence the king of Arakan sent an army across the mountains under the expelled commandant, who was also joined by some troops sent by the king of Prome. They came down the Irâwadi and invested Syriam, and being joined by a large body of the Talaing population, continued the siege for eight months. Ribeyro was acting governor, and determined not to surrender. To prevent his countrymen from thinking of escape while suffering from hunger, he burnt three ships he had in the port. At length relief was sent by the viceroy, and the investing force withdrew. Ribeyro took prudent measures to conciliate the Talaing chiefs, who now offered to accept de Brito as king of Pegu. He, in the meantime, had married the viceroy's niece and returned to Pegu with the title of captain-general.

Philip de Brito appointed agent to the king.

De Brito seizes the port.

[1] The story of this adventurer is told in De Sousa's History, vol. iii., and in the native histories of Arakan and Burma. He is mentioned in the narrative of the Hollander traveller Floris, and in the letters of the Jesuit Fathers Boves and Fernandez. One of these Fathers states that he went from Arakan to Pegu with De Brito in A.D. 1600 (Purchas' Pilgrims, vol. ii. p. 1746).

Is supported by the Portuguese Viceroy of India.

He had with him six ships, and proclaimed his reception of the kingdom in the name of his sovereign He put the fortifications in order, built a church, and marked out the limits of the city, which, with prudent management, might have become the capital of a great province under the crown of Portugal.

The king of Arakan attacks Syriam and is defeated.

The king of Arakan was not disposed to allow his former servant to remain quietly in his usurped position; but knowing that de Brito was now supported by the viceroy, he temporised, and sent him a complimentary message. De Brito forwarded a rich present to his former master. But this false courtesy on both sides, was soon changed to open war. The king of Arakan entered into a league with the king of Taungu, and sent a force to Pegu under his son Meng Khamaung. The army, embarked in several hundred vessels, approached Syriam, and the Arakanese flotilla was at once attacked by a few Portuguese ships commanded by Pinnero. The Arakanese were defeated, and the prince was taken prisoner and carried to Syriam. De Brito had the good feeling to treat the son of his former master with great respect. Nevertheless, he demanded a ransom of fifty thousand crowns for his release. The king of Arakan, sooner than submit to these terms, determined to make another attempt to take the port. Leagued with the king of Taungu, they brought a more formidable host to the attack by land and sea. Pinnero gallantly went out to fight the assailing vessels, but failed, and perished by blowing up his own ship rather

A.D. 1604.

than be taken prisoner. The allied force was unable to capture the town, and the king of Arakan having paid the ransom demanded, the young prince was released.

De Brito offends the Talaings by his evil deeds.

De Brito was now secure. The Talaing chiefs sought his friendship, and even the king of Taungu entered into alliance with him. Bassein and all the western side of the delta was independent. But de Brito's son,

Simon, married a daughter of Binya Dâla, the king of Martaban, who was tributary to Siam, and the Portuguese interests were thereby secured in that important province. The captain-general, however, instead of endeavouring to conciliate the native population, from prudent self-interest, if not from a sense of justice, by showing respect to their religious feelings, wantonly outraged them. The native historians, Burmese and Talaing, record with intense bitterness that the pagodas round the city of Pegu were dug into and plundered of the golden images, and precious stones, which Bureng Naung had enshrined in those fabrics. The people, deeply moved at this sacrilege, murmured among themselves that their race and religion would be brought to an end. The perpetrator of these outrages vainly sought to strengthen his government by pressing Buddhists to become nominal Christians; for the Portuguese historian speaks of a hundred thousand converts to Christianity. While the foreign intruder, by his arrogance and oppression, was digging a pit for his own fall, a power was rising in the country of the upper Irâwadi which was destined to avenge his deeds of injustice.

Ngyaung Ram Meng, king of Burma, son of Bureng Naung.

After the destruction of the capital of Pegu, and when the supreme king had been carried as a captive to Taungu, his younger brother, Ngyaung Ram Meng, refrained from interfering in the affairs of the lower country, and sought to establish his own authority in the ancient kingdom of Burma. The country in the valley of the Irâwadi to the north of Pugân submitted to him. His nephew, the king of Prome, seeing danger to himself in this consolidation of power, determined to invade Ava, but was assassinated by one of his own officers, who then declared himself king of Prome. Ngyaung Ram Meng having strengthened the defences of his capital, marched against the chiefs of Mogaung and Monyin, who had refused to pay tribute. He was unsuccessful in this expedition, but punished the chief

of Bamoa, and extended his authority along the Upper Sittaung to Ramêthen. The next three or four years were occupied in subduing the Shân states, including the two strongest, which before had repulsed him, and
A.D. 1605.
while so employed, the king died.

His son, Mahâ Dhammâ Râjâ, destroys Syriam and reigns in Pegu.

He was succeeded by his son, who took the title of Mahâ Dhammâ Râjâ. His father, when on his death-bed, had solemnly charged him to re-establish the empire of Bureng Naung, and to recover Prome without delay. The northern and eastern Shân states had at
A.D. 1608.
this time been brought under control, but it was not until three years later that Prome was taken, after an investment of eight months. The usurper's life was spared, and the king appointed his own brother governor of the town. He then returned to Ava, and received friendly messages from the kings of Arakan, Taungu, and Zimmè, who saw that he was likely to become
A.D. 1610.
master of all. He next marched against Taungu. The king of that state, named Nâtsheng, was the son of him who had taken the capital of Pegu. He agreed to become tributary to his cousin, and yielded some of his family as hostages of his fidelity. By this act he broke faith with de Brito, who, with the king of Martaban, led an army to Taungu and made Nâtsheng prisoner.
A.D. 1612.
They plundered the city, burnt the palace, and then retired.

The Burmese king determined to punish this insult to his authority, and at once prepared to attack de Brito in his stronghold. His arrangements were made with great care, as he knew the enterprise would be one of difficulty; but he would allow of no delay, and sending forward all his forces by land and river on their way to Pegu, he himself left his capital early in December of the same year. Before the close of the year the Burmese hosts had gathered round Syriam by land and water. The king was chiefly anxious that the hated de Brito should not escape, and all the outlets on the

sea-coast were vigilantly watched. The Portuguese governor, though he had been so recklessly aggressive, was utterly unprepared to resist attack. He was short of powder; he had lately allowed many of his Europeans to go to India; and had only one hundred Portuguese in the garrison.[1] The plan of the Burmese king, who had no guns to batter the fort, was by strict blockade to starve the inhabitants; and so effectually was this performed, that after thirty-four days de Brito sent to beg mercy. No answer was given. The king of Arakan sent a fleet of fifty boats, hoping yet to recover his authority in the port, but these were all taken by the besiegers. At length a Talaing chief in the town, opened one of the gates, and the besiegers entered at night during the first week of April. De Brito, the sacrilegious wretch A.D. 1613.
who destroyed pagodas, as is remarked in the Burmese history when his punishment is related, was impaled on a high stake before his own house, and so lived for three days in dreadful agony. Most of the leading Portuguese were executed, and the remainder, as well as de Brito's wife, and many of mixed race, were sent as slaves to Ava. Their descendants are still to be found there, and are known as native Christians. The Burmese king took care that de Brito's son Simon, who was at Martaban, should not escape, and he was put to death. The king of Taungu, no doubt, was similarly disposed of, though it is said he died a natural death. A few days after the surrender, five ships laden with arms and powder, sent by the viceroy from Goa, arrived to relieve Syriam. Somewhat later a ship belonging to de Brito's wife came in from Achin laden with provisions. All but one of these were taken by the victors, and the fortune of Mahâ Dhammâ Râjâ prevailed on every side. The king of Martaban submitted, and for the present

[1] The siege of Syriam is described in detail by Faria de Sousa, who condemns the evil conduct of de Brito as well as his neglect to provide against an attack.

was allowed to continue as tributary king. The king of Siam had sent a force to watch events, which advanced to Yê. But that kingdom could no longer contend with A.D. 1605. Burma. The warrior-king Byanarît had died at Zimmè, when he was believed to be on his march to attack Ava. His brother, who succeeded him, reigned only five years, after which a disputed succession and civil war, kept the Siamese employed at home for some years.

CHAPTER XVI.

PEGU AND BURMA—STRUGGLE FOR SUPREMACY —BRIEF SUCCESS OF PEGU.

Mahâ Dhammâ Râjâ recovers the empire of Bureng Naung—Communication with India—Thado Dhammâ Râjâ succeeds—Ava again made the capital—Bengtalè succeeds—Refugees from China enter Burma—Mahâ Pawarâ Dhammâ Râjâ succeeds to the throne—A junior member of the royal family made king—Decline of the empire—Reign of Mahâ Dhammâ Râjâ Dibati—Invasion from Manipur—Rebellion in Pegu—Mengtarâ Buddha Kèthî elected king of Pegu—Prome taken by the Talaings—Abdication of the king of Pegu—Binya Dâla elected king of Pegu—War carried on languidly—Grand invasion of Burma—Ava captured.

Mahâ Dhammâ Râjâ recovers the empire of Bureng Naung.

A.D. 1615.

AFTER the capture of Syriam the king of Burma established himself in a camp near the city of Hansâwadi. He was determined to recover the whole dominion which had been ruled by his grandfather. Towards the end of the year he marched to Martaban, from whence he sent a body of troops under his brother, which occupied Tavoy, and a detachment was sent to the town of Tenasserim. The latter place was defended by some Portuguese in the service of the king of Siam. They had four galliots, from the fire of which the Burmese suffered considerable loss, before they could enter the town.

A.D. 1578.

The king next turned his attention to Zimmè. The great Bureng Naung had made one of his sons tributary king of that state. On the death of Tharâwadi Meng, his three sons disputed the throne, and the youngest, Thadogyoa, apparently by acknowledging the supremacy of Siam, was successful. The king, in pursuance of his plan to restore the empire, marched on Zimmè from Martaban, and reached that city in the summer. A.D. 1615. Thadogyoa made but a feeble resistance, was taken prisoner, and being a traitor, is no more mentioned. Most of the leading officers of the state were sent prisoners to Pegu, and the king remained there for a year, settling the country, and devising measures for further operations. He prudently abstained from interfering with Laos, and returned to Pegu, leaving one A.D. 1616. of his sons as governor with the title of Mengrè Dippa.[1] He again took up his abode in camp, and when the city had been thoroughly put in order, entered it towards the A.D. 1617. end of the year. He diligently attended to the affairs of the kingdom, appointing Burmese, Shâns, and Talaings to administer the districts. Burma proper, Prome, Taungu, and Zimmè, were governed by tributary kings or viceroys; Martaban and Tenasserim by governors; and Pegu was under the direct government of the supreme king himself.

Communication with India.

According to the Mahâ Râjâweng, an ambassador arrived from the emperor of India, Jehangir, and at the same time an envoy or agent from the governor of Bengal. He brought a letter, written apparently in the Persian language, and was received with great honour. There is no distinct statement as to what were the objects of this mission, but it is probable that they had reference to contemplated action against the Portuguese adventurers and the Arakanese, who troubled the south-eastern districts of Bengal. In order more readily to protect those districts, the seat

[1] In Purchas' "Pilgrims," vol. v. p. 1006, is the story of an Englishman, named Thomas Samuel, who had been sent to Zimmè from Siam "to discover the trade of that country." Being there when the city was captured, he with all other strangers was carried to Pegu. He died; but in a letter from one William Methold, it appears that his property was given up by order of the king, who signified his desire that the English should trade with his country. An order to that effect, "written on a palmitto leaf," was brought to Masulipatam in April 1619 by two Englishmen from Pegu.

of the Bengal government had been removed to Dacca, and Ibraham Khan was appointed governor. But no further measures were then taken to assert the supremacy of the emperor over the districts east of the Megna near its mouth.[1] The supreme king himself sent an envoy to the viceroy at Goa, making explanations as to Syriam, and offering to assist the Portuguese against the Arakanese. The viceroy sent a return mission, but no result followed. The sultan of Achin likewise sent an envoy, desiring to form an alliance against the Portuguese. These advances showed that the neighbouring rulers felt that Mahâ Dhammâ Râjâ had restored the power of the kingdom. A.D. 1618

During the remainder of this king's reign no great public events are recorded. He continued to hold his court at the ancient capital of Pegu. His younger brother, Mengrè Kyoaswâ, was tributary king in Ava. Another brother, Thado Dammâ Râjâ, was tributary king in Prome. The supreme king himself occasionally held his court in Ava. Some of the Shân states at intervals gave trouble, and an expedition against Kyaing Hung or Yun was made, the chief of which state had withheld payment of tribute. The king sincerely desired to do justice to all. A handsome bell was cast and hung at the palace gate, on which was an inscription in the Burmese and Talaing languages, exhorting complainants to strike the bell and the king would hear their cry.[2] Yet this beneficent king met his death in consequence of a palace scandal in which his own son was concerned, and who, in the words of the Burmese chronicler, "committed an unutterable crime." The deed was perpetrated at a temporary palace on the west bank of the river of Pegu, from whence this king is now best known as

[1] See chapter xviii.

[2] For the curious subsequent history of this bell, see note at the end of this chapter.

Anaukphet Lwun Meng, or the king who passed away on the west side.

Thado Dhammâ Râjâ succeeds.

At the time of his death his two brothers, Thado Dhammâ Râjâ and Mengrè Kyoaswâ, were employed in settling affairs with the chief of Kyaing Yun. The son, styled Mengrè Dippa, was born of an inferior woman, and the nobles were averse to acknowledge him as king. As great delay was likely to occur in the arrival of the brothers, to prevent disturbance he was consecrated. The two tributary kings, on learning the death of their brother, marched rapidly to Ava. Though deeply suspicious of each other, they joined their forces together. They reached Pânyâ, and found that a son of Ngyaung Ram Meng had already been appointed governor of Avà. Thado Dhammâ Râjâ now took post at Tarukmyu, while the other brother proceeded to meet an army which was marching up from Pegu to fight them, but with the leaders of which Mengrè Kyoaswâ was in communication. The soldiers of this army were Burmese of the upper country; their families were in the power of the two brothers; and they were not well disposed towards the parricide king. The king of Arakan had marched an army across the hills in support of Mengrè Dippa, but effected nothing. Thado Dhammâ Râjâ overcame all opposition at Ava, and entered that city. His brother loyally supported him, and he, as acknowledged successor, then marched south. Before he could reach the city of Pegu, Mengrè Dippa had been seized by the commander of the palace guard.

March, A.D. 1629.

September, A.D. 1629.

Thado Dhammâ Râjâ at once assumed the government, but would not then be consecrated. He proceeded to Zimmè, and was absent for two years. On his return he was solemnly consecrated king according to the ancient ceremonies, in the presence of Burmese, Talaing, and Shân nobles. This ceremony took place in a grand pavilion put up for the purpose, for the

April, A.D. 1632.

palace had not been rebuilt since the destruction of the city more than thirty years before. Although the king sought to conciliate his Talaing subjects, a conspiracy among them was discovered. Many were put to death and many fled to Siam and Arakan. After two years the king proceeded to Ava, and was consecrated there also. His brother Mengrè Kyoaswâ was declared heir-apparent. A.D. 1634.

Ava again made the capital.

He now decided on making Ava the capital of his dominions. In celebration of this event he founded a great pagoda in the ancient hemispherical form, copied from the shape of the dagobas in Ceylon. It is known as the Kaungmhudoa, and is on the right bank of the Irâwadi, about five miles from Sagaing. The king's weight of gold was devoted to cast an image of Buddha, which was enshrined in the lower relic-chamber.[1] It is also obscurely hinted that a heavenly messenger descended at Taungu and gave a relic of Buddha to a holy man, which was enshrined in a second or upper relic-chamber. It is not stated what the relic was; but Taungu was probably mentioned as the scene of this miracle, as being the city from whence the royal family had sprung, and partly because the tooth-relic received by Bureng Naung from Ceylon, was believed to have been carried there from the city of Pegu, by the king of Taungu, when he returned with the plunder of that place, A.D. 1599. A.D. 1636.

The conduct of Thado Dhammâ Râjâ appears to have been irreproachable. Nevertheless his life was endangered from a conspiracy, the leading features of which have been repeated in recent times. The heir-apparent having died, his son was discontented that he was not appointed to succeed to that office. He suddenly assembled a band of armed desperate men, and

1 For particulars as to this pagoda, see Crawfurd's Embassy to Ava, vol. i. p. 346, and Yule's Mission, Appendix B. The work was not finished when the king died. The official name of the pagoda is Râjâ Muni Sula.

forced his way into the palace. The king fled by the western gate, and took refuge in a monastery. He then crossed the river and entered a stockade near Sagaing, which was guarded by soldiers. The rebel prince having no influence in the country, a large body of men rallied round their sovereign. The prince came out of the city and was killed fighting. The king then returned to his palace, and all the men of rank who had been forced to join the rebels were with their wives and children burnt as traitors. Thado Dhammâ Râjâ died after a reign of nineteen years. He is called in the Burmese history Sâlwun, because he increased the territory he had received from his father; but this was in the outlying Shân states rather than in the provinces constituting the wealth and strength of the empire.

A.D. 1648.

Bengtalè succeeds.

He was succeeded by his son Bengtalè, surnamed Gnâhtâp daragâ, who completed the great pagoda begun by his father. Not long after this pious duty had been performed, alarming reports reached the capital from the Chinese frontier, where armed bodies of men appeared to threaten an incursion into Burma. To understand this hostile movement it is necessary to refer to events in China.[1]

Refugees from China enter Burma.

Early in the seventeenth century, Tienming, chief of the Manchu Tartars, had commenced to attack the Chinese empire, and dying in 1627, left his conquests and his designs to his son Tientsung. Hwaitsong, the last emperor of the Ming dynasty, in despair committed suicide in 1643, and Tientsung dying soon afterwards, his son Shunchi became emperor in 1644. The Burmese history represents that the son and lawful successor of Hwaitsong was Yunhli; and on the death of his father he assumed the title of emperor, and established

[1] Du Halde's China, vol. i. p. 226, London, 1638; Modern Universal History (China), p. 299; History of the two Tartar Conquerors of China, by Père P. T. d'Orleans (Hakluyt Society, 1854).

himself at Nankin. Being driven from thence, he retired to Yunnan, and retaining the title of emperor, demanded the revenue from the Shân states west of the Salwîn river. This alarmed the Burmese court, as denoting a revival of the superiority exercised by the Mongols nearly four hundred years before. Troops were sent to Thinnî and to the Upper Shwèlè, where Chinese officers had appeared and demanded payment of tax. They withdrew without enforcing compliance, but in 1651 a similar demand was made in the state of Kyaingyun. A Burmese force was sent there under the king's brother, and an action occurred with Chinese troops, in which the Burmese were defeated. These encroachments were made by the adherents of Yunhli; but gradually there were signs of the appearance of more powerful enemies. To add to the terror of the Burmese court, earthquakes and storms, which were believed to portend disaster, began to occur; while to every eye in Ava, two suns, typical of rival emperors, shone in the sky. So threatening were the omens, that the king, following an ancient custom, built a Tabengdaing palace, in which was placed his eldest daughter, ready to be presented to appease the wrath of a conqueror. In 1658 the pseudo-emperor Yunhli, being driven out of Yunnan by the Manchus, fled to Momein,[1] the frontier town of Burma, on a branch of the Upper Tapeng river. He addressed the chief of Bamoa, saying he desired to take refuge in Burma, and that he would present an offering of one hundred viss of gold to the king. After some delay he was allowed to proceed, and was provided with a suitable residence at Sagaing. He had a large body of followers, and an officer who had been governor of Yunnan was with him.

The Burmese history attributes to Yunhli the perfidious design of conquering the country. A Chinese

[1] Shân name, Mungmyen; Chinese, Têng Yüeh.

army, in two great divisions, entered the country and marched, one by the Thinnî route and the other more southerly, on Ava. The invaders plundered and cruelly treated the inhabitants. Yunhli being questioned, stated that his officers did not know that he had become a subject of the king of Burma, and when they did they would throw down their arms. The Chinese having united in one body, drew near to Ava, burning the villages and monasteries without

May, A.D. 1659. mercy. They attacked the city, but were repulsed, chiefly by the good service of the native Christians, (descendants of the Portuguese captives), who served the guns on the walls. They retired, but returned again later in the year without any defined object, and finding a difficulty as to supplies, moved southward. It is not likely that these bodies of plunderers entered Burma at the instigation of Yunhli. They were probably marauders who gathered in Yunnan during the war with the Manchus, and on the triumph of the Tartars saw in the weakness of Burma opportunity for plunder.[1]

The occupation of the country by these bands interfered with agriculture, and a scarcity of rice existing in

May, A.D. 1661. the city, the people accused the king of indifference to their sufferings and of allowing the inmates of the palace to profit by the sale of rice which was stored therein. The king's brother, the prince of Prome, headed the insurrection, took possession of the palace, and the king and his family were sent away and drowned in the Hkyengdweng river. The prince followed up the Chinese, and by the end of the year they had been driven out of the country.

Mahâ Pawara Dhammâ Râjâ succeeds to the throne.

The prince of Prome was consecrated king, with the title of Mahâ Pawara Dhammâ Râjâ. He appointed new governors to all the districts of Pegu, where, during

[1] See remarks in Anderson's Expedition to Western Yunnan, p. 20. Calcutta, 1871.

the troubles in the north, there had been signs of rebellion. Suspicious of Yunhli, he determined to separate his followers from him, though they were much reduced below their original number. He assembled them at a pagoda, on pretence of swearing them to bear allegiance to him. Yunhli was also summoned. He and the Chinese officers, thinking they were to be put to death, snatched swords from Burmese soldiers, and in the scuffle which ensued, all but Yunhli and some of his family, were killed. Only one month after this tragedy a Manchu general appeared with an army; he was unopposed, and encamped at Aungpenglè, a day's march from the capital. He announced his terms in the stern words, "Give Yunhli or take war." The pseudo-emperor and his family were surrendered without delay. In the Burmese history there is a persistent attempt to justify the slaughter of the Chinese and the surrender of Yunhli, because of the designs of the refugee against the kingdom. But there is no sound reason for believing in the truth of the accusation. He was taken to Pekin and put to death by strangling. According to Du Halde, his wife and children had become Christians. They persevered in the faith, and were allowed to live at the capital.

January, A.D. 1662.

While the king of Burma was harassed by his Chinese enemies, the southern provinces had become disturbed. The Siamese had many adherents in Martaban, and that city was for a time in the hands of Talaing insurgents. Towards the close of 1662 a Burmese force reoccupied the place, and also Tavoy, but Zimmè fell to the Siamese. Two years later the people of Zimmè forced the Siamese garrison to retire, and the Burmese once more entered. The king having survived through a period which threatened the downfall of the throne, left the kingdom at his death in a better position than it had been since the death of his father.

A.D. 1672

A junior member of the royal family made king, Mahâ Dhammâ Râjâ.

His son Narawara succeeded him, but died within the year. The nobles then consulted as to his successor, and, passing over several elder princes, selected the youngest son of the prince of Prome, who was proclaimed king, with the title of Sri Pawara Mahâ Dhammâ Râjâ. His elder brothers and other members of the royal family showed signs of active opposition to the young king, and many of them were secretly put to death by the party in power.

This king reigned for twenty-six years. From the absence of powerful enemies, internal and external, the kingdom, under vigorous rule, might have been restored to the position it had under Ngyaung Ram Meng and his son. But the young king, as years passed, showed no qualities fitted to rule an empire. Though the

Decline of the empire.

monarchy suffered no great disaster, its power gradually declined. The chief of Manipur occupied the Kubo valley without any real effort being made to check the encroachment. Other outlying districts were lost. The king, devoid of energy, failed to assert the power of the

A.D. 1698.

kingdom, and dying, was succeeded by his son, who did nothing to retrieve the losses which had occurred. The reign of the next king, Hsenghpyu Sheng, lasted thirty-

A.D. 1733.

five years, and is only remarkable for the further decline of the monarchy. A Burmese army was defeated on the frontier of Manipur, and a force which had been sent to occupy Zimmè was driven out. An uncle of the king, Pugân Meng, indignant that his nephew should be under the control of a palace faction, raised a rebellion, but was overpowered and fled to Pegu. He passed a wandering life among the Karens and other border tribes; and his son, nurtured in hardy mountain life, was destined to achieve for a short time a high position, while his career had a mysterious ending.

Reign of Mahâ Dhammâ Râjâ Dibata.

The son of Hsenghpyu Sheng took the title of Mahâ Dhammâ Râjâ Dibati. The Manipuri people advanced into Burmese territory, destroying villages and pagodas in the district of Tabayin. They retired rather to carry off their plunder than to avoid meeting a Burmese force. Two years later they again invaded Burma in great strength, and defeated an army sent against them. So threatening was the danger, that a strong stockade was built at Sagaing, and one to defend the Kaungmhudoa pagoda, as all Buddhist buildings were destroyed by these Hindoo invaders. They marched down by the route between the Mu and Irâwadi rivers, and took by assault the stockade at the pagoda, but could make no impression on that at Sagaing. After four or five days they retired to their own country. It is probable that they retreated because they were unable to cross the great river; but in the Burmese history it is stated that they had come to fulfil a prophecy of their great Brahman, that if their chiefs bathed in the Irâwadi at Sagaing, all evil would cease in their country. Their object apparently was plunder, and not permanent conquest. Invasion from Manipur.

The long-continued degradation of the Burmese monarchy prompted a rising in Pegu. The immediate result of this revolt was surprising by its unexpected success; but the final consequence was a revival of Burmese power under a new dynasty. It will be interesting briefly to review the condition of Pegu at this period. After the removal of the seat of government from Hansâwadi to Ava by Thado Dhammâ Râjâ, A.D. 1634, the Talaing chronicle seldom mentions events occurring beyond the limit of Pegu. The successive appointments of Burmese governors are noted with sullen monotony, and the only interest shown in passing events, is in the record of damage to the national pagodas from storm or lightning, which appeared to show the displeasure of the powers of nature, or tutelary genii, with foreign rulers. There was a deep conviction among the Talaings that the guardian angel of their ancient city demanded the residence of the Rebellion in Pegu.

king within the walls; and Hsenghpyu Sheng had been persuaded to try and restore prosperity to the land by living there. But he was soon wearied with life in a ruined city, and returned to Ava. The people of Pegu in this reign sunk to the depth of misery. Nothing escaped taxation. Even the women's looms were not free. The same rigid exactions were continued in the next reign. The governor, Maung Thâ Aung, was intensely hated; yet he sought to make himself independent, and seeing his opportunity in the confusion during the incursion of the Manipuris, he proclaimed himself
A.D. 1740. king of Pegu. The leading men among the Talaings longed for the ascendancy of their own race, and determined to be rid of him. The hated governor was killed; but the leaders seeing as yet no chance of establishing the independence of their country, petitioned the king, professing their loyalty, and attributing the murder of the governor to a sudden rising against his tyranny. The king of Burma, waiving punishment for the present, appointed as governor his father's brother, Mengrè Aung Naing. He was deemed an honest man, but was received with haughty reserve by the Talaing nobles; and after a few days all his followers were massacred. An insurrection commenced among the people of the Shân colony, whose ancestors had been brought from their own country during the wars of Bureng Naung, and had been settled to the north of the capital of Pegu. They are called by the Burmese, Gwè
A.D. 1740. Shân. Towards the close of the year they marched to the city, and being supported by the Talaing chiefs, seized the governor and put him to death.

Mengtarâ Buddha Kèthî elected king of Pegu.

There was at this time in the city a man who had been a Buddhist monk, and is said, in the Talaing history, to have been by race a Gwè Shân. He joined the men of his tribe in the city, and was declared king of Pegu, with the title of Mengtarâ Buddha Kèthî. He was supposed by some to be a son of Pugân Meng, who had rebelled in the reign of his nephew, Hsenghpyu Sheng, and had fled to Pegu. The son had been brought up among the Karens and Gwè Shâns, and had made himself popular among the Talaings, whose language he spoke. Whatever may have been his origin, he was soon firmly established in power, and by his devotion to the people and kindliness of disposition satisfied the expectations formed of him. An army had been dispatched from Ava to suppress the rebellion. It was commanded by Mengrè Kyoagaung, but before he could reach the delta he was recalled to defend the north-western frontier against the Manipuris. The Gwè Shân king entered into communication with the chief of Zimmè, whose daughter he married. The Talaings soon forced their king, against his own judgment, to march against Prome, and the king of Burma, alarmed at the preparations against him, made his brother joint king, with his palace and court at Sagaing. The Talaing army, unable to take Prome, marched up by the eastern bank of the river, and ravaged the country nearly to the gates of Ava. In this rash expedition it was attacked by the Burmese from the north and south, and had to retreat with great loss. A force sent up the Sittaung river was, however, successful in occupying Taungu.

It would have been well for the cause of Talaing independence had the leaders of the nation been content with making preparations for defence. The occu- A.D. 1743-44. pation of Taungu rather weakened their resources, and the governor of Prome, Thado Meng Khaung, suddenly went down the river and took Syriam by surprise.[1] The place was quickly recovered, but great loss had been sustained, and the country along the river-banks ravaged. The Talaings, however, followed up the Burmese in their retreat, and succeeded in entering Prome. The

Prome taken by the Talaings.

[1] At this time there was a British factory at Syriam, which had been re-established about twenty years before. It was destroyed on this occasion, it is said, by the Peguans. See Syme's Embassy to Ava, p. 5, and Dalrymple's Oriental Repertory.

war was now carried on in the valley of the Irâwadi, and in that of the Sittaung, with varying fortune; and at the close of the next year the Talaings still held the towns of Prome and Taungu.

A.D. 1745.

A.D. 1746.

In the following year a Siamese ambassador arrived at Ava, nominally to express the friendship of his master for his brother king, but really to report, from appearances, what might be the issue of the struggle, and so to enable the former to decide what part Siam should take. The Talaings, probably advised from Siam, made a third advance up the Irâwadi, but sustained such heavy losses that they were compelled to retreat to Prome. Soon after an unlooked-for event occurred, more strange than any in the changing fortunes of this war. The Gwè Shân king suddenly left his capital, attended by ten leading nobles, with an escort of two thousand men, and proceeded to the town of Sittaung, ostensibly to hunt elephants in the neighbouring forests. Shortly after he sent for the queen and her attendants. He remained at Sittaung for some months, and then announced to the Talaing nobles that he had determined to retire from the kingdom. They entreated him to remain, for he was beloved by the people, but he left for Zimmè, accompanied by his queen and a strong guard. His after history may at once be told. Not allowed then to remain in Zimmè, he wandered through Laos and Cochin-China, and entered China. He returned after some years, and was permitted to settle in Zimmè. The only explanation of this conduct is given in the Talaing chronicles. It is there stated that the Gwè king was a proficient in astrology; that casting his own horoscope, the result portended disaster; and that in a self-sacrificing spirit he resigned the throne, hoping that the destiny of the Talaing people might be linked with one whose good fortune was assured.

Abdication of the elected king of Pegu.

As soon as his departure was known at the capital of Pegu the usual intrigues commenced, and a scribe in

Binya Dalâ elected king of Pegu.

the palace played for a few days the part of king. But among the officers who had accompanied the Gwè Meng to Sittaung one was pre-eminent in ability. He bore the title of Binya Dâla, a designation famous in Talaing history. His colleagues unanimously saluted him as king. He at once made for the capital, where no resistance was made, and the presumptuous scribe was put to death. This event occurred in the spring of the year. A.D. 1746.
The elected king was probably of Shân race. The Burmese history states that he had originally come to Pegu from Zimmè with elephants; was made master of the elephants under the Gwè king, and gradually acquired great influence. The Talaing chronicle is silent as to his race and early life, but, referring to the legend of the founding of the city of Hansâwadi, records that he was chosen king in fulfilment of the divine prediction regarding native rulers. He was consecrated with great solemnity, and proclaimed with the title of Phrâmindi Râjâ Naradibati. Among the people, however, he is now known by his first title of nobility. His younger brother was created Yuva Râjâ. After the ceremony of consecration, he made a stirring address to the assembled court. He spoke of the former prosperity and grandeur of the country; of the high renown of his predecessors; of the divine prediction at the founding of the city, that it was to be sacred and free for ever from the ownership and rule of foreigners; of the subordination of the kings of Ava and of other kings to the sovereign of Pegu; and announced that the empire of Bureng Naung would again be established with its ancient magnificence, and an army be raised, of which Talabân would be commander-in-chief. This is the first mention of a name to this day famous in Pegu.

Such an open declaration of plans by the king was unusual in the countries of Indo-China, but was probably considered necessary by Binya Dâla, in order to show his devotion to the interests of the kingdom to which he had been elected. He must have known, that a larger and better appointed army than had yet been embodied, would be required to accomplish the desired end; yet for three years a desultory warfare was carried on, from which no decisive result could be gained. The conquest in view could only be achieved by the capture of Ava, and to effect that, a large army and flotilla were essential, as well as a stock of provisions to supply the besieging army for at least six months. These requirements the Talaings appear to have been unable to fulfil. But having possession of the frontier towns of Prome and Taungu, mixed bodies of Talaings and Gwè Shâns made incursions, which, for the most part, the Burmese were unable effectually to resist. At one time they penetrated beyond Ava, apparently with the design of forming a league with the Shâns of the Upper Irâwadi. Some of the Gwè tribe had long been settled at Madarâ, a few miles from the eastern bank of the river above Ava. A party of the invaders, finding themselves isolated from their main body, entrenched themselves at that place, and were supported by the Gwè Shâns. They soon found themselves in dire extremity from scarcity of food, and sent messengers to Pegu imploring help.

War carried on languidly.

The king of Burma had sent envoys to the Emperor of China, representing the great danger which threatened his kingdom, and asking for support. In reply to this appeal two Chinese or Manchu officers arrived at the capital, with an escort of one hundred horsemen and a thousand foot. They suggested that an attack should be made on the Talaing stockade at Madarâ. This was done, and as it failed, the Chinese officers retired without making any promise of assistance.

A.D. 1750.

Grand invasion of Burma.

At length the king of Pegu had assembled an army, which, including all followers, numbered sixty thousand men. A numerous flotilla of war-boats kept command of the river, and was necessary to protect the hundreds of boats laden with provisions and other stores, essential to the success of the expedition. Symes, who gathered his information some forty-five years later from persons who had witnessed the operations of this war, states, that the Peguans procured firearms from European traders, and had in their service renegade Dutch and native Portuguese. The Talaing army would, therefore, have a considerable advantage over its enemies. The first move was made when the rainy season had somewhat abated. Yuva Râjâ nominally commanded A.D. 1751. the invading army, but the real leader was Talabân. The advance was made by the line of the Irâwadi only; and the Yuva Râjâ, passing Prome, proceeded with his army by land and water to Malwun. From thence the army, one division having been left with the flotilla, marched by the western bank of the river, where the districts had escaped occupation in the previous years and could now yield supplies. The invaders encountered no opposition, but at the Mu river met a body of Manipuris, which had come to observe events, and retreated without showing hostility. Early in the year the great A.D. 1752. Talaing army appeared at Sagaing, and the flotilla having arrived, crossed the river and invested Ava. The Talaing and Gwè Shân garrison of Madarâ came down, and joined the invading army. In the city the king, the court, and the citizens were in despair. No adequate defensive preparations had been made, and food soon became scarce. The soldiers of the garrison began to desert whenever they had the opportunity. In the latter days of March the besiegers entered the outer city. It was set on fire. The inner city, where was the palace, was surrounded by a wall, high and strong. But the soldiers who should have defended it, were disheartened by the neglect of their superiors, and weakened by hunger. After two days the besiegers were unopposed, and they forced the gates. The foremost Ava captured. soldiers rushed to the palace. The king of Burma, the last who could claim descent from the dynasty of Pugân, was found in a large hall, surrounded by his queens and their women attendants. He made no resistance, and the Burmese history admits that the invaders behaved gently. When the Yuva Râjâ arrived, orders were given for the accommodation of the royal captives, and they were put on board boats to be sent to Pegu. The king lived there, a prisoner but well treated, for two years, when he was put to death on suspicion of having conspired against Binya Dâla.

The city of Ava was burnt to the ground. The Yuva Râjâ, not foreseeing that any further resistance would be made by the Burmese people, returned after a few weeks to Pegu. He took with him the greater part of the army, and left Talabân in command, with orders to establish the rule of the Talaing king in the upper country.

Note regarding the bell mentioned at p. 133.

This bell, it appears, was carried to Arakan, when a raid was made by the king of that country into Pegu, some years after the death of Mahâ Dhammâ Râjâ. In the war of 1825–26 between Burma and British India, it was found in the precincts of a temple near the old capital, and was carried to India as a trophy by a Hindu officer of Irregular Cavalry. It now hangs in a Hindu temple in Zillah Alligarh. (See Journal of the Asiatic Society of Bengal, vol. vii. p. 287.)

CHAPTER XVII.

ALAUNGHPRÂ—TRIUMPH OF BURMA.

Early history of Alaunghprâ—Resists a Talaing armed party—The Yuva Râjâ leaves Ava for Pegu—Talabân marches against Alaunghprâ—Ava invested and occupied—The king of Pegu determines to reconquer Burma—Ava besieged by the Talaings for the second time—Talaing army retreats—Prome besieged by the Talaings. Alaunghprâ relieves Prome—Town of Rangoon founded—European traders in Pegu—British and French at Syriam—Syriam taken—The capital of Pegu taken by Alaunghprâ — Returns to his own city—Expedition to Manipur—Insurrection in Pegu—Invasion of Siam—Retreat and death of Alaunghprâ.

Early history of Alaunghprâ.

BEFORE the fall of Ava, a proclamation had been issued by the Yuva Râjâ, summoning the administrative officers in the country north of the city to submit, and swear allegiance to the king of Pegu. This order had been generally complied with. One officer, since known under the title of Alaunghprâ,[1] dared to disobey, and prepared to resist. No Burmese history now to be found contains what can be accepted as trustworthy information concerning the descent and early life of this national hero. The many narratives of his career which exist, set forth that though at the time of the Talaing conquest he was in a subordinate position, yet that he was of royal race, and that at his birth, signs and wonders in

[1] Alaunghprâ signifies "embryo Buddha," a title which the patriot hero assumed. It is the vernacular rendering of the Pali "Bodisativa," or Buddha elect. It is generally written by Europeans, Alompra.

heaven and on earth, had foreshown his future greatness. It is from European authors alone that the plain facts can now be gathered. He at one time followed the occupation of a hunter, not a respectable one in Burmese estimation. His native village, of which the original name is now uncertain, was situated about sixty miles north of Ava, and a few miles from the west bank of the Irâwadi. The village became famous as the home of the Muthsobo, or hunter-captain, as being the scene of his successful resistance to the invader, and eventually the capital of the kingdom. At the time of the Talaing conquest the hunter-captain was Kyêkaing, or deputy of the lord of the district in which the village was situated. As such he would be responsible for the collection of the revenue due to Government, and for the preservation of order. From the beginning of the troubles he was intensely national, and determined not to yield to the conqueror. It is related that when his father and mother entreated him to submit, he, with the deep reverence ever shown by Burmese children to their parents, bowed down to them on his knees, and said he never could swear allegiance to a Talaing king, adding, "When fighting for our country, it matters little whether our band is large or small; it is rather important to have a few comrades, with true hearts and strong arms, to will and work." These noble words are a key to his conduct in the early part of his career, before success aud irresponsible power had roused selfish ambition and hardened his heart.

Alaunghprâ resists a Talaing armed party.

After Ava had fallen to the invader, a Talaing officer was sent to the town of Singu, which is on the river to the north of the capital, to collect taxes from the surrounding country. He deputed a subordinate with a party of fifty men, who proceeded to a village near that of the hunter-captain, and summoned him as Kyêkaing to appear. Dissembling his purpose, he came with two-score armed men, surprised the Talaing party, and slew them all. A stronger body of men was now sent against him. He had already fortified his village, but he went out, met the enemy when on the march in the jangal, and defeated them with great loss. The hunter-captain was now joined by numbers of his countrymen. He again defeated a Talaing force, and fully recognising the national importance of his enterprise, gave orders to his men to spare the Burmese and Shâns who fought under the flag of the usurper. It is probable that at this time he adopted the name or title of Aungzêyâ—Victory, or the Victorious—as a rallying signal to his fellow-countrymen.

The Yuva Râjâ leaves Ava for Pegu.

The Talaing army in Burma had been much reduced. There were rumours of the king of Siam menacing an attack on Tavoy, of which, however, there is no proof. The Yuva Râjâ, apparently without the orders of his brother, the king of Pegu, on the ground of danger from Siam, and despising an insurrection headed by a petty village officer, determined to return to Pegu. He took with him not less than twenty thousand men, besides the greater part of the flotilla.[1] Talabân was left in command with an army numerically insufficient to support the invasion. He saw that it was necessary to crush the incipient rebellion, which his sagacity told him might prove to be serious. He therefore determined himself to lead a party against the hunter-captain. Leaving Ava and crossing the Irâwadi, he marched towards the stronghold of the rebel chief. Two months had scarcely passed since the Burmese capital had fallen to the Talaings, and already this head-man of a village had roused the spirit of his countrymen; and after the Yuva Râjâ had left, he, with daring self-confidence, or,

Talabân marches against Alaunghprâ.

May, A.D. 1752.

[1] Symes's information was that the king of Pegu himself commanded the army of invasion which took Ava. But this is contrary to Burmese and Talaing history. Symes also states that on the departure of the Yuva Râjâ the command devolved on his nephew, Dauhtautsh. He, however, accompanied his uncle to Pegu.

as the Burmese history expresses it, "inspired by the good Nâts who observe religion," assumed the designation of Alaunghprâ, and in a proclamation claimed to be a scion of the ancient royal race. Talabân appeared before the fortified village of the hunter, but though he had jingals—guns of small calibre—he could make no impression on it, and was obliged to relinquish the plan of capturing it by a sudden assault. He withdrew, suffering considerable loss in his retreat, but built a stockade to the north-west, in order to intercept the communication of Alaunghprâ with the district of Tabayîn, from whence supplies were drawn, and where dwell the choicest men of Burmese race. The stockade was garrisoned by Talaing soldiers under a chosen officer; but he abandoned it in a panic when attacked by Alaunghprâ in person. The king of Pegu, dissatisfied with Talabân, recalled him, and appointed the treasurer of Taungu, commander-in-chief, with Letyâpyânkhyi, already holding command, as his chief adviser. This change did not restore the fortunes of the invaders. They suffered more defeats, and by the end of the year almost all their Burmese adherents had deserted them. The Gwè Shâns still held the stockade of Madarâ and were hostile to Alaunghprâ. A son of the deposed king of Burma, who had been hiding in the mountains, now came into the camp of the victor, but finding he was not a welcome guest, he retired, and took refuge in the Gwè Shân stockade. Soon after Alaunghprâ attacked and drove out the Shâns. They fled to Momeit, and the Burmese prince went with them. The struggle proceeded with varying fortune, but the Talaings gradually lost ground. Though the war went on in a languid way for more than a year, no reinforcements arrived from Pegu. Alaunghprâ, with thorough confidence in the future, laid out his native village as the capital of his kingdom, and dignified it with the name of Ratanâthinga. A palace was built on the model

About the 20th of June, A.D. 1752.

of those erected by the ancient kings, and the whole Burmese people rallied to him whom they recognised as their native sovereign.

Alaunghprâ was now ready to attack the invaders in Ava. He had full command of both banks of the river, and had formed a strong flotilla, mainly with boats captured from the enemy. Towards the end of November, when the country was dry, the army under command of his second son, Thado Mengsoa, had nearly encompassed the city. The Talaing commander-in-chief, despairing of help from Pegu, and knowing that the Burmese and Shân citizens would turn against him, abandoned the city by night and retired so rapidly that he suffered but slight loss. Thado Mengsoa at once entered, and his father appointed him governor of the city. Alaunghprâ then moved down, and, surrounded by his great officers, entered and formally took possession. No suitable building remained within the walls, he therefore occupied a temporary palace outside. Ever careful to observe religious duties, he gave orders for the repair of the pagodas, and other sacred buildings, which had been injured during the war. In a council of his officers which he called to consider what should next be done, it was determined to settle affairs in the country to the north, as the Shân chiefs, unless subdued, might cause trouble. Alaunghprâ, therefore, after three months' stay in Ava, proceeded up the river in his state boat, while the army marched up both banks. The chiefs of Momeit and Bamoa came and swore allegiance to him. Commissioners were deputed to summon the chiefs of Monyin and Mogaung to the royal presence. They did not appear, though they sent messages of submission, and Alaunghprâ, professing to be satisfied, returned to his capital.

Ava invested and occupied by Alaunghprâ, December, A.D. 1753.

The king of Pegu, who, from the incompetence of his brother, the Yuva Râjâ, and his own neglect, had lost all that had been gained in the campaign of 1751–52, now

The king of Pegu determines to reconquer Burma.

determined again to invade Burma. No explanation is given in the native annals of the fatal delay which had occurred in forming this resolution. The army now assembled, though its strength is greatly exaggerated in the Burmese history, was probably not inferior in numbers to that employed in the first invasion. The men were drawn from the whole of the country south of Prome. But that important town had been allowed to fall into the hands of the Burmese. The Yuva Râjâ, in spite of his proved incompetence, was appointed commander-in-chief, with Talabân as his second in command. The Talaing army advanced from Lower Pegu by land and water early in the year. Arrived at
A.D. 1754. Prome, it was determined to blockade that place with a strong detachment, and the main army pursued its march. The invaders met with no resistance until they reached Tarukmyu. There they encountered a Burmese army under the command of Alaunghprâ's two sons, the elder entitled Thado Dhammâ Râjâ, and younger Thado Mengsoa. The Burmese were defeated. The elder son went to his father's city to entreat forgiveness; the younger entered Ava, and publicly washing his head as a token of grief and repentance, vowed to retrieve the disaster, and propitiated the tutelary Nât of the city with offerings.

Ava besieged by the Talaings for the second time.

The Yuva Râjâ quickly invested the city. With his numerous flotilla he had entire command of the river. Alaunghprâ remained at Muthsobomyu, but his scouts closely watched the besiegers. A Talaing force proceeded up the river in boats to reconnoitre. Alaunghprâ, leaving his capital, came to the river bank, and suddenly attacked and defeated the party with a great slaughter. He followed them down stream, and Talabân, who himself had advanced in support of the reconnoitering party, was forced to retreat. From this time the pusillanimous Yuva Râjâ remained passive within his entrenched lines. Alaunghprâ marched down to

Sagaing. The Yuva Râjâ having lost many men and many boats, began to feel the want of provisions, and with the approach of the rainy season and rise of the river, saw ruin before him. Thado Mengsoa made a vigorous sally, and the Yuva Râjâ utterly cowed, retreated hastily from his position before the city, a movement which soon became a hurried flight towards Prome. Arrived there, Talabân was left to rally the army and remain before the town, while the Yuva Râjâ fled by boat to Pegu.

Talaing army retreats, May, A.D. 1754.

In the delta the rainy season had set in, and Alaunghprâ delayed his march southward. He would have been placed in great difficulties there, and his flotilla was not sufficiently numerous. But the Burmese garrison in Prome was in dire distress, and made urgent appeals for relief. A strong force was sent which approached the Talaing army, and Talabân retreated to a position some miles down the river.

Prome besieged by the Talaings.

The king of Pegu, at last roused to the importance of the possession of Prome for the safety of his kingdom, determined once more to make an effort to take it. Again he gathered an army, of which one of his brothers, bearing the title of Binya Dâla, was commander-in-chief, and his son-in-law, Soabyâ, the second in command. Talabân was still to be the real general. Before the army marched the king of Burma, who had been carried away prisoner from Ava, was put to death, on the pretence that he had engaged in a conspiracy against the king of Pegu. This cruel deed injured the cause of the Talaing people, and Alaunghprâ when informed of it remarked that the event made his task easier. The Talaing army reached Prome and invested it. A strong corps was posted to the north of the town at the Naweng stream. A division occupied a position to the south, and some regiments were stationed on the bank of the Irâwadi opposite the town. Talabân, with 10,000 men and 200 war-boats, was entrenched at an advanced post on the east bank to meet the enemy coming to relieve the place. The Talaing commanders hoped to force the garrison to surrender before relief could arrive. Their measures for attaining this object were utterly wanting in vigour, and the cause of Pegu was lost before Prome.

Alaunghprâ relieves Prome, January, A.D. 1755.

Alaunghprâ, having dispatched his troops in advance down the river, left his capital to take the command. The first collision with the Talaing invaders occurred at Malwun, where their war-boats had gone to reconnoitre. Several of them were taken; and the Burmese army marching down the left bank of the river, the Talaings appear to have been panic-stricken by the presence of Alaunghprâ. Even Talabân retreated without making a creditable resistance. The position was abandoned, and the beleaguered town relieved. The Talaing commander-in-chief had built a strong earthwork a few miles to the south of Prome, where a depôt for provisions and warlike stores had been formed. This was occupied with a numerous garrison. Alaunghprâ, elated with his easy success, ordered an immediate attack. But the work was well constructed, and the Talaings had many guns and muskets which they had procured from Europeans at Syriam. The attack was repelled, and the Talaings were as secure in their earthwork as, remarks the Burmese chronicler, a "jackal in his hole might be against a noble lion." Alaunghprâ sternly ordered that this stronghold must be stormed, and his officers, dreading his anger, forced their way in,

Middle of February, A.D. 1755.

with great slaughter on both sides. Extensive stores of provisions, of muskets, and guns, were found. There was a large ship's gun, probably one of those which stood in front of the palace of Amarapura at the time of the mission from the Governor-General of India in 1855.[1] So much importance was attached to the pos-

[1] The largest piece of ordnance then seen was nearly thirty feet long. It was brought from Arakan. There was a smaller piece near it. See Yule's Mission to Ava, p. 136.

session of this gun, though of little practical use from its unwieldiness, that Alaunghprâ, though ostentatiously observant of the forms of Buddhism, allowed the gunner, a foreigner, to receive a daily allowance of flesh, spirits, and other articles of food, which were popularly thought to be offerings to the demon, who presided over the fortune of the gun.

Alaunghprâ devoted some weeks to the settlement of the surrounding country, and then proceeded down the river to Lwunhsè, where he marked out the plan of a stockade, and laid the foundation of a pagodâ. He changed the name of the town to Myanaung, "speedy victory." Moving down the river, his advance guard defeated the Talaings near Henzadâ, and took a number of boats, which he much required. His army then continued on to Danubyu, where he celebrated the new year about the middle of April. A few days later he occupied the position of Dagun, on the plain adjoining the great pagoda, from which a Talaing division was driven. Alaunghprâ, never doubting for a moment his final success, though the enemy's capital was still unconquered, laid out a new city, which he designed to be the future port of Pegu. The site chosen was admirably adapted for this object, and to proclaim his forecast of the immediate destruction of his enemies, he called the new city Rangoon.

Town of Rangoon founded.

April, A.D. 1755.

About the 5th of May, A.D. 1755.

The Talaing army had retreated before Alaunghprâ, and was concentrated at Syriam to defend the capital. That town was now the principal port of Pegu. The governor was Binya Dâla. Strong stockades had been built on both banks of the river to defend the passage. The governor hoped to have the assistance of the European merchants and of their ships against the invaders. After the destruction of Syriam by the king of Burma in A.D. 1619, European traders, Dutch and English, had settled there; but the English East India Company a few years later withdrew their agents. In

European traders in Pegu.

1695 a letter to the king of Burma was sent by the governor of Madras, soliciting protection for traders, and encouragement for their settlement in his dominions was given by the king. But it was not until A.D. 1709 that a commercial resident was appointed to attend to British interests.[1] From that time until the war of independence between the Talaings and Burmese, the British and other Europeans appear to have lived at Syriam, and to have carried on trade, with fair treatment from the Burmese Government. Alaunghprâ was well aware of the value of assistance which might be derived from Europeans, and he gave orders that they were not to be molested. There was at this time a British factory or trade depôt at Bassein, which was subordinate to the establishment at Negrais. This island had been occupied two years before as a depôt by order of the governor of Madras, without apparently any communication with the government of the country.

February 23, A.D. 1755. Early in the year, according to the British reports, a Burmese detachment came down the river in boats to Bassein. The Talaing garrison fled, and the Burmese burnt the town, but did no damage to British property. A month later a Burmese officer arrived at Bassein deputed to communicate with Mr. Brooke, the chief of the settlement at Negrais, from whom it was expected that muskets and gunpowder would be procured. The officer proceeded to Negrais, accompanied by Captain Baker; but during their absence a Talaing force, estimated at three thousand men, reoccupied Bassein. The victory of Alaunghprâ near Danubyu made the Talaing detachment evacuate Bassein, and by the end of April a Burmese detachment again occupied that port. Some military stores were now supplied to the Burmese by Mr. Brooke.

[1] Dalrymple's Oriental Repertory, vol. ii., and an account of the East Indies by Captain A. Hamilton, vol. ii. London, 1744.

At this time there was at Syriam a French as well as a British factory. The East India Companies of the two nations, after open war in the Carnatic during five years, made peace. Dupleix, the governor of the French possessions, was recalled, and was succeeded by M. Godehen. The two nations, while at peace in Europe, had been at war in India; and though hostilities were now suspended, the officers of the two governments continued to intrigue to gain commanding influence with the native powers. The state of affairs in Pegu produced similar action there. The French at first favoured the Peguans, while the British leaned to the Burmans.[1] It is not to be wondered at that European traders, entirely dependent on the favour of the native rulers, should, when a struggle for empire was going on, be in perplexity as to the side they ought to take. Nor is it surprising that the native authorities, seeing the fluctuating conduct of the Europeans, should accuse them of treachery. When Alaunghprâ reached Dagun, the chief of the French factory at Syriam was M. Bourno. Though inclined to support the Talaing cause, he endeavoured to avoid committing himself to a distinct line of action. Under pretence of more effectually helping the Talaings, but really to watch events, he embarked on board a ship under French colours, and, with two others, dropped down from Syriam and anchored in the Rangoon river. After some days, considering that Alaunghprâ was likely to be victorious, he proceeded to the royal camp, where he was graciously received. During his absence from his ship, his second in command, from some unexplained cause, took his ship back to Syriam. This act roused the suspicions of Alaunghprâ, who suspected treachery, but he allowed M. Bourno to depart, on his

British and French at Syriam.

August, A.D. 1754.

[1] The best authority for the conduct of the French and British at this time in Pegu is Symes in his "Embassy to Ava." London, 1800.

promise to bring back his ship. The chief of the British factory at Syriam had openly joined the Burmese by proceeding with four ships into the Rangoon river. Early in the following month, a vessel belonging to the English company, the "Arcot," arrived. The Yuva Râjâ, who was at Syriam, opened a secret correspondence with the master, captain Jackson, and there began to be symptoms of sympathy by the British, with the Talaings. This may have been brought about by doubts as to the final success of Alaunghprâ, for at this time he left his camp and proceeded up the Irâwadi. This apparently retrograde movement was made in consequence of reports of attack likely to be be made by the northern Shân chiefs on his capital. He therefore deemed it advisable to proceed there. As it was now the rainy season in Pegu, he knew that operations in the field must be suspended for some months, and he left the bulk of his army, strongly intrenched and well provisioned, under a trusted officer, confident that the position was safe from attack by the Talaings. No sooner had Alaunghprâ gone than an attack was made by the Talaings on the Burmese camp. It failed. The British vessels, though anchored within gunshot, gave no support to the Burmese. A few days later another attack was made by the Talaings on the Burmese position, which was supported by the fire of both British and French ships. This fire obliged the Burmese to abandon their war-boats, but the Talaings did not land to attack the fortified position. Some irregular skirmishing occurred for a few days, and the Talaings then retreated to Syriam, to which port the British and French ships now returned. The action of the British in this affair was disapproved by Mr. Brooke, and he directed the ships to proceed to Negrais, except the "Arcot," which remained at Syriam for repairs. The chief of the settlement at Negrais was placed in an awkward predica-

May, A.D. 1755. June.

September 17, A.D. 1755.

ment by the action of his subordinates. He had dispatched Captain Baker and Lieutenant North up the Irâwadi with presents to Alaunghprâ, in the hope of concluding with him a treaty of friendship and commerce. Captain Baker reached Muthsobo, and was received in audience by the Burmese king. Considering the treacherous conduct of the British at Rangoon, Alaunghprâ behaved with magnanimity. He granted permission for factories to be established at Rangoon and Bassein. Syriam he had determined to destroy. While these negotiations were going on, the "Arcot," with two British ships and one French ship, joined the Talaings in another attack on the Burmese entrenched position. This also failed, and the Talaings made no further effort. Alaunghprâ, having settled affairs in the upper country, was able to send down reinforcements to Rangoon; and a Shân army of twenty thousand men was about the end of the year set in motion to march by the Taungu route to Pegu. In the beginning of the year he left his capital, confiding January, A.D. 1756. it to two of his sons, and arrived at Rangoon towards the end of February. At once he determined to attack Syriam. The British ships had left, but some subordinates were at the factory. One French ship under M. Bourno still remained. It was moored close to the factory. The Burmese army advanced by land and water and invested the port. The French ship had taken the ground, and was disabled by the fire from a Burmese battery. M. Bourno secretly made offers of submission to Alaunghprâ, and the Talaing commandant, suspecting treachery, removed him and his men into the fort. Alaunghprâ took possession of the ship and occupied the factory building, which was near the shore. During several months the port was strictly blockaded. The Burmese were masters on land and water. On a night in July, when the heavy rain dulled all noise, a band of chosen men rushed on

Syriam taken.

one of the gates. The garrison, weakened by famine, made but feeble resistance. The Talaing officers for the most part escaped; the Europeans remained prisoners. The conqueror found considerable supplies of warlike stores in the fort, and fortune threw in his way increased means for carrying on the war. The governor of Pondicherry, the capital of the French settlements in India, had, on the recommendation of M. Bourno, determined to support the king of Pegu.[1] He dispatched for this purpose two ships laden with large supplies of military stores. One of these vessels, the "Galetée," arrived at the mouth of the river two days after the fall of Syriam. Alaunghprâ made Bourno, now a prisoner, write to the captain of the "Galetée," inviting him to bring his ship up the river. He fell into the trap, and the vessel was seized. The ship's papers proved that the warlike stores on board were intended for the king of Pegu, and Alaunghprâ in his rage put to death M. Bourno, and also the captain and officers of the "Galetée." The subordinates of the British factory had been put into prison by the Talaings, and were now released. Several European seamen were sent up the country. Their descendants, and those of the Portuguese whose lives were spared at the sack of Syriam in the previous century, constitute the community known as native Christians at the present time in Upper Burma. They have been preserved in the Christian faith by the pastoral care of Catholic missionaries, who, to the credit of the Burmese Government, have been allowed, through all disturbances, to reside unmolested among them.

The capital of Pegu taken by Alaunghprâ.

The king of Pegu was now left without foreign support. The rainy season having abated, the troops of his dreaded enemy began to swarm round his capital.

[1] Symes ascribes this measure to M. Dupleix; but, as has already been mentioned, he had left India two years before.

Coming in thousands by land and water, they appeared before the city about the middle of October. The Shân contingent, which had marched down by Taungu, occupied Sittaung by the end of September, and awaited further orders. The Talaings in the city made sorties, and still fought with the courage of men of spirit, who struggle for national independence in its last place of refuge. The outworks were all taken, though with considerable loss to the assailants, and by the end of October the whole of Alaunghprâ's army, including the Shâns, had closed round the devoted city. The king of Pegu had no resource left but to appeal to the mercy and the religious sentiment of his enemy—an expedient of which several instances are mentioned in the histories of the wars of Burma. The deeply revered Rahâns, the brotherhood who devote their lives to the observance of the law of Buddha, headed by their venerable superior, appeared in the camp of the invader, and in the name of religion besought him to put an end to the war, and to live as elder and younger brother with the king of Pegu. In other words, the kingdom was to be held as tributary to the king of Burma. The chief Rahân in his address, with sincere or artful allusion to the conqueror as a destined Buddha, referred to the satisfaction he would feel in after ages, when that high and holy state had been attained in his last birth, and when he could look back with pure delight on a noble act of generosity and mercy, which would give relief to millions of human beings. Alaunghprâ replied in terms which evaded the appeal to his clemency. In all ages, he said, with a ready assumption of the exalted character he claimed, Bodhisatwas who reigned as kings had observed the duties, and good works, incumbent upon rulers. He would be careful to follow their example; to obey the dictates of his heart; to secure the happiness of his subjects, and of all sentient beings. The poor had nothing to fear from him. He would respect and uphold existing laws and customs, and so with respect and friendship he imparted this information to the venerable Rahân.

This reply being reported to the king, Talabân and other Talaing officers represented that submission would be destruction. It was determined to defend the city to the last extremity. Alaunghprâ, to show to the whole country his determination to persevere, built a temporary palace with a lofty seven-storied spire, and excepting in the capital, was supreme throughout Pegu. A line of works being drawn round the city, no supplies of food could enter, and all signs of resistance by the garrison had ceased. The citizens were reduced by famine to the deepest misery The king assembled his council. They recommended that he should offer his maiden daughter, Maikum, to the conqueror, and again appeal to his mercy. This princess had been betrothed to Talabân, and they were to be married whenever he succeeded in expelling the Burmese army. In vain he now protested against the proposition of the council, which was supported by the king's brother, the Yuva Râjâ. Overborne by this influence, he determined to leave the city. With a devoted band of followers, the members of his family being mounted on elephants and horses, he went forth by night from the eastern gate, and forcing his way through the besieging lines, made good his escape to Sittaung. A wail of despair now arose among the citizens. The Talaing king forthwith wrote a humble letter to the conqueror, which was presented by the chief Rahân. He offered his daughter in marriage, that he might secure peace to his people, and prayed that he might be left as tributary in his kingdom. According to the Talaing chronicle, this petition was granted, while the Burmese history records the verbal reply as merely expressing the desire of Alaunghprâ to promote the happiness of all beings. To a noble, who accompanied the chief Rahân, he

January, A.D. 1757.

gave two bunches of orchid flowers, saying enigmatically, one is an offering, and one for adornment. The message being conveyed to Binya Dâla, the trembling suppliant again indulged hope. One nosegay was offered at the great pagoda; the other was given to the princess, who placed it in her hair. Without delay she set out for the camp of Alaunghprâ, borne in a palanquin, and surrounded by a hundred maiden attendants. The Yuva Râjâ with many Talaing grandees had preceded her, and they remained as hostages in the Burmese camp. The princess was received in open court, the conqueror sitting on his throne; she knelt down and made obeisance, and was then conducted into the interior of the palace.

For several days hostilities were suspended. Festivals were held in the city and in the besiegers' camp, all of both nations except a few of the leading men believing the war to be ended. From the palace of Hansâwadi came some princesses of the deposed royal family of Burma, whom Alaunghprâ was anxious to gain. Some officers of the Gwè Shâns, and Burmese who had taken service with the Talaing king were surrendered, and at once put to death. It was next demanded that the king's brother Binya Dâla, his nephew Doabanyâ, and his son-in-law Soabyâ, should be given up. They knew the fate that awaited them, and the demand was resisted. Alaunghprâ, who never intended to fulfil the hopes he had inspired, now no longer concealed his design. He had managed to introduce into the city a band of chosen soldiers, who remained hidden apart from each other, but ready on a given signal to attack the palace. They were discovered and put to death, and again hostilities were resumed. The Yuva Râjâ, who had made himself acceptable to Alaunghprâ, appeared at one of the city gates and called on his relations to come, as they had promised, to the Burmese camp. The famine in the city became more intense; quarrels arose among the royal family; and the wretched king sent secret proposals to surrender, asking only that his life should be spared. The Burmese king now made a night assault on one of the city gates. The defenders fled; the besiegers rushed in. The houses near the gate were set on fire, and amidst the terror and confusion no combined resistance was made. The city was given up to plunder, and the soldiers were allowed to keep as booty all they took, except warlike stores and the jewels, valuables, and equipage which had been carried away from the palace at Ava. The conquered king was taken prisoner in the palace. Most of the leading men, even Rahâns, according to the Talaing chronicle, were put to death; and thousands of men, women, and children were sold as slaves.

About the 2d May 1757.

Returns to his own city.

Remaining in Hansâwadi for some weeks, Alaunghprâ then went down to Rangoon, taking the captive king with him. All the artificers of the city were sent to his own capital. The buildings in Pegu were destroyed. He appointed a governor to Martaban, and officers to all the districts of the delta. He then left for Muthsobo. Proceeding up the Irâwadi, when a little above Danubyu, Ensign Lester, who had been deputed by the chief of the settlement at Negrais to ask for a treaty of commerce, was received in audience. He was told to follow on, and was again received a few days later at Myanaung. Alaunghprâ spoke severely of the conduct of the British in supporting the Talaing rebels, but issued a decree granting, among other favours, the island of Negrais, and ground for a factory at Bassein to the East India Company. Considering past events, his treatment of the British merchants was liberal; but the envoy was meanly treated by the subordinate officers of the court. He proceeded on to his capital, where he held a grand festival, and, surrounded by his court, went to worship at the pagodas. He also founded a

About 9th July.

23d July, A.D. 1757.

new pagoda, depositing immense treasures in the relic-chamber, and liberally rewarded all his officers, especially those who had been his companions in his first resistance to the Talaing king.

A small expedition was sent to punish the Gwè Shâns, some of whom had taken refuge in the Momeit states. This caused a collision with the Shân chiefs of Maingmaing, who were tributary to China, and was the remote cause of trouble to Burma a few years later. Determined to make his power felt among the neighbouring states, Alaunghprâ next announced in open court that an appeal had been made to him by one of the sons of the Râjâ of Manipur, and that he intended to settle the succession to the throne in that country. (Manipur.) His army marched westward from the capital, while he himself went by water down the Irâwadi, and marched on Langthabal, then the chief city of Manipur. Arrived there, he found no Râjâ and no inhabitants. (November, A.D. 1758.) All had fled to the mountains. Some chiefs came in and submitted, and Alaunghprâ contented himself with setting up a stone pillar as a token of conquest. He then returned to his capital, and occupied himself in directing works for bringing water to the city sufficient for the increased number of inhabitants. While engaged in this useful occupation, news reached him of an insurrection having broken out in Pegu. (Insurrection in Pegu.) Without delay he assembled an army, and having dispatched it by land and water, followed himself. His eldest son, now Ainshêmeng, was left as his deputy at the capital. (July, A.D. 1759. August.) The Talaing insurrection was feebly sustained. Though the Burmese governor of Pegu, Nè Myu Noarahtâ, had at first been surprised and obliged to retreat on Henzadâ, he recovered ground and again occupied Rangoon. But affairs were unsettled, and events occurred which seemed to point to foreign intrigue with the rebels. Before the rebellion had been entirely quelled, the ship "Arcot" arrived at Rangoon, having on board Mr. Whitehill, who

was in the service of the East India Company. He had been at Rangoon four or five years before, at the time of the siege of Syriam, when the "Arcot" had fired on the Burmese war-boats. It is not surprising, therefore, that he was now arrested and the ship seized. Mr. Whitehill was sent up the river to Prome, where Alaunghprâ then was. He was treated more leniently than he probably expected after the fate of M. Bourno, and was allowed to depart upon paying a heavy ransom. Alaunghprâ, on arriving at Rangoon, received what he no doubt considered to be correct information, that the agents of the Company at Negrais had sold arms and ammunition to the rebels. This report, which probably was well founded, could not fail to make a barbarian despot give full vent to his rage. He ordered that the settlement was to be utterly destroyed. The Government of Bengal had intended to withdraw the establishment from Negrais. At this time Mr. Southby arrived as chief of the
5th October. factory.[1] The following day a sudden attack was made by armed Burmese on the building where the Europeans were assembled. Ten of them, and nearly one hundred natives of India, were murdered. Two British ships were in the harbour, to which some Indians fled; and a few Europeans, who had escaped the massacre, were sent prisoners to Rangoon.

Invasion of Siam.

Alaunghprâ now determined to invade Siam. Pretexts for this measure were not wanting. Thousands of Talaings had taken refuge in Siamese territory, and bands of that race had made incursions on the Tavoy frontier, which had lately been re-occupied by the Burmese. The conqueror, it is stated, was also incensed against the king of Siam because he had refused to give him one of his daughters in marriage. He decided to march by the coast route to Ayuthiâ, as he had ships which could sail down the coast with provisions, and keep up

[1] Dalrymple's Repertory, vol. i. p. 343.

communication with the army. Before he left Rangoon his principal officers advised him not to undertake the expedition; and the astrologers represented that the aspect of the planets foreboded evil. Disregarding these warnings, the army marched. Alaunghprâ took with him his second son, Myêdu Meng. Moving by Hansâwadi and Sittaung, the whole force, including the ships, assembled at Martaban. A Talaing officer had been appointed governor of that city. He was suspected of being in secret correspondence with Talabân, who was in the Zimmè territory during the late rebellion. The governor was now put to death. The army crossed the Salwin river, and marched down the coast to Tavoy and Mergui. The port of Tenasserim, then occupied by the Siamese, was next entered; and a day's march in advance occurred the first skirmish with the Siamese forces. Alaunghprâ, traversing the low mountain range at this narrow part of the peninsula, debouched on the shore of the Gulf of Siam at or near the village of Banlaym. From thence marching northerly, a severe engagement with the enemy occurred at the Mayklaung river. The Siamese were defeated with heavy loss in killed and prisoners, elephants and guns. Alaunghprâ took up a position before the capital, Ayuthiâ. He soon found himself in dangerous plight. The Siamese king rejected all offers of peace, and was determined to hold out until the rise of the river should flood the camp of the besieger. Alaunghprâ was not prepared to support his army during a long siege. In vain he sent conciliatory messages, declaring that he came not to destroy the city, but as a Bodhisatwa to preach the law of holiness and deliverance from earthly desire. He would enter the city as his predecessor Goadama had entered Kapilawastu, his father's city, and subdue men's hearts by kindness. The Siamese, in reply, ridiculed his pretension and defied his power. While a glorious anticipated apotheosis was thus being announced, a

December, A.D. 1759.

About 10th April, A.D. 1760.

grievous downfall was at hand. The destined Buddha revealed to his confidential attendants that he felt stricken by mortal disease. He had only been five days before the city he came to conquer, when a retreat was ordered. The route selected was the valley of the Menâm river. The dying king was carried in a litter. The retreating army, much harassed by the Siamese, pushed on rapidly; and when near Rahaing, turning westward, reached Myawadi in the upper course of the Thaungyin. When half-way to the Salwîn, Alaunghprâ died. He was forty-six years old. The death was concealed as long as possible. The body was borne to Hansâwadi and Rangoon. The Myêdu Meng proceeded without delay to the capital, and the body was conveyed there by the river. It was burnt with the funeral rites of a Chakravarti or universal monarch.

Retreat and death of Alaunghprâ.

Middle of May, A.D. 1760.

CHAPTER XVIII.

ARAKAN.

The king of Arakan becomes aggressive—Takes Chittagaon—Arrival of Portuguese ships—European pirates—Alliance between the pirates and the king of Arakan—The Portuguese Viceroy sends a fleet to attack Arakan—Attack fails—King of Arakan occupies Dacca—Invades Pegu—Fate of Shah Shujâ—Arakanese driven from Chittagaon—Kings of Arakan at the mercy of foreign guards—Authority of the king restored—Great earthquake.

King of Arakan becomes aggressive.

IN a former chapter, the affairs of the kingdom of Arakan were traced up to the march of Tabeng Shwèhtî on the capital in 1546–47. The narrative of events in that country will now be resumed, and continued to the time of the death of Alaunghprâ. For many years after the retreat of Tabeng Shwèhtî, Arakan was left undisturbed. Situated between Bengal and Burma, and far inferior to either in extent and resources, the strength of Arakan lay mainly in woods and swamps, which opposed the passage of an enemy, and offered a safe refuge for the people. Trusting to these natural defences, the kings of Arakan might long have remained secure against foreign foes. But they were not content to exist in obscure independence at home, and they encroached northward or eastward, as they found opportunity from the weakness of either neighbour. The rulers of Arakan had extended their territory northward during the time of the feeble kings of Bengal. But a vigorous race coming from Central Asia now possessed the imperial throne at Dehli, and the time was not far distant when the kings of Arakan were to be driven within their ancient boundary.

Takes Chittagaon.

In Upper India, what is called the "Mughal or Mogul Empire" had been established by Baber in 1526, at which time Nusserit Shah, the son of Syud Hussein, reigned in Bengal. He was assassinated in 1539, when Sher Shah, the Affghan, became king, and ruled for six years. The general of Akhbar, the grandson of Baber, did not conquer Bengal until thirty years after, and the south-eastern districts were for some time later still unsubdued. Amidst these troubles in Bengal, the kings of Arakan, who had held portions of what is now the Chittagaon district about the middle of the fifteenth century, firmly established their authority there during the greater part of the sixteenth century.[1] The English traveller Fitch, who was at Chittagaon in 1585, expressly states that "it is oftentimes under the king of Ruon." The first appearance of Europeans in this part of India was in 1517, when, according to the Portuguese historian,[2] John de Sylveryra entered the port of Chittagaon, which then appears to have been held by the king of Arakan. The Portuguese were invited to trade with that country. In the native chronicles, however, the first arrival of the Portuguese in Arakan is stated to have been in 1532, when they came "from the great ocean in big ships."

Arrival of Portuguese ships.

[1] In vol. ii. of the "Researches of the Asiatic Society of Bengal," p. 383, is a paper which was read before the Society in 1790 by Sir John Shore. It refers to an inscription in what is called "the Maga language" (either Pali or Arakanese), on a silver plate found in what is called "a cave," near Chittagaon. From the account given it is evident that the silver plate was found in the relic-chamber of a pagoda. The relic-chamber had been constructed in the ground beneath the pagoda, and in it, together with the silver plate, were found numerous images of Buddha. It is the general practice in Arakan and Burma to deposit images in relic-chambers. The pagoda now in question was, according to the inscription, built in the year 904 (A.D. 1542) by Chandi Lah Râjâ, as a place of worship for the Magas. That name Maga, it may be remarked, has no doubt been given by the translator to the Arakanese people, as it is not likely to have been used in the inscription. The translation as printed is indeed evidently a rough paraphrase of the original. The name Chandi Lah Râjâ is no doubt an attempt at rendering the title of the Arakanese governor in a Bengal form.

[2] De Faria y Sousa. English translation, vol. i. p. 220.

Bitter complaint is made that not long after they wantonly plundered villages near the coast.[1] In 1538 an envoy from the Portuguese Viceroy at Goa landed at Chittagaon, and proceeded to the king of Bengal, Sher Shah, who held his court at Gour.[2] Meng Phalaung, who was king of Arakan for twenty-two years until 1593, held all Chittagaon, part of Noakhali, and of Tippera. He assumed the Muhammadan title of Sikunder Shah. Meng Khamaung, grandson to Meng Phalaung, who succeeded in 1612, is glorified as a hero in the native annals. His bold enterprise in proceeding to Pegu, where he was taken prisoner by his former slave, de Brito, has already been narrated. There were at this period numerous Portuguese adventurers in Arakan, and de Brito, who came to the coast as a cabin-boy, was for some time a menial in the palace.

Among other settlements which the Portuguese had formed was one called Dianga, situated on the sea-coast south of the mouth of the river Kurnaphuli, about twenty miles south of the present town of Chittagaon. There was a considerable European population at this port. They had a thriving trade with the ports of Bengal, but made themselves odious to their Asiatic neighbours by their piratical attacks on the native vessels which their galleys fell in with at sea. The king of Arakan on this occasion, and because of the ungrateful conduct of de Brito at Syriam, who had also designs to gain Dianga, attacked the settlement by land early in 1607.[3] The town was taken and the inhabitants slaughtered without mercy. A few Europeans escaped by sea. Among them was

European pirates.

[1] They are called in the Arakanese chronicle Phalaung. This at first was probably a corruption or adaptation of Feringi (as the Tibetan tribes, according to Hodgson, have changed the same word into Philing), and as the word is Burmese for tadpole, it was continued to be used in derision. The name is still called out to Europeans by children in the streets of Akyab.

[2] See Hunter's Statistical Account of Bengal, vol. v. p. 119, and vol. vi. p. 110.

[3] For the events of this period see the History of Manuel de Faria y Sousa, vol. iii.; Hunter's Statistical Account of Bengal, vols. v.

Sebastian Gonzales, who had lately arrived from a port of the Megna with a cargo of salt. His history was like that of many Portuguese adventurers at this time in India. He had come from Europe two years before and enlisted as a soldier. Afterwards he became owner of a small vessel with which he traded on the coast of the Bay of Bengal. After escaping from Dianga, he for some time lived by plunder on the Arakan coast, and found refuge when necessary in the mouth of the Megna. There lay the small territory of the Râjâ of Batecala or Bakla, in what is now the district of Bakirgunj, with whom the Portuguese were on friendly terms. Sundeep (Sandwip), the most eastern of the habitable islands off the mouth of the Megna, had at one time been occupied by the Portuguese, and was now in the possession of Futteh Khan, an Affghan. This chief appears not to have made his submission to the Mogul Government of Bengal, but to have set up for himself. He was very active against the Portuguese pirates, though at one time in league with them, and at length was killed in a fight at sea. Gonzales, who was selected to lead these sea-wolves, collected a flotilla of forty sail, manned by four hundred Portuguese sailors, and attacked and took the port of Sundeep after a long resistance. The whole of the garrison, and the inhabitants without distinction, were put to the sword. Gonzales now not only refused to acknowledge the authority of the Râjâ of Bakla, who had helped him to besiege Sundeep, but took possession of the island of Deccan Shabazpur and of another island adjoining. About this time the governor of Chittagaon having offended his brother the king of Arakan, fled to Sundeep. Gonzales received him and married his sister; but

March 1609.

and vi.; and Stewart's History of Bengal; also Marshman's. The Arakanese history mixes up the account of the destruction of Dianga with the subsequent rebellion of the king's brother. The massacre of the inhabitants is thus concealed by a short general description of events which were spread over three or four years.

he died suddenly, not without suspicion of having been poisoned. The piratical chief then seized all his treasure.

Alliance between Portuguese pirates and the king of Arakan.

The Mogul governor of Bengal, Sheikh Islam Khan, now determined to subdue the country east of the Megna, which had submitted to the king of Arakan. Gonzales and the king, though lately deadly foes, leagued for their own defence, and the Arakanese fleet, which consisted of a number of well-appointed galleys, was placed under the command of the Portuguese adventurer, who had also his own ships. The king of Arakan marched with his army from Chittagaon as far as Lakshmipura or Lukeepur, in the district of Noakhali, and expelled the Mogul detachments which had occupied the towns. Gonzales, who looked only to securing his own power, gained possession of the whole fleet of his ally, by the simple plan of calling the Arakanese captains to a consultation and murdering them. The vessels then fell an easy prey. The Moguls soon reappeared in force, and the king of Arakan with difficulty escaped across the river Fenny in his flight to Chittagaon. Leaving a strong garrison in that town, he returned to his own capital, and there a nephew of Gonzales, who appears to have been given to him as a hostage, was put to death by impalement. Gonzales in revenge entered the Arakan river with several ships, plundered the villages, and even captured some European merchant vessels—probably Dutch—which were lying there. The king of Arakan, Thado Dhammâ Râjâ, died in 1612, and was succeeded by his gallant son Meng Khamaung. The young king determined to attack Gonzales in his stronghold. He marched to Chittagaon, his fleet at the same time keeping as near the coast as was practicable, in order to preserve daily communication with the army. But he came into collision with the forces of the Râjâ of Tippera, and was obliged to retire without effecting his object.

The Portuguese Viceroy sends a fleet to attack Arakan.

Gonzales, fearing there would be a combination against him, and being no longer supported, as he once was, by a considerable number of his countrymen, determined to apply for aid to the chief of his nation in India. He sent messengers to the Viceroy at Goa, urging that all he had done was to revenge the murder of the Portuguese at Dianga, and offering, if supported, to pay a yearly tribute to the crown of Portugal. He suggested that Arakan should be attacked; declared that the conquest would be easy, and that great booty would be found. The Viceroy did not disdain to approve of the plan proposed by a freebooter. He sent a fleet of fourteen galliots under Don Francis de Meneses, which reached the mouth of the Arakan river at the close of the rainy season. By some defect in the arrangements for combined movement, or perhaps by the design of the admiral, Gonzales had not arrived. The admiral, however, at once took his fleet up the river, on a branch of which the capital of Arakan stands. There happened to be lying there some Dutch vessels, and they joined the Arakanese flotilla to resist the attack. A furious battle ensued, and the Portuguese fleet was forced to retire to the mouth of the river. After a few days Don Francis was joined by Gonzales with fifty sail, for the most part small craft. The admiral now sailed up the river and attacked the Dutch ships. They were anchored so as to bring their broadside guns to bear on the assailants, and were supported by earthen breastworks on shore, manned with Arakanese musketeers. The Portuguese had the best of the fight, due mainly to their superior numbers and the reckless onslaught of the pirate chief. Suddenly Admiral Don Francis was killed, and the galliot of Gaspar de Abreu was taken. He escaped capture but died of his wounds. The Portuguese fleet, much discouraged at these losses, drew out of fire, floated with the ebb tide down the river, and sailed for Goa. Gonzales re-

A.D. 1615.

Attack fails.

turned sullenly to Sundeep. Meng Khamaung made another attack on that island about two years later. He took it, putting most of the inhabitants to death, and destroyed the fortifications. Gonzales escaped, and is heard of no more; but, in the words of the Portuguese historian, "His pride was humbled and his villanies punished." Meng Khamaung, emboldened by success, extended his territory in Bengal by occupying a part of what is now the district of Bakirgunj, and for a time the city of Dacca. This movement, which is boastfully termed in the Arakanese chronicle the "conquest of the middle land," was rendered possible from the confusion which then existed in the Mogul empire. Shah Jehan, in rebellion against his father, Jehângir, had killed in battle Ibrahim Khan, the Subadar of Bengal, and had then marched towards Delhi. The south-eastern districts of Bengal were left without a master. Meng Khamaung did not long enjoy his success, which could only gratify a vain ambition, and not be of any lasting advantage to his country. He died in 1622. His name is still remembered with pride and affection by the people of Arakan.

King of Arakan occupies Dacca.

His son succeeded to the kingdom, and took the title of Thiri Thudhammâ Râjâ. He enforced payment of tribute from Dacca, and marched on a marauding expedition into Pegu, where, after the death of Anoukphetlwun Meng, affairs were for some time much confused. He brought from thence as a trophy a bell which had been cast by the king of Pegu, and set it up at a temple near the capital.[1] He reigned until 1638, in which year, says Stewart,[2] "the Mug chief Makat Rai,"[3] who had fallen under the displeasure of his

King of Arakan invades Pegu.

[1] This is the bell before mentioned, which is now in a Hindu temple in the Doab. See Journal of the Asiatic Society of Bengal, vol. viii. for 1838. The inscription, in Burmese and Talaing, is of considerable historical value. See p. 148.

[2] History of Bengal, 1813, p. 245.

[3] Makat Rai is apparently a corruption of Meng Rè, signifying "Bold Chief," a title held by the Arakanese governors of Chittagaon. It appears on some of the coins they issued.

master, came to Dacca, which had been recovered to the empire by Kasim Khan, the governor of Bengal. It is stated that this chief made over the sovereignty of the territory of Chittagaon. That district, however, did not then pass to the officers of the Mogul emperor, and apparently remained subject to Arakan for several years longer. In 1652 Sânda Thudhammâ succeeded to the throne. In his reign Shah Shujâ fled into Arakan. The sad fate of this prince and of his wife and children, has excited deep compassion.[1] Appointed viceroy of Bengal in 1639, he made Rajmahal his capital. Engaged in war with his brothers, he was defeated by Mír Júmla, the general of Aurungzebe. Despairing of mercy from his brother, he sent his son to demand an asylum from the king of Arakan, and permission to embark for Mecca. The reply was satisfactory, and the prince with his retinue, together with his wife, sons, and three daughters, proceeded from Dacca to a port on the river Megna, where they embarked in galleys. As it was the season of the boisterous south-west monsoon, the galleys could not leave the river, and fearful of being taken prisoners, the whole party landed in what was then the territory of Tippera, and proceeded by land to Chittagaon. From thence they travelled through a difficult country to the Naaf river; crossing which, they entered Arakan, and arrived at the capital about the end of the year 1660. The prince was well received. He was anxious to leave for Mecca, but Mír Júmla sent emissaries, who offered large sums if the fugitive were delivered up. The king, desirous no doubt to have a

Fate of Shah Shujâ.

[1] For the story of Shah Shujâ after his flight into Arakan, see Bernier's Travels (Calcutta edition), vol. i. pp. 120, 127. Bernier derived his information from Mussulmans, Portuguese, and Hollanders who were at that time in Chittagaon and Arakan. The Arakanese chroniclers conceal the cruel conduct of their king. They lay stress on the attempt of the fugitive prince to possess himself of the palace, but omit to mention the previous provocation, of which there can be no reasonable doubt.

specious cause of quarrel, basely required the prince to give him in marriage one of his daughters. This demand was indignantly refused, and the king openly showed his resentment. Shah Shujâ foreseeing that force would be used, endeavoured to excite a rising in his favour among the Muhammadan population of the country. He made an attempt with his followers to seize the palace, which failed. He was then attacked by the king's soldiers at his residence, and fled to the hills, but was taken prisoner, and forthwith put into a sack and drowned. His sons were put to death, and his wife and two of his daughters committed suicide. The remaining daughter was brought into the palace, where from grief she died an early death. Those of the prince's followers who escaped slaughter, were retained by the king of Arakan for the same service as that they had held under the prince; a bodyguard of archers. They became the nucleus of a foreign corps, which later was notorious in Arakan for turbulence and violence, disposing of the throne according to their will. Later still, when by diminished numbers their influence was weakened, they were deported to Ramrî, where their descendants still retain the name of Kumânchi. Though using only the Burmese language, they are Mussulmans in religion, and their physiognomy and fairness of complexion still tell of their descent from Turks, Affghans, or so-called Moguls.

Arakanese driven from Chittagaon.

In Bengal, Shaista Khan succeeded Mír Júmla as Subadar. King Sânda Thudhammâ, with the assistance of Portuguese and other vagabond Europeans, again made incursions west of the Megna, and plundered the country to the very gates of Dacca. Shaista Khan, determined to drive these invaders out of Bengal, assembled a large fleet and army. By liberal offers he detached the Portuguese from the service of Arakan, and gave them land on a branch of the Megna south of Dacca, still known as Feringibazar. The Mogul army under Uméd Khan in 1666 laid siege to Chittagaon, and the Arakanese having lost their fleet, abandoned the city and endeavoured to escape. About two thousand were made prisoners and sold as slaves. More than twelve hundred pieces of cannon, most of them jingals carrying balls not exceeding one pound, were found in the city. Chittagaon, which the kings of Arakan had possessed for a century and a quarter, was lost, and since that time the Arakanese have never, except during plundering incursions, held any of the country north of Râmu.

Kings of Arakan at the mercy of foreign guards.

Sandâ Thudhammâ Râjâ reigned for the long period of thirty-two years, and in 1684 was succeeded by his son, who took the title of Thiri Thuriya Dhammâ Râjâ. For a century no external danger threatened Arakan, but the country suffered from internal disorder. The archers of the guard, whose numbers appear to have been maintained or increased by fresh arrivals of men, of the same race from Northern India, began to assert their superior energy. They gradually acquired power, and they exercised it without scruple for their own ends. The events of the next hundred years may be summarised in a few sentences. The king, Thiri Thuriya, the queen, and the inferior women of the palace were murdered by the guards, and the treasury was plundered. The brother of the murdered king was placed on the throne with the title of Wara Dhammâ Râjâ. He promised to give as monthly pay to each private of the guard four takâls of silver, about equivalent in value at the present time to twenty rupees. Being unable to fulfil his engagement, the guards mutinied. The palace was set on fire, and the puppet king with difficulty escaped. The bodyguard, after plundering the city, retired, and for some time maintained themselves in the country. A peace was at last agreed to, and the king returned to his capital. But once more he was
A.D. 92. deposed and contemptuously allowed to leave and go wherever he pleased.

His brother was placed on the throne with the title of Muni Thudhammâ Râjâ. Before long he was murdered, as also was a younger brother. For several years the guards deposed and set up one puppet king after another. The native chronicler laments that for more than twenty years the country was at the mercy of a band of foreign robbers. At length an Arakanese of determined character, styled Mahâ Danda Bo, gathered round him a body of devoted men and dispersed or expelled the guards, who from that time lost their power. The native chief became king, with the title of Tsanda Wijaya. He had the support of ten influential nobles. He again established the authority of Arakan towards the north, as, after the death of the Emperor Aurungzebe, the Mogul power east of the Fenny had declined. He had a war with the Râjâ of Tippera, and made an incursion as far as Sundeep and Hâttaya, returning with much plunder and many prisoners; but he only retained possession of the country as far as Ramû. He also made an expedition to the eastward across the mountains into the Irâwadi valley. His troops occupied Prome and advanced to Malwûn, while he himself remained in observation at Mendun. The object of this expedition appears to have been to take advantage of the weak state into which the kingdom of Burma had fallen under Maraung Ratanâ Dáragá and his successor. The king of Arakan, however, had to retire without having effected any object of importance. Soon after his return home he was deposed and put to death by his son-in-law, who became king with the title of Chanda Thuriya Râjâ. After him several adventurers took the throne in rapid succession, and even a foreigner called Kâtra for a few days held the palace. Next, Narâapaya gained the kingdom, and as his reign extended over nineteen years, he lived to see Arakan hemmed in on one side by the conquests of Alaunghprâ, and on the

Native authority restored.

A.D. 1710.

A.D. 1742.

other by the British, to whom the district of Chittagaon was ceded. In the Arakan chronicle the author records with awe repeated shocks of earthquake in the last year of this king's reign which seemed to forebode the downfall of the kingdom. So great was the terror that the king changed his name and abode, hoping by this childish expedient to elude the threatened vengeance of the occult powers of nature. But a more terrible shock came in the following year, when Parama Râjâ was on the throne. The sea retired (so the chronicler describes this great convulsion) along the whole coast to the extent of three cubits perpendicular. In some places the sudden elevation of the land far exceeded that amount. As if to fulfil the gloomy prognostications of the soothsayer, from this time there is nothing to record but change of dynasty or the struggles of aspirants to the throne. The ancient kingdom of Arakan, weakened by constant strife among her own children, was soon to be the prey of the successors of Alaunghprâ, and was destined only to find rest when annexed to the empire of British India.

January 1, A.D. 1761. Great earthquake.

Note on the Earthquakes of 1761 *and* 1762 *recorded in the History of Arakan.*

The great earthquake of 1762 is still known by tradition among the inhabitants of the country. There is an account of it in letters written during that year by Europeans, and the effect of it in raising the land along the sea-coast of Arakan, and depressing it farther north on the border of Bengal, have been described by geologists and other observers within the present century.

In the "Philosophical Transactions," vol. liii., there are two accounts of an earthquake, as observed at Chittagaon on 2d April 1762. One is a translation from the report of a Persian Munshi, and the other is contained in a letter from the Rev. Mr. Hirst, dated Calcutta, November 2, 1762. Both accounts state that the earthquake was very severe. In the latter it is mentioned that an English merchant, who was at the time at the metropolis of Arakan, described the effects "as having been as fatal as at Lisbon." These statements prove that the account in the Arakanese history is not exaggerated. For the evidence of upheaval of the coast, ancient and recent, the amount of the latter varying at different points from 6 feet to 22 feet, see the following works:—

"Asiatic Researches," vol. ii., report by Mr. Reuben Barrow, who surveyed part of the coast of Arakan, A.D. 1788.

"Journal of the Asiatic Society of Bengal," vol. x., 1841, report on Cheduba by Captain Halstead, R.N.

"Records of the Geological Survey of India," vol. xi., 1878, report by F. R. Mallett on the mud volcanoes of Ramrî and Cheduba.

CHAPTER XIX.

DYNASTY OF ALAUNGHPRÂ.

Naungdoagyî succeeds to the throne—Rebellion of Meng Khaung Noarahtâ—The governor of Taungu rebels—Death of Talabân—Death of Naungdoagyî—Hsengbyusheng becomes king—Preparations against Siam—Manipur—City of Ava reoccupied—Operations in Zimmè and Laos—March of the southern and northern armies on Siam—Capital of Siam invested—City taken—Origin of war with China—Chinese army appears at Kyaingtun—Chinese invasion by the Momien route—Burmese measures for resistance—Operations at Mogaung and in the north—Chinese main army retires from Burma—Burmese generals return to Ava—Third invasion by the Chinese—The Burmese armies meet the invaders—Burmese victory—Chinese retreat to their own country—Fourth invasion by the Chinese—The Chinese generals sue for peace—A convention agreed to.

Naungdoagyî succeeds to the throne.

ALAUNGHPRÂ, at his death, left six sons by his first wife. He had expressed a wish that those of his sons who survived him should succeed to the throne in the order of their seniority. The eldest son, who was Ainshêmeng, or heir-apparent, had remained at the capital as regent during the Siamese expedition. He is styled in Burmese history Naungdoagyî. Though at first there was in the attitude of Myêdu Meng some appearance of opposition, it soon became evident that he intended to be loyal to his elder brother; but resistance to the Ainshêmeng was made by the most trusty officer of Alaunghprâ, the cause of which has not been explained. When Myêdu Meng left the army to bear the body of his father to Motsobo, the command devolved upon Meng Khaung Noarahtâ. He led the remnant of the army to Taungu, where a brother of Alaunghprâ was governor. The governor, acting upon orders from the capital, where suspicion of the designs of the general had been excited, attempted to arrest him. He escaped the snare which had been laid for him, and seeing no safety for himself but in resistance, marched to Ava, and, expelling the governor of that city, occupied it.

Rebellion of Meng Khaung Noarahtâ.

A.D. 1760, about 25th of June.

The king sent him a friendly message, inviting him to come without fear to the royal presence. He, well knowing that forgiveness was impossible, refused. Naungdoagyî, without delay, marched on Ava, and, establishing his headquarters at Sagaing, closely invested the city. All attacks were repulsed by the garrison, but famine did its work, and the rebel general, seeing that surrender was inevitable, fled from the city, accompanied by a few horsemen, in December 1760. Not far from the city he separated from his escort and was shot in the jangal. The city surrendered shortly after.

About the 5th.

During the siege Captain Alves, who had commanded one of the English ships anchored off Negrais when the massacre occurred on that island, appeared at Sagaing with letters from the governors of Bengal and Madras. He was admitted to an audience, but was treated with great indignity, and all compensation was peremptorily refused, on the ground that Mr. Whitehill and the governor of Negrais were the aggressors, while the presence of Mr. Southby, who had lately arrived and was innocent of any offence, was an accident which could not have been foreseen. He was included with the rest just, it was said, with lofty indifference to casual suffering, as herbs are consumed along with noxious weeds when ground is cleared by burning for useful purposes. Some English prisoners who were still detained at Rangoon were ordered to be released, and permission was given for the East India Company to occupy land for a factory at Bassein.

August 23, A.D. 1760.

Governor of Taungu rebels.

In the following year the king's uncle, who still governed Taungu, fell under suspicion. He failed to obey a summons to submit himself, and the king marched with an army to reduce him to obedience. The city was encompassed by a high wall, beyond which was an earthen rampart with a broad and deep moat. The king himself remained in camp directing the operations. During the blockade the famous commander Talabân, who was now in the service of the king of Zimmè, entered the territory of Martaban with a considerable force, and for a time appeared to threaten an attack on the besieging army. It was not until January 1762 that the city surrendered. The king pardoned his uncle, and without delay ordered a march on Zimmè to punish the insult which had been offered by an invasion of Burmese territory. Talabân was still at the head of a force in the country between the rivers Salwîn and Thaungyîn. He, his wife, and family were captured; and though in the Burmese history it is stated that his life was spared, it is to be feared that the general who had nobly fought for the cause of the last king of Pegu, was secretly put to death. The expedition against Zimmè was successful. The capital of that state was occupied without much difficulty. The remaining months of the reign of Naungdoagyî passed without any important incident. He devoted himself to erecting religious buildings, and while so employed died suddenly about the end of November 1763.

Death of Talabân.

Death of Naungdoagyî.

Hsengbyusheng becomes king.

His next brother, Myêdu Meng, who has since become known as Hsengbyusheng, succeeded without opposition. He inherited his father's energy and military talent, and soon after his accession took preliminary measures for future operations against Siam, to avenge the insult which Alaunghprâ had received at Ayuthia. He reinforced the army at Zimmè with twenty thousand men under Thihapatè. New officials were appointed to the provinces in all parts of the empire, including the

Preparations against Siam.

February 7, A.D. 1764.

Shân states to the north of the capital. The same year, as the position of Muthsobo was felt to be inconvenient for the seat of government, orders were given to rebuild Ava. In November an army of twenty thousand men under Mahâ Noarahtâ, which had been raised in the lower provinces, marched from Martaban on Tavoy to operate against Siam from the south-west.

Expedition to Manipur.

Not content with the extensive preparations against Siam, the king, in boundless confidence in his fortune and resources, determined at once to punish the chief of Manipur for some incursions which his subjects had made on the frontier. At the close of the rainy season, an army marched from the capital westward to Kannimyu on the Hkyengdwen, and there waited for the king, who went by water. The army of Manipur was defeated. The Râjâ and his family fled to the hills. The chief city was taken, and hundreds of people were carried off as captives. The king returned to his capital in April 1765. While his armies were operating in the distant enterprise against Siam, the building of the palace at Ava was completed by the middle of April, when the king and his whole court proceeded to that city. The large population which soon gathered, and the numerous foreign traders who established themselves, showed the advantages of this site for the capital over that of the native city of the founder of the dynasty.

A.D. 1764. The city of Ava reoccupied. A.D. 1766.

Operations in Zimmè and Laos.

Thihapatè, who had been sent to command the forces in Zimmè, reduced the whole of the territory to obedience. In order to secure his rear when he should advance to the capital of Siam, he marched against the king of Lengzeng, whose capital was then Muanglim, on the river Mêkhaung, to the north-east of Zimmè.[1] The king at the head of his forces met the Burmese

[1] This is the town where the expedition from French Cochin-China under M. de Lagrée left the river and proceeded by land to Kyaingtun.

army some days' march from his capital and was defeated. Thihapatè marched on the city, and the king submitted and agreed to be tributary to the king of Burma. Returning south, the general fixed his headquarters at Lagwun, subdued all the Shân states eastwards, levied contributions, and forced the chiefs to supply auxiliary contingents to his army.

March of the southern army on Siam.

Mahâ Noarahtâ, who commanded the southern army, remained at Tavoy during the rainy season of 1765. He received reinforcements from Pegu, and resumed his march about the middle of October. Proceeding southward to within a few marches of Mergui, he crossed the mountain range of the peninsula nearly by the route which had been followed by Alaunghprâ, and reached Kamburî. Marching from thence direct on Ayuthia, he had a severe battle with the Siamese to the west of that city, in which he was victorious. He took many prisoners, elephants, and guns. Not hearing of the army marching from Zimmè under Thihapatè, he halted at Kannî, a village in the neighbourhood of the Siamese capital.

March of the northern army. A.D. 1765.

The northern army marched from Lagwun about the middle of August. Thihapatè had under his command more than forty thousand men, chiefly Shâns. As he proceeded south he was much delayed by the resistance of the towns of some petty chiefs. At length all opposition was overcome, and the army having received additional Shân troops, assembled at Pitsalauk, a town on a branch of the Menâm in its upper course. The route was pursued down the valley of the river. The Siamese attacked the invaders, but were repulsed with heavy loss; and Thihapatè, continuing his march, took up a position on the east side of Aynthia about the 20th of January 1766. Mahâ Noarahtâ moved his camp to the north-west of the city, where communication with his colleague was more easy. The centre of his new position was at a pagoda which had been built by Bureng Naung.

Capital of Siam invested.

Progress of the siege.

The king of Siam had made careful preparations to defend his capital. The fortifications consisted of a high brick wall with a broad wet ditch. There were numerous guns or jingals mounted. The king, advised by his minister, Bayâ Kuratît, attacked the force under Thihapatè before the junction of the two armies had been effected. The attack failed, and a few days later, when a sally was made against the army of Mahâ Noarahtâ, a desperate battle ensued, in which the Siamese were defeated with the loss of several thousand men killed and made prisoners. The two Burmese armies now completely hemmed in the city with a line of works. The place was too strong and too well defended to be taken by assault, and as time passed and no signs of surrender appeared, the approach of the dreaded rainy season with the rise of the river, which more than once in former times had saved the city, caused alarm among the besiegers. Many officers of high rank advised Mahâ Noarahtâ to retreat to another position until the dry season; but he firmly refused, and was supported by his colleague Thihapatè. When the water rose and flooded the country, the besiegers occupied such bits of high ground as there were, and threw up dykes to keep out the water. They had collected hundreds of boats, which were kept fully manned, but the line of intrenchment round the city was for the time rendered useless. The Siamese made attacks, both by land and water, on the Burmese, who now were broken up into separate corps; but these attacks were unsuccessful.

When the waters subsided, the Burmese commanders, with steady persevering labour, again began the construction of earthworks round the city, and gained more complete command of the river than before. The citizens became straitened for provisions. A body of Shâns from the north attempted to relieve the city by an attack on the besiegers, but were repulsed and dispersed. The king of Siam, with his family and a number of the leading inhabitants, attempted to escape, but were driven back. The king, in despair, wrote to the Burmese generals offering to become tributary to Burma. The reply was in contemptuous terms, and required unconditional surrender. Just at this time Mahâ Noarahtâ died. But this event did not affect the operations of the war. Reinforcements and orders to persevere came from Ava. The Burmese, having command of the whole resources of the country, successfully prevented food supplies from entering the city. The garrison, unable any longer to defend the walls, yielded to a general attack by the besiegers. The city was entirely destroyed by fire.[1] The king, Ekâdatha Râjâ, was killed in the confusion. His brother, Brâun Soasân, recognised the body near the western gate of the palace. The queen and the whole of the royal family were taken prisoners and carried away captive. Immense treasures and stores of war material were found in the palace. The conquest was effected at a critical moment for Burmese interests. Thihapatè had received orders to return home, for the Burmese monarchy was once more threatened by a Chinese invasion. The army, marching rapidly, reached Ava in July; the Shân auxiliaries were allowed to return to their own countries.

City taken, April, A.D. 1767.

Origin of war with China.

A series of petty misunderstandings on the frontier of China had led to an invasion of Burma from that country. In the spring of 1765 a Chinese merchant named Loalî arrived on the frontier, coming by the Momien route, with a large drove of oxen laden with merchandise. In order to cross the river Tapeng, he wished to construct a bridge at the village Nânbâ, and applied to the governor of Bamoa for permission to do

[1] In the history of Siam it is correctly stated that this siege occupied nearly two years, 1766 and 1767 A.D. In a brief history of Siam published in the Chinese Repository, and said to have been written by the king of Siam, this siege is confused with that by Alaunghprâ in 1760. The date for the capture of the city is given as March 1767. See Bowring's Siam, vol. i. p. 58, and vol. ii. p. 347.

so. The merchant, annoyed at the delay which occurred in attending to his application, uttered some words in his own language which were interpreted to the governor as being disrespectful. The governor sent him to Ava as a prisoner. The authorities there released him, and gave orders that he might build the bridge and pursue his vocation. On returning to Bamoa, where his merchandise had been left, he complained that some of the packages had been opened and a portion of the goods abstracted, and he demanded compensation. The officials replied that his own men had remained in charge of the bales, and they refused to inquire into the complaint. Loalî then departed, and, on arrival at Momien, complained of the treatment he had received. He went on to the city of Yunnân, where the governor received his statement and noted the facts. Soon after another dispute took place at a distant point of the frontier. A Chinese merchant named Loatârî arrived, with several followers, at a mart in the territory of the Shân state of Kyaingtun, and there sold goods on credit.[1] Payment was refused by the purchaser, a quarrel arose, and in the affray which ensued a Chinaman was killed. At that time the Soabwâ of Kyaingtun was in Ava. The Sitkê, who was the next in authority, received the complaint of the merchant, who demanded that either the manslayer or a substitute, to be made responsible for the crime, should be delivered up to him. The Sitkê replied that he would give the amount of fine payable according to Burmese law in such cases. The Chinese merchant refused this offer, and left for his own country. He proceeded to the city of Yunnân and complained to the governor. Some Shân nobles and a nephew of the Soabwâ of Kyaingtun, who had offended the Burmese government, were at this time refugees in that city.

[1] Captain W. C. M'Leod heard the same story when at Kyaingtun in 1837. See his Journal, p. 60.

They excited the Chinese officials to demand satisfaction with a threat of making war should it not be given. The general of the frontier petitioned the emperor, who ordered that Kyaingtun was to be attacked and justice enforced. A document was posted at a ford on the Tâloa river,[1] making a formal demand that the homicide or a substitute should be surrendered. No reply having been sent to this summons, a Chinese army advanced and surrounded the town of Kyaingtun. The Soabwâ of Kyaingtun had joined the invaders. An army had marched from Ava in December 1765 to support the Sitkê of Kyaingtun. It was under the command of Letwêwengmhu. He approached the town and forced the Chinese investing army to retreat. It retired towards the Mêkong river, and in a combat there the Chinese general was killed. The chief of Kyaingtun now made his submission, saying that he had been coerced by the Chinese. A garrison was placed in Kyaingtun and the bulk of the Burmese army returned to Ava.

Chinese army appears at Kyaingtun.

April, A.D. 1766.

The king of Burma, viewing with alarm the state of his relations with China, determined to place a garrison at Kaungtun, a town on the Irâwadi, a few miles below Bamoa. This precautionary measure had not long been adopted when it was reported that a large Chinese army had appeared on the frontier near Momien. It marched into the Burmese territory and took up a position at the Mwêlun mountain, which lies to the south of the Talo branch of the Tapeng river. The army of invasion was under two leading generals, Yîng Khun Târeng and Hseng Tâ Loareng. The Burmese garrison at Kaungtun was reinforced and the stockade strengthened. The commander there was Balamenhteng, a bold

Chinese invasion by the Momien route.

[1] This is the name given to the river in the Burmese history. It is however the name of a town on the Melem or Melâm river, fifty-four miles north of Kyaingtun, on the road from that town to Kyainghun. Kyaingtun is still a great thoroughfare for Chinese traders going to the Shân states west of the Salwin. M'Leod's Journal, pp. 59 and 65.

and active officer. The plan of the Chinese generals appears to have been to occupy Bamoa; to advance from thence on Ava; and to collect boats in order to gain command of the river Irâwadi. At the same time they appear to have been in communication with the Soabwâ of Mogaung, who was disaffected towards the Burmese king, and from whom they might receive important assistance. The Burmese Government, though knowing the general objects of the invaders, had not been sufficiently on the alert, and with the Siamese war on their hands, to support which constant reinforcements were required, must have felt a difficulty in raising men. But though attacked by so powerful an enemy, they met the invader with a determined spirit which deserves high praise.

The Chinese generals, in pursuance of their plan, detached from their position at the Mwêlun mountain a column under Rengsutâreng by the Mowun (Muangwan) route to Bamoa. A division was also posted at the intermediate position of Thinzanwêlim to keep up the communication with the headquarter army. At Bamoa the commander built a stockade on the bank of the river, and leaving there a part of his force in garrison, pushed on to Kaungtun. Balamenhteng had, with unwearied diligence, strengthened his post, and being well supplied with fire-arms, awaited the onset of the enemy with confidence. The Chinese commander made desperate efforts to capture the post, but failed, suffering a heavy loss of men, and finally drew off. But success here was of too much importance for the enterprise to be abandoned, and he entrenched himself in a camp near the fort waiting for reinforcements.

Burmese measures of resistance.

The king of Burma had dispatched a force by water up the Irâwadi under Letwêwengmhu to proceed to Bamoa, while a column under wungyî Mahâ Sîthu marched by the western bank of the river on Mogaung. These bodies started from the capital about the middle

A. D. 1767.

of January. Letwêwengmhu on the way up, hearing that Kaungtun was invested, threw some reinforcements and a supply of ammunition into the place from the river face. He then sent a division to Bamoa, which attacked and carried the Chinese entrenched position there. With the bulk of his command he remained in observation on the west bank of the Irâwadi, while by his superior flotilla he held command of the river. He next attacked the Chinese entrenched post near Kaungtun and forced the garrison to retire on the fortified position at Thinzanwêlim. He followed them up and dislodged them from that position, inflicting upon them a heavy loss in men, arms, and horses. They retreated to Mowun. The Chinese invaders had now been driven from the posts they had occupied on and near to the Irâwadi, south of Bamoa, and had lost the boats they had collected for operations on the river.

Operations at Mogaung and in the north.

The corps under the command of Mahâ Sîthu, by a rapid march reached Mogaung before the Chinese could arrive. He made such arrangements for the defence of the town as time allowed. He then advanced to meet the invading force, which, under Hsengtâloareng, was marching by Sanda in a north-westerly direction to a point on the Irâwadi in order to cross that river. The Chinese commander had no boats and took post at Lisoa hill, arranging means to pass to the right bank. Mahâ Sîthu did not allow him time for this, but marching from Mogaung, crossed the Irâwadi to the left bank, and sent on a reconnoitring party of five hundred musketeers. This party fell in with a body of a thousand Chinese horsemen. The musketeers retired to a mountain defile. The Chinese cavalry followed headlong, and, cooped up in a narrow pass blocked with boulders, sustained a heavy loss from the fire of the musketeers. The Burmese commander, finding the Chinese position on the Lisoa hill too strong to be attacked in front, halted on the Nânmyin stream, and sent two divisions to circle round it right and left. This movement was concealed by the thick woods, and the Chinese general, leaving one-third of his force on the hill, marched to attack the Burmese on the Nânmyin. The force left on the hill, supposing the enemy to be only in front, and to be held in check by their main body, was careless, and allowed itself to be surprised and cut up by the two Burmese divisions. The main body of the Chinese under Hsengtâloareng retired hastily to Sanda. Mahâ Sîthu then took post with his whole army at Muangla, which would enable him to intercept the retreat of the Chinese to their own country. He had conducted the operations successfully, but being ill, was now succeeded in the command by Letwêwengmhu. The Chinese army was suffering from want of provisions. The main body, which had originally been posted at the Mwêlun mountain, had been reduced, by continued requisitions to supply reinforcements, to a small number; and this, with the remnant of the division under Hsengtâloareng, retreated to the Chinese territory.

Chinese main army retires from Burma.

Burmese generals return to Ava.

At a late period of the campaign a Chinese column had appeared on the Thinnî frontier, and menaced the capital by that route. This column was attacked on two sides: by a force under Mahâ Thîhathura, marching from Kyainghun, where he had held command during the Siamese war; and by the troops of Letwêwengmhu moving down from the north. The invading column was driven back, and the two victorious generals arrived in Ava with the captured guns, muskets, and prisoners, early in May. The eight Shân states in the basin of the Tapeng river, which had for centuries, though not continuously, been included in the Chinese empire, were now reunited to Burma.

A.D. 1767.

The Chinese generals had grossly mismanaged the campaign. They divided their forces into detached bodies which could not support each other, and thus exposed them to be separately attacked and overpowered. The late appearance of an isolated column at Thinnî was not likely to retrieve failure elsewhere, and the movement itself was feebly made. The Burmese commanders, with inferior numbers in the field, skilfully took advantage of the blunders of their opponents. They are entitled to great praise for their energetic defence of their country against an invader who not only had a numerical superiority in the field, but enjoyed the repute of former conquest and long acknowledged ascendancy. But the Burmese history, which states the original number of the enemy to have been 250,000 men and 25,000 horses, greatly exaggerates the strength of the invaders.

The emperor of China, Kienlung, a competent civil administrator, but no warrior, was determined not to allow what he considered a petty barbarian power, successfully to resist the armies of the son of heaven. To the dismay of the Burmese king, towards the end of the year a Chinese army, more numerous than that which had invaded the country in the previous year, crossed the frontier and advanced to Thinnî. It was under the command of two generals, the emperor's son-in-law, Myinkhunrè, and the emperor's younger brother, Sutâloarè. This was the main army of invasion, and smaller columns, intended apparently to divert attention, were marching, one on Bamoa by the route south of the Tapeng river, by way of Thinzanwêlim, and a second on Momeit, by the route south of the Shwèlè river.

Third invasion by the Chinese, A.D. 1767.

The main army entered Thinnî without opposition. The Soabwâ at once submitted, and furnished whatever the enemy required from him. The Chinese generals commenced the construction of a stockade to the southwest of the town, as a depôt for stores and station for reserves.

Burmese armies meet the invaders, A.D. 1767.

An army under Mahâ Sîthu left Ava about the middle of December to oppose the main body of the invaders. It marched by Thonzè and Thîboa, the object being to operate on the front of the Chinese. A second army under Mahâ Thihathura marched two days later, taking an easterly route to oppose the same body, by intercepting their supplies and circling round to attack them in rear. A column under Letwêwengmhu also marched north to oppose the invaders advancing by the valley of the Shwèlè on Momeit.

When the army under Mahâ Sîthu had advanced beyond Thîboa they encountered the Chinese under Myinkhunrè. The invaders were far superior in numbers and the Burmese were defeated. Mahâ Sîthu then retreated down the line of the Myitngè. Considerable alarm prevailed in the city, but the king was undaunted, and calmly issued his orders for defence.

The column under Mahâ Thihathura marched by the route south of the Myitngè. The Chinese army drew large supplies of provisions from the country east of the Salwîn, and had a depôt in a stockade at Lashô, west of that river. This stockade was taken and many convoys intercepted. A detachment was also sent, which occupied the Taku ferry on the Salwín, where a large number of laden horses and mules were captured. Mahâ Thihathura with his main body pushed on to Thinnî, where the Chinese general, Sutâloarè, commanded in the stockade. The Burmese entered the city and the Soabwâ fled to the stockade. The Chinese garrison soon became straitened for provisions—the arrival of which had been intercepted—and the Burmese commander cut off their water supply. The Chinese soldiers began to desert. The general, a younger brother of the emperor, according to the Burmese history, seeing only death or surrender before him, committed suicide. The garrison, utterly disheartened, ceased to make resistance, and the Burmese entered the stockade. The Burmese general, leaving a garrison

Burmese victory.

in the place, marched without delay on Thiboa, in order to operate on the rear of Myinkhunrè.

That Chinese general had not followed up his first success with vigour. In his march on Ava, which he hoped to enter, and so close the war, he found the Burmese army under Mahâ Sîthu in position at Lunkâpyingyî. About the same time he heard of the defeat and death of his colleague. This news made him irresolute. The Burmese general, dreading the anger of the king, and burning to retrieve his former defeat, made a night attack on the Chinese. It was successful; and Myinkhunrè, abandoning the line by which he had advanced from Thinnî, retreated to Taungbaing. There he took post on a hill. Mahâ Sîthu followed him up, and was soon joined by the victorious column of Mahâ Thîhathura. The Chinese general now made no further attempt to carry out the original object of the invasion, but retreated precipitately from the Burmese territory. The invading divisions which had marched against Bamoa and Momeit had effected nothing, and retired by joining the main body under Myinkhunrè. By the middle of March the last of the enemy's troops had been driven across the Salwîn, and the Burmese generals returned to the capital.

The Chinese retreat to their own country.

A.D. 1768.

Fourth invasion by the Chinese.

But Burma had to struggle once more against the attack of a powerful and persevering foe. It was with a heavy heart that the king again prepared to resist invasion; for the dreaded omen of the great national pagodas being rent by earthquake seemed to portend coming disaster. Vast treasures were lavished in repairing damage to the htî or crowns of the Shwezîgun at Pugân and of the Shwè Dagun at Rangoon; while in these shrines were deposited gold and silver images in thousands, in hope that the threatened vengeance of the invisible powers might thereby be averted.

Hardly had the solemn ceremonies with which these offerings were presented been completed, when the governors of Bamoa and Kaungtun reported the appearance of a powerful Chinese army on the frontier. It was commanded by three principal generals, whose names or titles, as given in the Burmese history, are Sukunrè, Âkunrè, and Ywunkunrè. They moved down the valley of the Tapeng to the Yoayî mountain, where they halted and detached a division under Hsengtârî, to march on Mogaung. In an adjoining forest they felled suitable trees, which were shaped into planks, and were then conveyed to a suitable spot higher up the Irâwadi, where boats were to be built. They had brought many carpenters for this service, and the duty of carrying out their orders was intrusted to Loatârî, with an adequate force at his disposal. Having made these arrangements, the three generals proceeded on towards Bamoa.

To meet this formidable invasion the king sent an army under the master of the ordnance, Thihathu, which left Ava in the last week of September, and A.D. 1769. marched on Mogaung by the west bank of the Irâwadi. A second army, of which Mahâ Thihathura was commander-in-chief, moved in boats up the river, designed to meet the invaders at or near Bamoa; while the elephants and the cavalry, under the Momit Soabwâ and Kyoateng Râjâ, marched north by the east bank of the river.

The Chinese plan of operations was generally similar to that of the campaign of 1767. The three generals, marching in the direction of Bamoa, did not enter that town, but constructed a strong stockade at Shwèngyaungbeng, twelve miles east of Kaungtun. Ywunkunrè was left in command there, while the other two generals proceeded with the bulk of the force to invest Kaungtun. Balamenghteng commanded there. The Chinese generals made many attacks on the place, both from the land side and from the river face, by means of the boats they brought down the river. Balamenghteng well sustained the reputation he had gained, and the Chinese were repulsed with great slaughter.

Mahâ Thihathura had been somewhat slow in his movement up the river, but at length he reached Tagaung. He sent on a division in light boats to throw reinforcements of men and ammunition into Kaungtun, which service was effected, and many of the Chinese boats were destroyed or taken. A Burmese officer, Sânhlâgyi, built a stockade on the river bank below Kaungtun, while the remainder of the division occupied an island on the west bank opposite Kaungtun. The Chinese had now lost command of the river. Mahâ Thihathura, continuing his progress by river from Tagaung, joined the division on the island, directing operations from that station, and keeping his own force as a reserve to be used when required. The elephants and cavalry, with a strong division under Letwêwengmhu, who now took command of this column, continued marching by the east bank on Momît, there to await further orders. The commander-in-chief also sent a column under Tingyâ Mengkhaung to the east bank of the river above Bamoa, to cut off supplies coming to the Chinese force, which was still investing Kaungtun on the land side. The column under the Letwêwengmhu marched boldly on towards Kaungtun, and defeated a Chinese detached force sent against it. Tingyâ Meng Khaung, approaching from the north, was equally successful in an attack on him. The result of these engagements was, that the Chinese generals Sukunrè and Akunrè fell back on their line of retreat by the Tapeng with half the force, while the remainder were compelled to withdraw into the great stockade at Shwèngyaungbeng. The division under Hsengtârî, which had marched on Mogaung, did not reach that town, and was held in check on the east of the Irâwadi by Thihathu.

Letwêwengmhu now combined the several divisions

which were on the east of the Irâwadi to attack the great stockade. The assault was made simultaneously on the four faces of the work, and was successful. The Burmese forced an entrance, but, from the great extent of the works, they were unable to prevent the escape of the Chinese general, Ywunkunrè, who, with those of his men not killed or disabled in the attack, fled and joined his two colleagues. Several more boats belonging to the Chinese were now destroyed, and the Burmese having taken immense stores of arms, powder, and lead, were enabled to arm several battalions more efficiently than they were before.

The Chinese generals sue for peace.

The commander-in-chief, Mahâ Thihathura, now took measures to complete the discomfiture of the invaders. He sent several thousand fresh men across the river, and established his own headquarters on the eastern bank. The Chinese generals, discouraged by defeat and straitened for provisions, determined to negotiate, in order to secure an unmolested retreat. They addressed a letter to Mahâ Thihathura, in which they attributed the war to misunderstanding caused by the intrigues of the Soabwâs of Thinnî, Bamoa, Mogaung, and Kyaingyun. They proposed that these officials, then in Chinese territory, should be exchanged for the Chinese officers who were prisoners, and that the relations of the two countries should be established as they were before the war. Mahâ Thihathura called a council of his principal officers and asked their opinion. They replied that the Chinese had invaded the country with a vast army, evidently intending to conquer it. The enemy had been defeated, and were now surrounded like cows in a pound. In a few days they would be still more helpless from hunger, and the officers unanimously recommended that no terms should be granted. The commander-in-chief observed it was true that the Chinese had wantonly invaded their country, but China was a powerful empire, and could send even more men than the vast hosts which had already appeared. If these men now at their mercy were destroyed, the quarrel between the two countries would be perpetuated, and great evil would result to future generations. He therefore considered it advisable to come to a settlement with the Chinese generals, and should the king disapprove of this course, on him alone would the blame rest. The council did not oppose this wise resolution, and a conciliatory reply having been sent to the letter of the Chinese generals, and preliminaries having been agreed to, fourteen Burmese and thirteen Chinese commissioners, appointed by the commanders-in-chief of both armies, met in a temporary building near to Kaungtun. A document styled "a written contract of settlement" was drawn up and agreed to by all present. It stated in general terms that peace and friendship were to be established as of old between the two great countries, and the gold and silver road, or commerce, to be open as before; presents were exchanged between the commissioners of both nations, and, in accordance with former custom, it was agreed that letters of friendship were to be sent every ten years from one sovereign to the other. The question of boundary between the two countries, which had formed a subject of correspondence, was not mentioned in the document, nor was the surrender of the Ṡoabwâs and prisoners inserted therein.

A convention for peace, friendship, and commerce agreed to. December 13, 1769.

The Chinese appear to have still had some boats in their possession at the time of the negotiations, but no distinct arrangement regarding them had been come to. After having used the boats to convey stores to Bamoa, they burnt them, instead of giving them up to the Burmese, as was expected. This act gave rise to some sharp altercation, but the Burmese general contented himself with remonstrating. The remnant of the invading army retired by the route of the Tapeng river, watched or escorted by a Burmese corps. Thousands of

Chinese soldiers died in the mountains of fatigue and hunger.

The campaigns of Chinese armies in Burma from 1765 to 1769 are noticed very briefly in the histories of China which I have had the opportunity of consulting, and Gutzlaff alone tells the truth without disguise.

The war is not noticed in the "Modern Universal History," published at London in 1781, which professed to narrate the history of China from sources then available in Europe. The valuable work of Father de Mailla,[1] being a translation from Chinese authors, brings the history of the empire down to A.D. 1780. The war with Burma during that century does not appear to have been mentioned by the Chinese historians, and the reverend father adds in a note information supplied to him from another source, in the following words :—

"Le Comte Alikouen, général de l'armée et ministre d'état, ne rendit dans le Yunnan pour commander les troupes, que Kienlong faisoit defiler dans cette province, dans le dessein de venger les insultes que les peuples de royaume de Mien ou Mienfeï actuellement soumis au roi du Pegou, etoient venus faire dans quelques endroits du Yunnan, province limitrophe du Mienfeï."[2]

Gutzlaff writes as follows :—

"A numerous army of Chinese and Mantchoos invaded Birmah in 1767. The Birmahs attacked them vigorously, slew a great number, and took many thousand captives. Only a few of the invincible soldiers returned to give an account of their total defeat. Keenlung was not dismayed. Another army, under the celebrated Akwei, was sent. His soldiers were destroyed by jungal fever, and he was glad to retreat unmolested, after having concluded a treaty with the king of Birmah."[3]

The origin of the war as narrated in the Burmese history is probable, while the events are told clearly and apparently truthfully. But the strength of the invading armies is greatly exaggerated.

Father San Germano states that the success of the Burmese in this war resulted "principally, perhaps, by the aid of their heavy artillery, served by the Christians, who had established themselves in these parts." In other words, the descendants of Portuguese and French captives.

[1] Histoire de la Chine, Paris, 1778. Eleven volumes.
[2] Vol. xi. p. 581.
[3] Gutzlaff's China. London, 1834. Vol. ii. p. 53.

CHAPTER XX.

DYNASTY OF ALAUNGHPRÂ—CONQUEST OF ARAKAN.

The king disapproves the convention made with the Chinese generals—War against Siam—Expedition to Manipur and Kachâr—The king goes to Rangoon—Unsuccessful invasion of Siam—Death of Hsengbyusheng—Succession of Singgusâ—Plots—Palace seized by conspirators—Succession of Bodoahprâ—Plots against him—Site for a new capital selected—Burmese Doomsday book—Distracted state of Arakan—Conquest of Arakan—Invasion of Siam—Plan of operations—March to the frontier—Heroic defence by the king of Siam—Bodoahprâ commences religious buildings—Events in Arakan—Envoy from British India to Burma—Further communication between the British and Burmese Governments—Attempt to arrest the British Resident at Rangoon—Burmese intrigues with native princes of India—Disturbances on the frontier of Arakan—Events in Assâm—Manipur—Death of Bodoahprâ—Great reservoirs constructed—Capture of a white elephant—Character of Bodoahprâ.

The king disapproves the convention made with the Chinese generals.

THE invading army having retired, the Burmese general dispatched to the capital a report of his proceedings, and forwarded the presents which he had received from the Chinese commanders. Hsengbyusheng, indignant that the enemy had been allowed to escape, rejected the offerings, and ordered the families of the principal officers of the army, including the wife of the commander-in-chief, to remain kneeling at the western gate of the palace, bearing the presents on their heads. For three days and nights they were unnoticed, after which they were allowed to withdraw. But when Mahâ Thihathura returned to Ava, he and the principal officers were banished from the city for one month. From China no direct communication as to the convention was made;

but Chinese caravans began to arrive according to former custom, and the Burmese court allowed trade to go on as formerly.

When the Burmese army was recalled from Siam to oppose the Chinese invaders, the general, Thihapatè, carried away the members of the Siamese royal family, who had fallen into his hands. There then arose in Siam a man named Phayâ Tâk, said to be the son of a Chinaman, who gathered round him a body of armed men, and attacking the retreating Burmese, inflicted on them severe losses.[1] Having gradually increased his followers, he assumed the title of king, brought several of the Shân states again under Siamese dominion, and for greater security for the future, established his capital at Bankok. He next conquered Viang Chang, called also Chandapuri, then the capital of the principal state of Laos, on the Mekong. Later, a Burmese force occupied Zimmè, where Thadô Mengteng was appointed governor. When the opportunity appeared favourable, Hsengbyusheng determined to recover what he had lost in Siam, and an army under Thihapatè marched to Zimmè. The general there assembled the contingents of the Shân chiefs, and proceeded to Viang Chang, the king of which state had implored protection against the Siamese. The Burmese governor of Zimmè, by his contemptuous treatment of the Shân chiefs, had roused their indignation, and three of them, whom he intended to forward as prisoners to Ava, fled from the territory. He next disputed the authority of the commander-in-chief, Thihapatè, who was on his march into Siam proper. The general was obliged to halt, partly from want of due support from the governor of Zimmè and partly from the determined front shown by the Siamese troops. Meanwhile disasters threatened to paralyse the Burmese operations at other points.

War against Siam.

[1] Bowring's Siam, vol. i. pp. 58-60; also vol. ii., Appendix A, pp. 349-363.

The governor of Martaban, Kâmani Sânda, had embodied a force, composed principally of Talaings, intended to move by Tavoy and Mergui. After a few days' march the Talaing troops mutinied. Kâmani Sânda with difficulty escaped, and, escorted by a bodyguard of Burmese soldiers, retired to Martaban. Not venturing to remain there, he fled to Rangoon. The Talaing mutineers under Binya Sin followed him up and besieged the stockade. They failed in an attempt to storm it; and as a Burmese army under the governor of Myânaung began to appear, they withdrew, and returning to Martaban, fled into Siam with their wives and children. Hsengbyusheng now raised an army of thirty thousand men, composed of Burmese and northern Shâns, to which Mahâ Thihathura was appointed general. He moved down to Martaban, and prepared to march on the capital of Siam.

Expedition to Manipur and Kachâr.

These extensive preparations to recover lost ground in Siam did not interfere with the king's design to extend his dominion towards the north-west. Under the pretence that the ruler of Manipur had repaired the defences of his capital since they had been destroyed by Alaunghprâ, an army was sent, which not only ravaged that state, but pushed on into Kachâr, and thence northwards across a high mountain-range into Jaintia. The invaders suffered immense loss, but the Râjâ of Kachâr had to submit for the time. The remnant of the Burmese army returned home after two years, having gained no advantage to the empire.

The king goes to Rangoon.

While this predatory excursion was still in progress, the king determined to go himself to Rangoon, both to be nearer to the scene of operations against Siam, and to place a new htî or crown on the great pagoda, Shwè Dagun. This was a religious act, which by force of its own merit might bring the reward of victory, and it was hoped would favourably impress the Talaing people. The king left Ava and proceeded in grand state down the Irâwadi. The deposed king of Pegu and his nephew, who had remained prisoners for fourteen years, were led in the royal train. Hsengbyusheng delaying on the way while he worshipped pagodas at Pugân and Prome, only reached Rangoon after a progress of three months. He adorned the great pagoda with a magnificent golden jewelled crown, and after this display of religious zeal, the captive king of Pegu was with a mockery of justice put on his trial before a special tribunal. He was declared guilty of having excited the Talaing people to rebellion, and was publicly executed. Hsengbyusheng after this cruel deed set out to return to his capital.

Middle of December, A.D. 1774.

April, A.D. 1775.

Unsuccessful invasion of Siam.

Mahâ Thihathura, having many difficulties to overcome in preparations for the campaign, did not commence his march from Martaban until the close of the rainy season. The route he selected lay eastward, so as to gain the upper waters of the Menâm. He reached Rahaing with little opposition from the Siamese. Dissensions among officers of high rank, now the curse of the Burmese armies in the field, soon broke out. The second in command, Zêya Kyo, protested against the plan of operations, and returned to Martaban with a portion of the troops. Mahâ Thihathura persevered in his march. He was successful in occupying Pitsalauk and Thaukkatai, but suffered a severe defeat from the Siamese, and was compelled to make an ignominious retreat towards the frontier.

Death of Hsengbyusheng. Succession of Singgusâ, June, A.D. 1776.

In the midst of these disasters Hsengbyusheng died at Ava, and was succeeded by his son Singgusâ at the age of nineteen years. He was determined to put an end to the Siamese war. But Zêya Kyo by court favour was allowed to return to the army, and having succeeded in a skirmish with the Siamese, was considered to have atoned for his mutinous conduct. The armies in the Upper Menam and in the Zimmè territory were ordered to withdraw from the Siamese territory, where they no longer could remain with safety. Several officers suffered death for alleged misconduct before the enemy, and Mahâ Thihathura was disgraced and deprived of his office of Wungyî.

Plots against Singgusâ. Palace seized by conspirators.

Singgusâ, suspicious of plots, put to death a younger brother of his own, and also his uncle, the fourth son of Alaunghprâ. The fifth son, then known as Badun Meng, an astute prince, was sent to live at Sagaing, where he was closely watched. The son of Naungdoagyî remained. Maung Maung, who was a child at the time of his father's death, became an object of anxiety to the court party as a probable tool in the hands of conspirators. He had been brought up in a monastery, and was now placed in the village of Phaungkâ, where it was supposed he would be less dangerous than elsewhere. The king seemed to be satisfied with the precautions taken against conspiracy, and wearied with the monotonous life in the palace, all warlike expeditions being suspended, made frequent pilgrimages to distant pagodas. He was accustomed to leave the palace, and return suddenly after an interval without warning. A conspiracy, which was joined by several influential men, was formed against him, and was supposed to be secretly supported by Badun Meng. This plot was formed on the plausible ground that if the rule of succession in favour of the sons of Alaunghprâ were departed from, then the son of the eldest, Naungdoagyî, had the best claim. As possession of the palace is the chief manifestation of right to the throne in Burma, the frequent absences of Singgusâ soon offered a favourable
About 8th February, A.D. 1781. opportunity to the conspirators. The young king had gone with his chief queen, his mother, and sisters to worship at a pagoda about fifty miles up the Irâwadi. The young prince, Maung Maung, came suddenly at midnight to the palace gate, and his followers demanded admission for the king. The guard at the outer gate admitted the party without .delay At one of the inner gates the guard resisted, but was overpowered. The

prince at the head of his followers gained possession of the palace, and forced the high officials in charge therein, to swear allegiance to him as king. In the morning several men of rank, old servants under former kings, being summoned, arrived at the city and were appointed to office. Mahâ Thihathura took command of troops to defend the palace. The Badun Meng and other members of the royal family came to the capital, and remained apparently passive.

Singgusâ was at this time at a village about fifty miles distant. The next day he heard of the event. He at once, with all his retinue, crossed the river to Singgumyû, intending to march down to the city. Hearing later that the whole of the capital had turned against him, he retired farther north to Sanpênago. There his retinue gradually left him, and at last the crews of the royal boats deserting, he was left with only a few followers and his own relations.

Succession of Bodoahprâ.

In the palace, the Atwen Wuns, ministers for personal affairs, quickly came to the conclusion that the boy Maung Maung was utterly unfit to rule. All who had abetted the conspiracy looked to the Badun Meng as the fittest to occupy the throne. He, prepared for the occasion, at once referred to the declaration of Alaunghprâ on his deathbed, that his sons should succeed him according to their seniority. Already he had collected a body of armed men, and found no difficulty in entering the palace. Maung Maung, after a six days' reign, was seized and put to death. He was only eighteen years of age. Badun Meng was forthwith proclaimed king. He assumed various titles afterwards, especially that of Hsengbyu Mya Sheng, but is now usually known as Bodoahprâ. The unfortunate Singgusâ, and those who remained with him, were sent to the city as prisoners, and all, including children and attendants, were ruthlessly burnt to death.

March, A.D. 1782.

Plots against Bodoahprâ.

Bodoahprâ, still pretending ignorance of the conspi-

racy by which he had profited, put to death those who had gained the palace for Maung Maung. The disclosure of his perfidious nature, seems to have surprised many who had supported him. Plots began to be formed against him.[1] One, said to have been supported by Mahâ Thihathura, had for its object to place on the throne an illegitimate son of Alaunghprâ. The old general, who, though unsuccessful in his last campaign, had long led the Burmese armies to victory, was executed. Another conspiracy was headed by Myatpun, said to be a son of the last king of Burma of the ancient race, who had been carried away as prisoner by the Talaing king. This youth, after a life of adventure among the Shâns and Red Karens, found a few desperadoes ready to support him. They boldly scaled the
December, A.D. 1782. wall of the palace in the dead of night, and cried aloud that "the true branch of the royal stock" had appeared. The palace guards were panic-stricken by the suddenness of the attack. The conspirators gained possession of the guns and powder in the palace-yard, but finding no balls, could not use the cannons. They might have fired the palace, but did not. As soon as it was daylight, and the small number of the assailants was seen, they were seized and put to death. Myatpun for the time escaped, but was speedily taken. Bodoahprâ now gave full rein to his fury. Hundreds of both sexes, and even some Buddhist monks, on vague suspicion that they had been privy to the conspiracy, were burnt alive upon an immense pile of wood. The village where the plot had been formed was razed to the ground; the fruit-trees were cut down, and the fields left to grow wild. In Pegu an insurrection broke out, having for its object to restore the Talaing monarchy; but this was easily suppressed.

[1] These plots are briefly hinted at in the Mahâ Râjâweng. Details are given by Father San Germano, pp. 51, 52, and by Colonel Symes, pp. 99, 102.

Bodoahprâ having sated his rage, commenced building a pagoda at Sagaing, where he had lived for some years. He poured vast treasures into the relic-chamber, and made suitable offerings to the monks. Having thus, as he believed, expiated the bloodshed he had caused, he thought to escape the evil influence which might cling to the palace, which had been the scene of so much slaughter, by changing the capital to another position. After careful search, the site selected was on a plain about six miles north-east from Ava, and bordered to the west by a branch of the great river. The new city was laid out as a square of about two thousand five hundred yards, according to the traditionary rules for the capital of a Burmese king. It was named Amarapura. The palace was in the centre of the city. The king, with his whole court, came in grand procession to occupy the new palace, which a few days afterwards was consecrated. The same year a complete register of the kingdom, showing the number of families in each village, with the amount in weight of silver payable from each village circle to the royal treasury, with the boundaries of the villages, townships, and provinces, was completed. This great work, as a record of the financial resources of the empire, was carried on simultaneously by the local officers of each district, who were sworn to report truly, and deserves commendation. But the first use made of it, was a requisition on all the principal cities and towns for an extraordinary payment, to be applied to the restoring and gilding of pagodas and other religious buildings of royal foundation throughout the empire. Payment of this demand was promptly enforced, but whether the amount received was expended for the pious purposes set forth in the royal order, is uncertain. Bodoahprâ, however, was too firmly seated on his throne to give heed to any murmurings. All dangerous men of influence had been got rid of; but he allowed no adverse remark on his measures to pass un-

Site for a new capital selected.

May 10, A.D. 1783.

Burmese Doomsday-book

punished. Having created his eldest son Ainshê-meng, or heir-apparent, one of his younger brothers was said to have quoted his own reply, as to the declaration on succession to the throne of the great founder of the dynasty. He was at once executed.

Distracted state of Arakan.

Bodoahprâ was now entire master of the country included in the basin of the Irâwadi. The chiefs in the districts east of the Salwîn as far as the Mekong acknowledged his supremacy. The sea-coast, as far south as the port of Tenasserim, was subject to his government. Fortune laid open to him a kingdom which had been subject to Burma some centuries before, but afterwards had recovered independence, and had not been subdued by Alaunghprâ. The distracted state of Arakan at this period has already been narrated.[1] For many years past, discontented nobles from that country had flocked to Ava, beseeching aid to restore order. Singgusâ had no ambition for warlike expeditions, and paid no attention to these applications. So terrible, from the tyranny of faction and the desolation of civil strife, was the state of that country, that even foreign interference,—the last resource of despair to lovers of their country,—was accepted as promising relief from greater evil.

After the destructive earthquakes which seemed to portend the overthrow of the kingdom, Sanda Parama was dethroned by his brother-in-law, who ascended the palace, and took the title of Apaya Mahâ Râjâ. He in his turn was put to death by one of his officers, who then reigned as Sanda Thumanâ. Bodoahprâ sent emissaries to inquire as to the state of the country; and the king not daring to resent this act of interference by his powerful neighbour, humbly represented by letter that all disturbance had subsided. But resistance to the nominal king soon broke out once more, and Sanda Thumanâ fled from his capital. He became a Rahân, but this did not save his life. One

[1] See chapter xvii.

of the rebel chiefs seized the palace. Immediately there was a combination of faction leaders against him, and he fled. A chief in Ramrî, Aungzun, a man of resolute character, was called by a majority to occupy the throne. He took the title of Sanda Thaditha Dhammarît Râjâ. Some chiefs still persisted in resistance to his authority, and as he pursued them into the mountains with untiring determination, they fled across the border into Burma. One of them, Hari, the son A.D 1781. of Apaya Mahâ Râjâ, invited Bodoahprâ to take the country. The time did not appear suitable, and nothing was done. In the meantime, Dhammarît Râjâ honestly endeavoured to quiet the kingdom. His efforts were in vain. Village fought against village, and robbers plundered everywhere. In the midst of this confusion the king suddenly died. The husband of his niece A.D. 1782. succeeded, and took the pompous title of Mahâ Thamadâ, the name of the first king, the Nimrod of the Buddhist world. Bodoahprâ saw that the time had come. His scouts kept him well informed, and he knew that Arakan would be an easy prey.

Conquest of Arakan.

The conquest having been determined on, Bodoahprâ made ample preparations to ensure success. An army of twenty thousand men, two thousand five hundred horses, and over two hundred elephants, was assembled at and near Amarapura. It was composed of four divisions, three of which were to march to Arakan by land. The fourth, still incomplete in numbers, would, when joined by boatmen and landsmen drawn from the lower country, proceed by sea. The three divisions which formed the land columns were under the command of the king's three sons, the Ainshêmeng, who was also commander-in-chief, Thado Mengzoa, and Kâma Meng. The army having moved in advance, the Ainshêmeng left the capital and proceeded down the river. The division under Thado October, A.D. 1784. Mengzoa disembarked at Mengbu, with orders to cross the mountains by the Talâk pass. The two other divisions continued on, passing Prome to Padaung. The plan was, so to arrange the march of the three land columns, that the flotilla should have time to come round by sea, and enable the land columns to occupy Sandoway, Ramrî, and Cheduba; after which a general advance would be made on the capital in Arakan proper. The division under Kâma Meng went down the river as far as Kyankheng, from whence it marched to cross the mountains, and debouch on the plain of Sandoway. The flotilla of armed vessels under Nê Myu Kyohteng and Tarabyâ, a Talaing officer, went on to Bassein. Joined there by more vessels, and men raised in the delta, it passed Pagoda Point and Cape Negrais, and began to work up the coast towards Sandoway and Ramrî.

The Ainshêmeng halted at Padaung for twelve days, and then commenced his march leisurely, by the pass which led to Taungup on the sea-coast. Thadô Mengzoa reached Talâk after some opposition from an Arakanese force. The flotilla made extraordinary exertions, and a few days after the Ainshêmeng had arrived at Taungup, it was reported to be at the mouth of the Sandoway river, and in communication with the column of Kâma Meng. The town of Sandoway was occupied without opposition, and the whole force was combined under the commander-in-chief at Tanlwai. He proceeded against Ramrî. The island was held by a son of Dhammarît Râjâ, who was defeated without difficulty. The Ainshêmeng then proceeded northwards, and mustered his forces at the mouth of the Talâk river. Moving his army, chiefly by means of his flotilla, into the great river of Arakan, two chiefs with their followers made submission. At Laungkrek the Arakanese fleet was defeated, and there being no adequate means for the defence of the capital, the chiefs and Rahâns entreated Mahâ Thamadâ

About 2d December, A.D. 1784.

to submit. He fled to the jangal, and the Ainshê-meng entered the city. The fugitive king was brought in a prisoner a month afterwards. About 28th December, A.D. 1784.

Bodoahprâ recalled his sons, and sending Meng Khaung Gyô as governor of the conquered province, directed that ten thousand men should remain as garrison, and the rest of the army return home. The great national image of Arakan, called Mahâmuni, was sent across the mountains by the Taungup pass; was received by the king with great honour; and was set up in a building specially erected for it to the north of the city. The king of Arakan, his queens, and his whole family; the chief officers, the Brahman astrologers and soothsayers with their families, and numerous prisoners, were sent by the same route. All the arms and muskets, with the great guns, one nearly thirty feet long, which had been found in the city, were sent by sea.

Invasion of Siam.

The conquest of Arakan had been achieved so easily that Bodoahprâ, ambitious of military glory, determined himself to lead an army to subdue Siam. The pretended cause of war was to exact tribute asserted to be due, and to avenge the defeats inflicted by the valiant Phaya Tâk. A preliminary expedition was sent by sea, which took possession of Junk Seylon, but after a few weeks the force was driven out by the Siamese, and obliged to return to Mergui. The advantage to be derived from this isolated attack is not apparent. Success could have had little effect on the main object, which was to occupy the capital. Junk Seylon could not be made the base for operations against Bankok, and the only benefit to be derived from the occupation of that island by the Burmese, would be to intercept the supply of firearms coming from Indian ports, of which traffic however there is no evidence. The expedition was a very expensive one, and caused a great loss in men. Early in A.D. 1785.

Bodoahprâ determined to throw an overwhelming

Plan of operations. invading force into Siam, at several points simultaneously. Meng Khaung Gyo was sent to Martaban to collect boats, cattle, and provisions, and to explore the road for a march by the route known as that of the three pagodas. An army of one hundred thousand men was assembled and divided into six corps. It was composed of men drawn from Mogaung and the northern Shân states; from the eastern states; and from September, A.D. 1785. other parts of the empire. One corps was dispatched in advance from Martaban to Tavoy to be in readiness to act from that quarter. One was assembled at Zimmè, and three at Martaban. One body of choice troops was headed by the king himself. Leaving his eldest son in charge of the palace, he marched from the capital to Taungu, and reached Martaban after thirty-Middle of October, A.D. 1785. nine days. There he combined four corps into a grand army under his own command, to move by the route of the three pagodas, but detached a division to create a diversion towards Rahaing. His own projected line of march was to cross the Salwîn from Martaban; to proceed up the valley of the Attarân river by the branch which leads to the three pagodas, at the summit of the mountain range which separates the two countries; from whence, crossing the Siamese border, the route would be pursued down the course of the Menam or Khwaynauey to the town of Kanburî, from whence the march to Bankok would be easy. The grand army, commanded by Bodoahprâ, consisted of not less than fifty thousand men. It soon appeared that the provisions and transport collected, were utterly inadequate for the wants of such an army. The king, in his self-sufficient ignorance and impatience, had issued orders without allowing sufficient time for due arrangements to be made. In his rage he now threatened with death the whole of his principal officers, or, in his own words, "to burn them all in one fiery furnace." The unfortunate Meng Khaung Gyo, who was chiefly responsible, had gone in command of the corps of Tavoy. He was ordered to be sent back in chains. The king persevered in his march. When near the three pagodas, the prisoner arrived and was forthwith executed. The army, now in a difficult mountainous country, was repeatedly attacked and severely handled by the Siamese, and already thousands of the invaders were dying for want of food.

March to the frontier.

Phaya Tâk had been succeeded on the throne of Siam by Phaya Chakkri, the ancestor of the present king of that country. For greater security against Burmese attack, he removed the inhabitants of Bankok from the west to the east bank of the river. Being a man of ability and courage, he had led the Siamese armies in many actions since the fall of Ayuthia in A.D. 1767, and had revived the spirit of the people, which, after the conquest by Bureng Naung, had been cowed under the superior force of the Burmese. The confidence thus infused into the Siamese was manifested by the vigorous attacks made on the invading army. By the middle of January, news reached Bodoahprâ that the column marching from Tavoy had been almost annihilated beyond Mergui. His own advance met with the same fate, and those who escaped fell back in disorder on the main body. The king, terrified for his own safety, was only anxious to escape. He issued orders for all the invading columns to retreat. That which was advancing from Zimmè had met with some success, but all the others had suffered from the enemy and from hunger. Bodoahprâ, fearing lest his own retreat should be cut off in the difficult country in which he was entangled, fled back to Martaban, leaving the scattered remains of his army to escape as they could. Ordering his queens and children to meet him at Rangoon, that all might worship together at the great pagoda, he proceeded to the

Heroic defence by the king of Siam.

A.D. 1786.

ancient capital of Pegu. From thence he came by river to Rangoon and returned to his own capital. The following year the Siamese in revenge laid siege to Tavoy, but were unsuccessful.

Bodoahprâ commences religious buildings.

After this disgraceful campaign, the king was consoled by an embassy from the Emperor of China. A Burmese envoy accompanied the Chinese ambassador on his return; and this was considered the first establishment of friendly relations with the elder brother, since the succession of the house of Alaunghprâ. For some years there was a lull in warfare. Bodoahprâ's martial ardour had received a severe check. He now determined to show his religious zeal by raising a pagoda which should surpass in bulk, if not in beauty of design, all that had hitherto been accomplished in the buildings of the world of Buddhism. The site for this huge fabric of brick and mortar was selected at a spot, since called Mengun, a few miles above the capital, on the western bank of the river. The foundation was laid by the king himself with great ceremony. He had a temporary palace erected in the vicinity, in order that he might

November, A.D. 1790.

see to the work, and acquire the more religious merit by personally assisting therein. He made his eldest son his deputy for the transaction of ordinary affairs, and lived for some years in the temporary palace, but returned to the capital on some occasions. He came into Amarapura to grant audience to Colonel M. Symes,

September, A.D. 1795. February, A.D. 1797.

envoy from the governor-general of India; but he received Captain H. Cox at Mengun. The lower storey of the pagoda had several chambers for containing holy relics, and objects of value or supposed rarity, the offering of which would be esteemed an act of devotion. The principal chamber had an area of ten cubits square and seven cubits in height. It was lined with lead, and was filled with a number of articles, valuable and paltry, after which a metal lid, covering all, was sealed up. It is probable that from the main chamber and the others, which formed large cavities in the structure, not having been built with arched ceilings, and the masonry being of inferior quality, was the cause of the collapse of the building during a severe earthquake some years later. After this great pile had occupied the work of many years it was abandoned, although it had been carried up only to about one-third of the intended height, which was to have been about five hundred feet. The bell which was cast to match this immense fabric still exists, and weighs about eighty tons. It is supposed that the great discontent throughout the country, consequent on the vast number of men pressed to labour on the work, was the reason why it was abandoned. The warning conveyed by the fate of the last king of Pugân in the thirteenth century, of whose proceedings in a similar undertaking a saying arose, "The pagoda is finished and the country is ruined," made even Bodoahprâ pause. He enjoys the dubious fame of having left a ruin which is pronounced by Colonel Yule to be one of the hugest masses of brick and mortar in the world.

The work at Mengun, peaceful in name, but hateful to the people, was interrupted by news from Pegu that the governors of Martaban and Tavoy had rebelled, and that the latter had delivered up the town to the Siamese. A force of ten thousand men was hurriedly sent off from the city with Nêmyu Thengkharâ, who was appointed governor of Martaban, and Thetdoashê, commander-in-chief. Arrived at Martaban, a part of the force was sent on to Tavoy under the command of Mankyîdun. He found the town occupied by the Siamese, while outside, and strongly entrenched, were several corps commanded by the king's son and other members of the royal family. Mankyîdun, anxious to fulfil the expectations of his superiors, rashly made an attack on one of the entrenched positions, and failed. He was compelled to retreat, and returned with the

March, A.D. 1792.

remnant of his force to Martaban. He and four of his officers were afterwards executed. By this time large reinforcements under the Ainshêmeng, who fixed his headquarters at Rangun, had reached Martaban. They were sent on to the south by sea and land under Gun-

December, A.D. 1792.

nerâp Kyoathu. With his superior force he retook Tavoy, and then marched on and relieved Mergui, which the Burmese governor had successfully held. The Siamese invaders having been expelled, the Ainshêmeng returned to the capital, a portion of the troops being left to guard the districts on the south-eastern frontier.

Events in Arakan.

While on the whole of the eastern frontier, from whence the Burmese kings had long been accustomed to expect attack, all danger was quelled, there arose in the opposite quarter commotions, at first despised as insignificant, which were destined to produce fatal effects to the successors of Bodoahprâ.[1] The conquest of Arakan had promised to bring quiet to that country. The people rejoiced at the prospect of relief from desolating civil war; but cruel oppression and severe exactions by the Burmese officers destroyed their hopes, and roused them to revolt. The fact of thousands of men being forced from their country to labour on the "works of merit" undertaken by Bodoahprâ, of whom none returned home, is recorded with bitter resentment in the history of Arakan. The chiefs who headed the insurrection maintained for some years a guerilla resistance. Thousands of the people abandoned their country, and took refuge in British territory, where they were permitted to settle on unoccupied land. Three chiefs, after having bravely maintained the struggle for independence, were compelled to fly across the border. The

[1] For events on the frontier of Arakan the authorities consulted are the native chronicles; Historical Review by Bayfield, revised by Col. Burney (Calcutta, 1835); Symes, pp. 117, 122; and History of British India, H. H. Wilson (continuation of Mill), vol. ix. pp. 8, 16.

arrogant aggressiveness of the Burmese officers, prompted by orders from the capital, produced collision with the British authorities of the district of Chittagaon. The river Nâf separates the territory of Arakan from that of Bengal. The Burmese general, Nandakyoazô, crossed that river near its mouth, at the head of five thousand men, to demand the three fugitives, who were charged with rebellion, robbery, and murder. He entrenched his force in British territory. A detachment of troops under major-general Erskine was sent from Calcutta to oppose this aggression. The two commanders met, and the Burmese officer consented to withdraw, on the assurance that inquiry would be made into the charges brought. The result was that the three chiefs were delivered up as fugitive criminals, and two of them were executed. Their real crime was, that they had led their fellow-countrymen in resistance to the Burmese conquerors, and in their wild warfare had probably been as unscrupulous as their oppressors of the lives of their foes. The surrender of these patriots must be condemned as an act unworthy of a civilised power, having an armed force at command. In the hope of preventing a recurrence of such an aggression, and of establishing some order in government action towards the trade existing between the two countries, Captain Symes was deputed by Sir John Shore, the governor-general of India, as envoy to the king of Burma. He was received with dubious courtesy. He obtained a delusive royal order as to trade, but no treaty; and no reply from the king was sent to the governor-general's letter.

A.D. 1794.

Envoy from British India to Burma.

A.D. 1795.

The British Indian government, desirous of maintaining if possible friendly relations with the court of Burma, deputed captain Hiram Cox, towards the close of the following year, to be resident at Rangoon, under the supposed treaty of the previous year. He was well received at an audience by Bodoahprâ, then residing at

A.D. 1796.

February, A.D. 1797. Mengun, who was pleased with a carriage and other presents from the governor-general. After this unusual condescension the resident was treated with insulting neglect. For nearly nine months he remained in attendance at court, and then withdrew in disgust. In this instance also no reply was sent to the governor-general's letter.

A.D. 1797–98. On the frontier of Arakan events similar to those of 1794 again occurred. Thousands of Arakanese emigrated into the district of Chittagaon. Once more a Burmese military force crossed into British territory to compel the fugitives to return. The invaders entrenched themselves, and repulsed an attack made on their position by the local or police battalion of the district. But Bodoahprâ, occupied at this time with designs on Asâm, and unwilling to commit himself too far, for already he designed to effect alliances with some of the native states of India, withdrew his troops, and sent an agent to Calcutta to negotiate for the restoration of the fugitives; in other words, that they should be expelled from British territory. The marquis Wellesley now governed British India. The known designs of the malignant sultan of Mysore, supported by France, with a threatened invasion of India by Zemân Shah, king of the Afghâns, prevented that great ruler from dealing effectually with Burmese aggression. The reply to the agent was, in general terms, that the immigrants should not be allowed to make raids into Arakan. This did not satisfy Bodoahprâ, who, through the governor of
A.D. 1800. Arakan, renewed the requisition for the extradition of the fugitives; and in a letter from that officer addressed to the governor-general of India, threatened an invasion if the demand was not complied with. Tippu sultan had now been crushed; but preparations for an expedition to the Isle of France, the departure of troops to Egypt, and disagreement with the Mahratta powers looming, would not allow of a war being undertaken in Indo-

China. The insolent threat passed unpunished. Colonel M. Symes was again deputed as envoy in order to require a disavowal of the threatening letter, and to conclude an improved treaty. Having arrived at Mengun, the envoy was treated with gross indignity. The only reply vouchsafed to the letter which the governor-general addressed to the king was a communication from the wungyîs sent at night to the envoy. The governor of Pegu gave a verbal disavowal in the name of the king of the insolent letter from the governor of Arakan. The other objects of the mission were treated with disdainful silence. A.D. 1802.

Further communications between the British and Burmese Governments, A.D. 1809-10.

The following year captain Canning was deputed to reside at Rangoon as agent, but was so ill received by the local officers that he left after a few months. Some years later he proceeded to Burma with a letter and presents from the governor-general. He was on the whole well received by Bodoahprâ, but no reply except from the ministers was sent to the letter he delivered. For some years nothing had occurred to increase the unfriendly feeling which existed between the governments of Burma and British India. But the Arakanese refugees began again to disturb the frontier. Khyengbyan, a restless chief, bearing intense hereditary hatred to the Burmese, after fighting desperately at the head of a few followers, fled into the district of Chittagaon. There he gathered a number of his fellow-countrymen, and entering Arakan, attacked Burmese detachments and outposts. The Burmese Government had just cause of complaint, for the weakness or the neglect by which the refugees who enjoyed British protection were left without control. Captain Canning was again dispatched to Burma to disclaim all sympathy or complicity with this inroad, which had been secretly prepared and suddenly made by the bold outlaw. The viceroy of Pegu, to whom this communication was made, declared the explanation to be satisfactory. Khyengbyan having

A.D. 1811.

A.D. 1811-12.

again taken refuge in British territory, the governor of Arakan marched with an army to the frontier, and required the surrender of the fugitives, using insulting menaces if the demand were not complied with. Negotiations took place between the governor and the British magistrate of Chittagaon, which ended in the Burmese troops being withdrawn from the frontier.

Attempt to arrest the British resident at Rangoon.

Bodoahprâ, convinced of the powerlessness and treachery of the British Government, determined to adopt an extreme measure to ensure the surrender of the rebels. Captain Canning, while still at Rangoon, was urged to proceed to the capital. Being suspicious of the motive for this invitation, he declined doing so; and the viceroy of Pegu having orders from his master to hold him as a hostage for the delivery of the Arakanese rebels, endeavoured to gain possession of his person. This design was frustrated by the escape of the envoy on board his ship, and an armed British vessel having arrived soon after, his safety was secured. Seeing no hope of a satisfactory arrangement, he left Rangoon.

September, A.D. 1812.

April, A.D. 1813. Burmese intrigues with native princes of India.

The following year Burmese envoys were sent to Calcutta, again to demand the surrender of the rebel chiefs. Not long after, a Burmese was arrested while on his way to Delhi, ostensibly in search of religious books. The British Government now gained information, apparently for the first time, that Bodoahprâ was actively engaged in intrigues with some of the native princes of India. The direct object of these secret negotiations did not appear until later. The conquest of Arakan had brought Burmese officers into more immediate contact with India than at any previous period, and the ambitious king was inspired with the desire of acquiring the districts of Eastern Bengal, at least as far as Dacca, which had once belonged to Arakan. Even a claim to Murshedabad was some years afterwards openly made. A preliminary mission had been sent to Benares to procure Sanscrit books. The emissary returned, and was accompanied by a learned brahman, said to have been selected by the râjâ of Benares. This deputation probably had for its main object the acquirement of books held in esteem by Buddhists, but others followed which can only have had political designs. A mission on a much larger scale was sent in the following year. Several natives of India were attached to it. They went through Arakan to Patna, where the party divided. Most of the Burmese officers went to Buddha Gayâ to make offerings in the name of the king; to execute a complete plan of the precincts of the temple and the holy tree; and to procure relics. The chief of the mission, in company with a learned brahman, went on to Benares and upper India. They visited Laknau, Dehli, Bhartpur, the Panjâb, and probably Kashmir. They were absent nearly two years, and brought back many Sanscrit books, images, and presents from various chiefs. More brahmans came from Benares, whom it was intended to employ, in conjunction with the descendants of Brahmans from Arakan, in translating Sanscrit works into Burmese. Missions from the court of Amarapura to various cities in India, extending even to Puna, went on for some years, apparently without the government of British India having any suspicion of their political significance. A flattering prospect was also opened to the ambition and the religious feeling of Bodoahprâ, by the arrival at his capital of a mission, real or feigned, from Ceylon. A deputation of notables, professing to come from that island, entreated him to revive religion, now desolated by foreign heretics. Bodoahprâ made a suitable reply, referring to the acts of "his great ancestor Asoka," whose example he intended to follow in support of religion.

A.D. 1807.

A.D. 1808.

Disturbances on the frontier of Arakan.

By the supineness of the British government, Khyenbyan was still allowed to raid on the frontier of Arakan.

He had established himself in a strong position in the interior of the hill country, where practically he defied both powers. The British government, with a discreditable disregard of its own character, allowed Burmese troops to enter the hills within British territory to attack the chief in his stronghold. At last the restless Khengbyan died. Bodoahprâ again sent agents to Bengal, nominally to demand the extradition of other refugees; but really to concert measures for entering into a league with some of the native princes of upper India. A discovery of the existence of such a plan was made by the magistrate of Chittagaon; and in little more than a year later, three natives of western India, one of whom was a British subject, came to Calcutta duly accredited from Amarapura. They demanded the surrender of the Arakanese fugitives, and permission to travel to Lahore, on the old pretence of procuring religious books. They were not allowed to proceed on their journey. It was discovered that the Burmese government was scheming to enter the confederacy which the Peshwa was forming against the British power. The hopes of Burma were extinguished by the battles of Kirkî, Mahidpur, and Ashtî; and the dispersion of the Pindâri hordes by the army under lord Hastings.

A.D. 1814. A.D. 1815. A.D. 1817. A.D. 1817 and 1818.

Events in Asâm.

While ambitious designs for the extension of dominion, which had their direct origin from the occupation of Arakan, were being actively prosecuted, the confidence of Bodoahprâ in his own high destiny led him to interfere in the affairs of another country, forming a portion of the extensive border-land between India and Burma. Since the thirteenth century of the Christian era, when the Shâns had conquered Asâm, there had been little or no intercourse between that country and the land of the Irâwadi. The descendants of the first Buddhist kings in the valley of the Brahmaputra had been received into the fold of Hinduism; and, forgetting the history of their race, had adopted the myths and traditions of their new teachers. In the eighteenth century[1] the râjâ of Asâm had lost much of the authority which had been exercised by his predecessors, and was controlled by three principal ministers termed Gohains. These were also governors of the three great divisions of the kingdom, who frequently acted as independent princes. The restricted power of the râjâ led him to struggle to regain the authority once held by his ancestors, and this brought about a perpetual succession of intrigues. In 1793 the râjâ Gaurinath was driven from his throne, and appealed to the governor-general of India, lord Cornwallis, for protection. That nobleman, then about to retire to Europe, sent captain Welsh with eleven hundred sipâhis. This small body of men was sufficient to restore the râjâ. The British troops then retired. The râjâ's minister, the Boora Gohain, assumed the chief authority, and placed his master in confinement. The râjâ soon died, and the Gohain then placed on the throne a youth named Kinaram, belonging to an illegitimate branch of the royal family. Another claimant applied to Bodoahprâ to assist him in enforcing his rights. The mission from this person, bearing presents and a princess, arrived at Amarapura, while captain Cox was there. Preparations were made June, A.D. 1797. to invade Asâm, but were countermanded, and for some years no further measures were taken for interfering in that country. When Chandra Kanta was on the throne, A.D. 1809. he became impatient of the thraldom in which he was held by the minister, the Boora Gohain. He entered into a secret engagement with the Bor Phokan, governor of the central province of the kingdom, to get rid of the powerful minister. The plot being discovered, the Bor Phokan fled to Calcutta, and implored help to rescue his master from this humiliating position. The government of British India, occupied with important affairs of in-

[1] See Francis Buchanan's Eastern India, vol. iii. pp. 607–663; and History of India, Mill and Wilson, vol. ix. pp. 17–19.

ternal administration, and with plans for expeditions beyond seas, refused assistance. The Bor Phokan then applied to Bodoahprâ. The king at once sent him back with a force of six thousand men. The Boora Gohain had died before their arrival, and Chandra Kanta, no longer in need of foreign support, dismissed his allies with valuable presents. The Bor Phokan now became an object of jealousy with his master, and was put to death. The son of the late Boora Gohain formed a plot against Chandra Kanta; deposed him, and placed on the throne, Purandar Sing, a prince of the dynasty. Chandra Kanta escaped to Bhutân. A Burmese army was sent to Asâm under the command of Kyoagaung. He rein-
A.D. 1816. stated Chandra Kanta, and returned home with the bulk of the army, Mahâ Thilawâ being left in command with the remainder. Purandar Sing now took refuge in Bhutân, and afterwards in British territory. The friendship between Chandra Kanta and the Burmese was of short continuance. He left the capital, then Rangpur, and proceeded to the border of the British territory, where with a body of his own retainers he defended himself against attack from the Burmese. Purandar Sing having procured arms and ammunition, entered Asâm, and attacked both the Burmese and Chandra Kanta. He was defeated by the latter, and the British government, anxious to prevent the Burmese from occupying Asâm, now gave support to
A.D. 1821. Chandra Kanta. Mahâ Thilawâ wrote to the governor-general, warning him not to assist Asamese rebels. By this time the reign of Bodoahprâ had come to a close, but his policy in Asâm was continued by his successor.

Manipur. The small country of Manipur had at an early period been subjected by Burma, and forced to pay tribute.
A.D. 1735. Once only had Manipur been able to retaliate, with an army which penetrated to the Irâwadi, opposite Ava, and for a time seemed likely to occupy that city.

Alaunghprâ invaded the country to assert the supremacy of his dynasty therein. After the death of that monarch the chief of Manipur applied to the governor of Bengal for protection.[1] This was promised, and somewhat A.D. 1762.
precipitately an alliance, offensive and defensive, was concluded by Mr. Verelst, then acting as governor. In pursuance of this treaty, six companies of sipâhis marched from Chittagaon with the object of expelling the Burmese from Manipur. The detachment only reached Kaspur, the capital of Kachâr, and had suffered so much from sickness that it was recalled. The râjâ again applied for assistance, but the government of Bengal, by this time aware of the difficulties to be encountered, refused to fulfil their engagement. Mani- A.D. 1764.
pur again suffered from a Burmese inroad, but after this for several years was unmolested. At length dissensions among the members of the royal family brought foreign interference and loss of independence. The A.D. 1799.
râjâ, Jay Sing, died, and his sons fought for the succession. Three survived this struggle, of whom the elder, Chorjit, became râjâ. The second brother, Marjit Sing, A.D. 1806.
sent presents to Bodoahprâ, soliciting his support. Chorjit also sent presents, and one of his daughters, in token of fealty. Marjit came and dwelt for a time at Amarapura. He returned to his own country, but again appeared with complaints against his brother. Bodoah- A.D. 1813.
prâ summoned the râjâ to his presence in order to settle the dispute. Chorjit refused to come; a Burmese army marched into Manipur; the râjâ was defeated, and fled into Kachâr; Marjit was placed on the throne, and the Burmese army was withdrawn. From this time the Kubo valley was annexed to Burma.

Bodoahprâ, as already narrated, had abandoned the work on the great pagoda he had commenced at Mengun. For some years afterwards he undertook no such work,

[1] H. H. Wilson, History of India, vol. ix. pp. 20–22.

A.D. 1816.

but later caused a small stone pagoda to be built at Thihadoâ, about fifty miles from the city up the river. When it was finished he went there to place the htî on the summit. Returning, he landed and went to the city of his father, but feeling ill, hastened back to Amarapura, where he died soon after his arrival, having reigned more than thirty-seven years.

Death of Bodoahprâ, May, A.D. 1819.

Great reservoirs constructed.

Among the public works of utility executed by Bodoahprâ, two great reservoirs deserve mention. One of these was formed by the enlargement of the ancient tank situated a few miles to the north-east of the capital, in which, on the completion of the work, water sufficient for the irrigation of some thousands of acres was stored. This artificial lake, which has a superficial area of about twenty square miles when full, was, with the exuberance of oriental imagination, named Aungpenglè, or the "pent-up sea." The other lakelet was formed at Mittila. It was of ancient construction, and the banks had been renewed by Alaung Sîthu in the twelfth century, but had fallen out of repair. The king went there with his whole court, and remained for three months superintending the work. The labourers were brought from all parts of the empire in thousands, and were embodied in battalions and companies under the command of the officers of their districts. The forced labour on these works caused deep discontent.

Capture of a white elephant.

Bodoahprâ probably considered that the greatest glory of his reign was the possession of a perfect white male elephant. This animal, caught in the forests of Pegu, was received at court with honours due to an object of worship. He lived in captivity for more than fifty years.

Character of Bodoahprâ.

The character of Bodoahprâ is drawn by Father San Germano, who during his reign lived in Burma for more than twenty years. The description, when compared with other evidence, including that in the royal history, does not appear to be too severely drawn.

"His very countenance is the index of a mind ferocious and inhuman in the highest degree, . . . and it would not be an exaggeration to assert that during his reign more victims have fallen by the hand of the executioner than by the sword of the common enemy. . . . The good fortune that has attended him . . . has inspired him with the idea that he is something more than mortal, and that this privilege has been granted him on account of his numerous good works. . . . A few years since he thought to make himself a god."

Notwithstanding his cruelty he was a man of ability, and, except in the great folly of heading an invasion of Siam, carried out his plans, for what he considered the glory of the kingdom, with prudence and perseverance.

The eldest son of Bodoahprâ had died more than ten years before his father. His son, Sagaing Meng, had then been appointed Ainshêmeng. He now performed the funeral obsequies of his grandfather, and succeeded to the throne at the age of thirty-five years. Succeeded by his grandson.

Silver medal of Bodoahprâ, supposed to be intended to be deposited in the relic-chamber of the pagoda at Mengun.

CHAPTER XXI.

DYNASTY OF ALAUNGHPRÂ—CONQUESTS TO THE WEST AND WAR WITH BRITISH INDIA.

Accession of Hpagyîdoa—Ava again made the capital—Expedition to Manipur—To Asâm—Kachâr invaded—Attack on the Chittagaon frontier—Action near Râmu—British plan of operations—Occupation of Rangoon—Failure of attack on Kyîmyisidaing—Operations in Asâm, Kachâr, and Manipur—Fighting at Rangoon—Coast of Tenasserim—Mahâ Bandula attacks the British position—Defeat of the Burmese—Occupation of Arakan by the British—The British army marches northward from Rangoon—Siege of Danubyu—Death of Bandula—Alarm of the Burmese court—Prome occupied by the British—Negotiations for peace—War resumed—British advance on Myedè—Malwun taken—Action at Pugân—British army at Yandabo—Treaty signed—The Burmese soldier—Commercial treaty—Hpagyîdoa dethroned.

Accession of Hpagyîdoa.

THE grandson of Bodoahprâ took possession of the palace without opposition. He assumed, according to custom, a distinguishing title, but is generally known as Hpagyîdoa. He commenced his reign well. He remitted some taxes for three years, and in a speech to his courtiers promised to rule justly, and to follow the precepts of religion. He made liberal presents to all public officers. But after a few weeks had elapsed, two of his uncles, the princes of Prome and Taungu, were suspected of treasonable designs, and were put to death, together with a number of persons supposed to be their adherents in conspiracy.

Ava again made the capital.

From causes which are uncertain, but which probably were the alighting of a vulture on the palace spire—ever regarded as an evil omen—and the burning of a large portion of the city, including the court of justice, the palace campanile, and other buildings pertaining to the palace, the king determined to return to Ava. The preparations proceeded leisurely. A new and more extensive palace was built upon the ancient site, which the king and queen entered in great state. Gradually the whole population followed the court. Pursuing the plans of his grandfather in foreign policy, Hpagyîdoa sent a mission to Buddha Gayâ with offerings. The chief brahman, who had formerly come from Benares, and became known to foreigners as the Râj Guru, accompanied the Burmese officers, and proceeded on to Benares. At this time there appeared no opportunity for making an alliance with any of the native princes of India, though this object was probably kept in view. Nearer home, prompt measures were taken to enforce the supremacy which had been established during the previous reign in Manipur.

February, March, A.D. 1823.

Expedition to Manipur.

The râjâ of that state, Marjit, had for some time past shown a disposition to evade the promise of fealty which he had made to Bodoahprâ. On being summoned to appear at the capital, where all the umbrella-bearing chiefs of the empire were to do homage to their superior lord, he made excuses. Hpagyîdoa at once determined to depose him. An army marched for Manipur at the close of the rainy season. In this force the officer afterwards known as Mahâ Bandula served as Sitkê, and by his skill and daring during the operations made himself conspicuous.[1] The râjâ escaped to Kachâr. The country having been subdued, a force was left to garrison it under the Kannî Myuwun, and the rest of the army returned home. Some thousands of the inhabitants were carried away. In Kachâr, Marjit found his

October, A.D. 1819.

[1] In Buddhist legends this is the name of a great warrior, son of the sister of a Malla king who reigned at Kusinârâ. Hardy's Manual of Buddhism, p. 280. Bishop Bigandet's Legend of the Burmese Buddha, 2d edition, p. 329.

brother Chorjit, who, by treachery and force, had acquired a portion of that country. Marjit and Gambhir Sing joined together and expelled their brother. The rightful râjâ of Kachâr, Govind Chandra, who was also a fugitive, after having been refused assistance by the British government, applied to the king of Burma. The Burmese troops left to occupy Manipur were insufficient to hold it. The son of Marjit began to make incursions from Kachâr, and before long the Burmese commander was shut up in a stockade near the capital. A relieving force marching
November, A.D. 1820. rapidly, arrived in time to save the garrison. The British government, alarmed at the progress of the Burmese on so many points of their eastern frontier, determined to take Kachâr under their own protection and to support Govind Chandra. The Manipur chiefs were conciliated by pensions, and were placed in command of an irregular levy, formed principally of fugitives from Manipur.

Expedition to Asâm.

The king of Burma prepared vigorously to pursue the policy of his grandfather in Asâm. Chandra Kanta having turned against his supporters, a Burmese army was sent, under the command of Mahâ Bandula, to reinforce Mahâ Thilawâ. The Asamese
A.D. 1821–22. chief was defeated, and fled into British territory, where his relative and rival, Purandar Sing, was also. Asâm was declared a province of the Burmese empire. The chief authority was vested in Mahâ Thilawâ, who was left with two thousand men, while Mahâ Bandula returned home with the rest of the
July, A.D. 1822. army. A Burmese agent arrived in Calcutta bearing letters from the Burmese generals, demanding the surrender of Chandra Kanta. This was refused. The Burmese contented themselves with demonstrations on the frontier, and some villages within the British district of Goalpâra were plundered, probably by local marauders.

The Burmese commander in Manipur had been informed that the British government would not permit him to interfere in Kachâr. A Burmese force, however, in two columns, one coming from Asâm and one from Manipur, entered Kachâr for the alleged purpose of reinstating Govind Chandra, whose cause the British government had already espoused. A combat took place with a British battalion of sipâhis, in which the Burmese were defeated. But their two columns having united, the battalion was forced to retire before superior numbers. The Burmese then pushed on with confidence, and threw up entrenchments on the banks of the Surma. They were driven from these, and the column from Asâm returned there, while that from Manipur retired to a strong stockade at Dudhpatli on the Barak river. An attempt was made to storm this stockade by a British force under Colonel Bowen, but the attack failed. The Burmese, however, soon after abandoned the position, and returned to Manipur.

Kachâr invaded

January, A.D. 1824.

The frontier of Chittagaon again became the scene of aggression by the Burmese authorities in Arakan. At the mouth of the Nâf river is the island of Shâpuri, which, from its proximity to the Chittagaon shore, the channel there being fordable at low water, and from long occupation by British subjects, was undoubtedly British territory. The Burmese officers began to exercise authority over it, and the right to overhaul boats of British subjects passing up and down the river. A guard of twelve men of the provincial battalion of Chittagaon was stationed on the island to protect British subjects residing there. The post was attacked by a Burmese armed party; six of the guard were killed and wounded. Two months later the island was occupied by a detachment of regular sipâhis. Hpagyîdoa had thorough confidence in his own strength and resources, and was not going to shrink from a struggle with the British. He was encouraged in his determi-

Attack on the Chittagaon frontier.

September 23, A.D. 1823.

nation by the ambitious Mahâ Bandula, who, after a showy review of his troops, left the capital early in the year with six thousand men, to take command in Arakan. His men were drawn principally from the district of Dibayen or Tabayîn, which is supposed to furnish the best soldiers in the empire. He had orders to advance towards Chittagaon, and there was confident expectation that the capital of Bengal would be taken. He crossed the mountains by the Aeng pass, and, proceeding to the old capital of Arakan, made arrangements to carry out his orders. He evidently saw greater difficulties than appeared when he was so full of confidence in presence of the king, and now paused in his enterprise. The British government had stationed a brigade, much too weak for the duty required, at the town of Chittagaon. War was formally declared against Burma. Colonel Shapland, who commanded the brigade, threw forward a detachment to Râmu, a village about thirty miles from the mouth of the Nâf. Mahâ Bandula at length commenced operations. He did not himself lead the invading force across the border, but, as if to test the strength and temper of the enemy, sent on a column under the governor of Arakan. This body, estimated by the British at eight thousand men, but which, from information afterwards received, was probably not more than half that number, crossed the Nâf and marched on Râmu. The British detachment there was commanded by Captain Noton of the 40th Bengal Native Infantry. It consisted of three hundred and fifty regulars, with six hundred and fifty of the police battalion and levy of Arakanese refugees. The Burmese attacked and drove the British force from its position with great slaughter. After this success the governor of Arakan awaited further orders from Mahâ Bandula; but events elsewhere induced the latter, with unexpected caution, to stay further operations, and the invading force, after a few weeks, recrossed the Nâf.

January, A.D. 1824.

March 5, A.D. 1824.

Action near Râmu, 17th May.

The British plan of operations.

The British government having declared war, decided on a plan of campaign which appeared likely to be the most effective. The Burmese had become dangerous neighbours by the occupation of Asâm, Kachâr, and Manipur; while for more than thirty years the Chittagaon district had been harassed by incursions from Arakan. To penetrate to the capital of Burma through any of those territories was difficult, far more so than the British government yet knew. The long distances to be traversed through jangal, swamp, and mountain; in countries sparsely populated, and yielding no supplies fit for an army of civilised men, presented formidable obstacles to the march of a European force. These countries had indeed been overcome by the Burmese; but the Burman soldier of that day, very lightly clad, bore on his back ten days' rice, found edible herbs in every jangal, and his drink was water. He did not reject the flesh of animals, even of those which died natural deaths, when procurable; but it was not essential for his wants. If he carried a musket, he was not trusted with more than ten rounds in pouch, and large bodies of such men moved rapidly through the wildest country. In view of the difficulties to be encountered in a march through the border-lands, in order to reach the Burmese country, the British government determined to drive the enemy from Asâm, Kachâr, and Manipur, but not to advance beyond them; and to guard Chittagaon against further molestation, by strengthening the frontier force in that district. The real attack, that which was meant to force the Burmese government to treat, was to be by the valley of the Irâwadi, after occupation of the chief seaport, Rangoon. In pursuance of this plan, troops were assembled at Madras and Calcutta, where they embarked in transports. The fleet had its rendezvous at Port Cornwallis, in the northern Andaman. It was convoyed by H.M. frigate "Liffey," and the sloops of war "Larne" and "Sophia." There was one small steamer. The troops from the two presidencies numbered about eleven thousand five hundred men, under the command of general Sir Archibald Campbell.[1] The whole fleet sailed, detachments being sent to occupy Cheduba and Negrais, and arrived off Rangoon. The town was situated on the river-bank, enclosed by a square stockade of teak timber about twelve feet high. A few old ship-guns were mounted at the wharf, which was outside the river-face of the stockade. Fire was opened from these guns on the leading ships, which was at once replied to by the "Liffey." The guns at the wharf were, after a few rounds, dismounted. The troops landed and took possession of the town without seeing an enemy. At this time the governor of Pegu had been summoned to the capital, and had died there. His successor had not yet arrived. The rêwun or chief of the flotilla was deputy-governor. He had no information of the intended invasion, and was completely taken by surprise. All he could do was to drive away the whole of the native inhabitants, of whom none remained in the town or suburbs. The few European and other foreign residents had been placed in confinement, but their guards fled and they escaped. The rainy season was at hand, and the British general had not sufficient transport for operations either by land or water. Boats, carts, and cattle had disappeared with the inhabitants. The great pagoda, which stands on a commanding height a mile and a half from the river, was occupied as the key of the position. So entirely was the invading force isolated, that general Campbell found it impossible to gain any intelligence of what was going on outside his lines. A reconnaisance by means of armed row-boats having been made to Kyîmyindaing, a village six miles by river from Rangoon, some

Occupation of Rangoon, May 11, A.D. 1824.

[1] BENGAL DIVISION.—H.M. 13th Light Infantry; 38th Foot; 20th Bengal Native Infantry; two companies of artillery. MADRAS DIVISION.—H.M. 41st and 89th Foot; the Madras European Regiment; seven regiments of native infantry; four companies of artillery; and one battalion of pioneers.

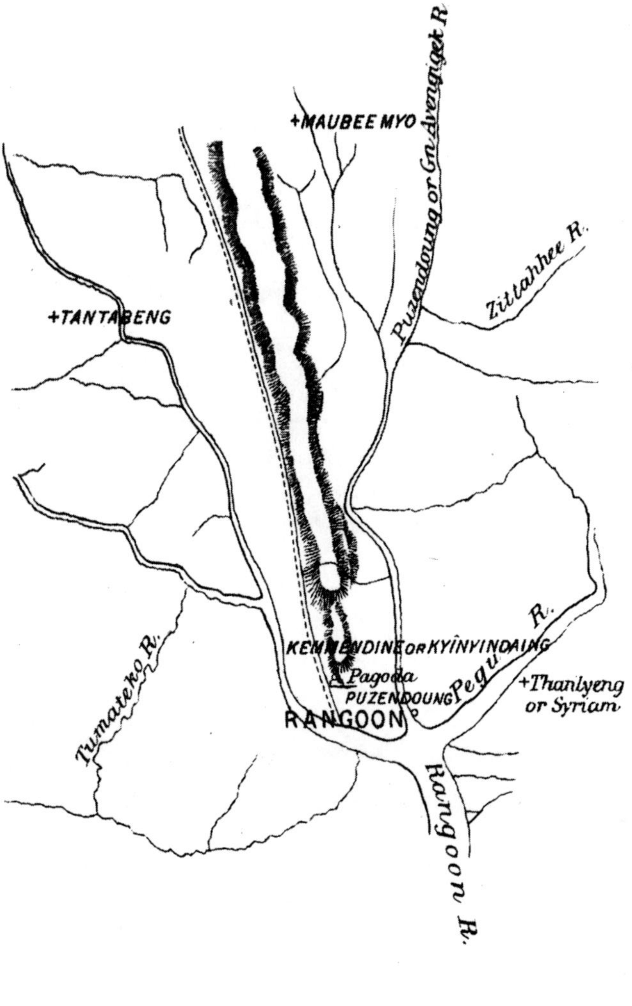

Sketch of Country round Rangoon.

Trübner & C°. London.

Vincent Brooks, Day & Son, Lith.

breastworks were seen on shore from which shots were fired. The next day these breastworks were attacked and carried by a small party of troops and seamen. The place was not occupied by the British general, and the rêwun found it a convenient spot to launch fire-rafts, which, floating down with the ebb tide, endangered the shipping. A few days later the general made a reconnaisance in person to the north of the great pagoda, with three hundred Europeans, some native infantry, and two guns. The rain fell in torrents; road there was none; the ground was knee-deep in water; the guns had to be left behind. The men pushed on, and at some five or six miles from the great pagoda came on two stockades. These were formed of palisades four feet high with an interior trench and a well-laid abatis. The muskets of the assailants were rendered useless by the heavy rain, and the works were carried by the bayonet. Some three hundred Burmese were killed. The British loss was ten killed and twenty-seven wounded. These stockades, which had been rapidly constructed, were garrisoned by fifteen hundred men, the crews of the war-boats stationed at and around Rangoon, who were as efficient soldiers as Burma could produce. In presence of the armed row-boats and the steamer, the war-boats had been laid up. The rêwun had the levies of the country in the vicinity of the stockades, but made no use of them.

16th May.

28th May.

Failure of attack on Kyîmyindaing.

The Burmese had never before encountered European troops, and the fierce dash of these white strangers into the stockades without firing a shot, astonished them. The rêwun, an old soldier and brave, did not appear to lose heart, but exerted himself to oppose the invaders until reinforcements should reach him from the capital. A new and stronger stockade was built at Kyîmyindaing, which extended half a mile along the river-bank. Fortune seemed to favour this resolution. The British general attacked the stockade by land and water. From a

3d June. rash contempt of the enemy no artillery accompanied the land force, and the fire from the armed vessels fell heavily on one of the columns. The attempt failed,
10th June. with considerable loss to the assailants. Heavy guns were now landed, and a second assault was made, with measures arranged to minimise loss, and ensure success. The guns, eighteen-pounders, field-pieces, and mortars, were dragged by the soldiers. About three thousand men marched out of the British lines. From the state of the country the progress was slow. A small outwork was met with and taken, but it was night before the main stockade was reached. The men had to bivouac in the mud and water as they best could. At daybreak the guns opened; all was silent in the stockade, and the storming parties found the work abandoned. The Burmese had full information as to the heavy guns, and knew that resistance would be hopeless. Kyîmyindaing was now occupied as a British outpost, and for some weeks there was a lull in hostilities. From this time commenced the terrible sickness which almost paralysed the British force. The expedition had been undertaken with imperfect knowledge of the resources of the country, and of the methods of defence which would be used by the Burmese government to confound their enemies. The exposure of the troops to the wet, day and night, brought fever and dysentery. No fresh meat or vegetables were to be had; much of the salted meat was putrid, and the biscuit served out had to be soaked in hot water to clear it of weevils. Fresh supplies could only be expected from India after a long delay. The troops endured this trial, before which ordinary hardships of a campaign are nought, with admirable fortitude.

While these operations were being carried on in the south, the campaign in the north was proceeding, as planned, at the several points of the frontier. On the border of Asâm the British force consisted of a brigade composed of local corps, with one battalion of regular native infantry, and some river gunboats. The whole was under the command of General M'Morine. The brigade advanced up the river Brahmaputra to Gowhati, where the Burmese were stockaded. They abandoned the works and retired up the valley eastward. The difficult nature of the country, sparsely inhabited, with extensive stretches of heavy jangal, and the setting in of the rainy season, prevented Colonel Richards, who had succeeded to the command, from following up the enemy. He retired to Gowhati, where he fixed his headquarters. It will be convenient at once to narrate the issue of the campaign in Asâm. The brigade was reinforced by two regiments of native infantry, and at the close of the rainy season Colonel Richards renewed operations. Bûra Râjâ, who had been appointed governor by Hpagyîdoa, was driven from Noagong, and the British brigade pushed on to Rangpur, then the capital of upper Asâm. This town was garrisoned by Burmese and Asamese. The chiefs of the latter wished to submit to the British. Shâm Phokan surrendered with his followers, and two thousand Burmese were allowed to return to their own country. Operations in Asâm were thus terminated except some fighting with Burmese detachments and Singpho tribes on the Dihing river.

Operations in Asâm, March 1824.

October.

January 29, A.D. 1825.

On the Kachâr frontier the Burmese reappeared from Manipur in great force. They stockaded themselves on their former ground at Dudhpatli and in other positions. The weak brigade stationed at Sylhet under colonel Innes was unable to cope with them, and failed in an attempt to dislodge them from an entrenched post at Talain. The troops on this part of the frontier were increased to seven thousand strong, under the command of general Shuldham. The Burmese had withdrawn from Kachâr. The division, composed of native corps, regular and local, marched to Banskandy, after a road had, with infinite labour, been made passable for guns.

June, A.D. 1824. Kachâr and Manipur.

November, A.D. 1824.

From that point to Manipur, though no enemy appeared, the advance of the division through swamp and jangal, persevered in during two months, was found to be impracticable. The occupation of Manipur was at length accomplished by a levy of Manipuris and Kacharis, unencumbered with baggage, led by Gambhir Sing. The Burmese troops had been recalled to oppose the British invaders advancing up the Irâwadi.

February and March, A.D. 1825.

June 1825.

Fighting at Rangoon.

The Burmese government made strenuous efforts to oppose the British army which occupied Rangoon. The plan adopted was simple. It was to prevent all communication with the people of Pegu, who were likely to favour the invader, and by overwhelming numbers to drive the invaders into the sea, or take them prisoners. A new governor, the Thekkya Wungyî, had been appointed to the province of Pegu a few days before the invasion. He was on his way down the river when he heard of the event. Being a man of pacific disposition, who had never served in war, he was overwhelmed with terror, and appears not to have reported the capture of Rangoon so promptly as he might have done.[1] He left all arrangements to the rêwun, and was superseded by the Thunba Wungyî, in whom the king and court had entire confidence. The new general, having under him large bodies of men levied from the country beyond the delta, rapidly built a strong stockade in a commanding position at the junction of the Hlaing and Panhlaing rivers, about seven miles above Rangoon.[2] Other stockades were constructed opposite thereto on the Rangoon bank, and were well placed to prevent any reconnaisance being made by the British. Both positions were attacked, the latter by a land column. The guns had to be left behind. The stockades on the

July 3, A.D. 1824.

8th July.

[1] The landing of the British army was not known at Ava until 23d May 1824. With due diligence the intelligence might have reached four or five days sooner.

[2] See sketch annexed of the country round Rangoon.

Rangoon river-bank were extensive, and were garrisoned by ten thousand men. The promptitude of the British general took the wungyî by surprise. The defences were as yet incomplete, and the resistance lacked vigour. The stockades were stormed with great slaughter to the defenders, and the Thunbâ Wungyî was amongst the slain. The works at the junction of the two rivers were at the same time captured by attack from the flotilla and a column of troops combined.

The British general now had time to turn his attention to places more distant from his position. The Burmese garrison was expelled from Syriam, a town of some importance on the Pegu river. Some of the fugitive inhabitants of Rangoon, seeing the Burmese troops everywhere defeated, began to return to their homes. Expeditions were sent to the coast of Tenasserim, and the towns of Tavoy and Mergui were taken possession of and occupied. Martaban was captured towards the close of the year, and the city of Pegu, the ancient capital, was entered without opposition.

Coast of Tenasserim.

4th August.

September.

November.

On the death of the Thunbâ Wungyî, the king and his advisers seemed to recognise the gravity of the crisis. Mahâ Bandula was recalled from Arakan with the greater portion of his army. Seeing that the British by means of their armed boats, and more especially the small steamer, would command the river Irâwadi, Burmese armies were posted on either bank. That on the right bank was under the command of the king's brother, the prince of Tharâwadi, and that on the left by the Kyî Wungyî. The former had his headquarters at Danubyu; the latter at Htantabeng, on the Hlaing river, about twenty miles above Rangoon. The rêwun had command of small bodies of troops, and was active in attacking the outlying British pickets to the north of the great pagoda, and cutting off stragglers. Bandula having returned from Arakan, proceeded to the capital. An army was raised there which was to be added to

October, A.D. 1824. the veteran troops he brought back with him, and he left Ava full of confidence. The British general sent a 4th October. combined force, naval and military, up the Hlaing river to Htantabeng, which destroyed the stockades erected by the Kyî Wungyî. A column composed of native troops, under colonel Smith, the same day marched northward by land, with the view of distracting the attention of the enemy. Several unfinished works were passed, and information was received of a strong stockade at Kyaikkalo, being about twelve miles from Rangoon, where the Sâdoa Wun, steward of the palace, with the rêwun as second in command, had a garrison of chosen men and guns mounted. Attack was made on the principal stockade in two columns, and failed. The whole force retreated in disorder after severe loss in killed and wounded. A column at once marched to retrieve this disaster. The stockades at Kyaikkalo were found to be deserted, and the troops, pushing on to a town six miles in advance, came there on a stockade also empty. From the destruction of the works at Htantabeng, the Kyî Wungyî deemed it imprudent to remain within striking distance of such active foes, and withdrew his troops from their advanced positions. But Bandula, in taking supreme command, viewed the whole condition of affairs as very favourable, and the king and his court were highly elated at the last success. The Kyî Wungyî, however, was deprived of his command, though not disgraced.

Mahâ Bandula attacks the British position. Mahâ Bandula was appointed by the king commander-in-chief in the southern provinces. He took over the command at Danubyu. The prince of Tharâwadi, vexed at being superseded, told him to be careful how he attacked the Kulâs. His reply was, "In eight days I shall dine in the public hall of Rangoon, and afterwards return thanks at the Shwè Dagun pagoda." The army under his command numbered, it was said, sixty thousand men; but only one-half were armed with muskets. A large proportion of this army acted as pioneers, working with light entrenching tools, according to the commendable practice of Burmese armies in the field, who never halt or encamp without throwing up defences. Bandula crossed the Irâwadi at Danubyu, (Last week of November.) and thence to the left bank of the Hlaing with the bulk of his army. He thus gained the ridge of high ground which led direct to Rangoon, and the country now was for the most part dry. A portion of the army went by water, but with caution, lest it should be attacked by the British gunboats. After four or five days' march (December 1.) the whole of the army was in position before the British lines. It occupied the space extending in an irregular semicircle from Kyimyindaing on the Burmese right, to the Pazundung river on the left. A numerous body of troops also crossed the Rangoon river to the Dalla side, and threw up batteries to fire on the shipping. On the river itself were war-boats, and what were much more dangerous to the British, fire-rafts ready to be launched. The Burmese front was everywhere protected by earthen breastworks, which had been constructed with astonishing rapidity. It was not without reason, calculating from his past experience, that Bandula felt sure of success. Of the British force, disease allowed not more than thirteen hundred Europeans to be present under arms, with about two thousand five hundred native troops. The key of the position to be defended was the great pagoda, which was certain to be the main point of attack. It was well garrisoned, and had twenty guns mounted on the upper terrace. The troops at Pazundaung and Dalla had been withdrawn. A brick building, known as the white house, about one mile south-east of the great pagoda, was held on the extreme British right; and on the left the stockade at Kyîmindaing, which was supported by the ships of war, the steamer, and gunboats. Reserves were posted in rear of the great pagoda and extending towards the town.

The object of the British general was to allow the enemy to establish himself close up to the position, whereby he could be readily reached; and to tempt him, if possible, to an engagement on open ground. Bandula rapidly developed his plan of attack. One division advanced to within a mile of the great pagoda, and threw up entrenchments, while a strong column established itself to the east of the pagoda, resting on the royal lake. The latter was at once attacked and driven from its position. A successful sortie was also made on the works in front of the pagoda. It was impossible to hold these positions when won, and on the following day the Burmese advanced their entrenchments to within three hundred yards of the great pagoda. The post at Kyîmindaing was vigorously attacked, and menacing fire-rafts, launched with the ebb tide at the

December 5.

ships of war, were with difficulty warded off. At last the left wing of the Burmese army deployed on the open ground adjoining the royal lake, and gave an opportunity to the British general to strike a blow. Gunboats worked up the Pazundaung creek to aid the attack, and two columns advanced eagerly to throw themselves on the enemy. The works were carried, the Burmese abandoning their guns, colours, muskets, and

Defeat of the Burmese, December 6.

much ammunition, and leaving many dead and wounded. The centre of the investing army renewed the attack on the pagoda, but was repulsed with great slaughter;

December 8.

and a similar result befell at Kyîmindaing. The division

December 10.

which was entrenched at Dalla was driven out two days later.

The Burmese army rallied close to the ground from which it had been driven, and the British force was too weak in numbers and from fatigue to attempt pursuit. An old stockade at Kokien, two miles from the great pagoda, had been repaired and strengthened, and Mahâ Thilawâ, formerly in Asâm, was in command. The

December 14.

town of Rangoon was fired by emissaries, who gained

entrance without attracting notice, in hope that the magazines might be destroyed. This design was frustrated, and on the following day the stockade at Kokien was stormed. Bandula, now despairing of success, retired rapidly with seven thousand of his best men to Danubyu, while Mahâ Thilawâ fled to Moabî. The greater part of the investing army broke up, and the men dispersed.

Occupation of Arakan by the British.

In consequence of the unforeseen difficulties which beset the advance of an army by the line of the Irâwadi, the British government determined to occupy Arakan, and to strike at the capital of Burma through that province. An army, numbering eleven thousand men, was assembled at Chittagaon, under the command of general Morrison. A numerous flotilla of gunboats and armed cruisers, on which two European regiments were embarked, sailed along the coast. A squadron of irregular cavalry and some of the native infantry marched by land, generally close to the sea-shore. The February 1, 182 whole force gathered in the Nâf river, and most of the native troops landed on the southern bank without opposition. It was nearly two months before the army March 29. reached the capital. The city of Myauku, or Arakan, is surrounded by low hills, which afford excellent means for defence. The first assault of the British at a narrow defile was repulsed, but on the following day the position was turned, and attack made in front under cover April 1. of a brisk cannonade. The enemy fled precipitately. The Burmese garrison, being the troops left by Bandula, easily escaped, concealed by the jangal, and retired across the eastern range of mountains to their own country. The southern districts of the province were now occupied by the British without opposition. A reconnaissance was made of the Talâk pass, being one of those by which the Burmese army had entered Arakan. It was found to be so difficult for guns and laden cattle that it was pronounced to be unsuitable for the object in view. The army was speedily stricken by disease, if possible more deadly than that from which the force at Rangoon had suffered. There was no want of wholesome food, but after the rain began to fall, exhalation from the soil made the climate fatal. The troops were distributed in cantonments along the sea-coast, the site known as Akyab, then an open grassy plain, being occupied; and the plan for invasion of Burma from Arakan was abandoned. Though there had been great natural difficulties to overcome in operating on the long line of eastern frontier, and many errors had been committed in the conduct of the war, yet by the end of the spring the Burmese had been driven from the whole of their conquests in Asâm, Kachâr, Manipur, and Arakan. The ancient port of Martaban was occupied by the British, as was the whole coast of Tenasserim as far south as Mergui. It now remained for the army at Rangoon, under Sir Archibald Campbell, to carry on the war by advancing up the river Irâwadi.

A.D. 1825.

The British army marches northward from Rangoon, December, A.D. 1824.

Towards the end of the year reinforcements reached the British general from India. His means for transport, whether by land or water, were still defective. The rainy season having ended, the health of the troops improved, but fresh provisions were yet scarce. Preparations were made to advance on Prome, where it was hoped the Burmese government would be disposed to treat. Mahâ Bandula had determined to make a stand at Danubyu, about sixty miles from Rangoon, but the British general had no information either as to the strength of his army, or the nature of the stronghold which he had constructed on the river-bank at that place. The British force, to move up the valley of the Irâwadi, was divided into two columns. One was to proceed by the river under general Willoughby Cotton; the other by land under the commander-in-chief himself. The former numbered eight hundred Europeans and a battalion of native infantry, with a flotilla of gunboats and one steamer. There were also numerous boats of various tonnage carrying heavy guns and mortars, ordnance stores and provisions. The land column was composed of thirteen hundred Europeans, one thousand sipâhis, three hundred of the governor-general's bodyguard, a troop of horse-artillery, and a rocket troop. The number of men seemed small for the enterprise of dictating terms to a haughty power, which for more than sixty years had triumphed over the neighbouring nations; but no one doubted of success. The surface of the country was now dry, and the land column marched northwards to Hlaing, and thence to Sarawâ on the Irâwadi. There had been no communication with general Cotton. That officer had proceeded up the Panhlaing river into the great river without much opposition. When near Danubyu he found that Bandula was with his army in an extensive stockade on the right bank of the river. There were also two smaller works below the larger one. The southernmost of these, which enclosed the town pagoda, was attacked and carried. The party which attempted to storm the next work was repulsed with severe loss. General Cotton re-embarked his men the same night. It was reported that the garrison of the main stockade amounted to fifteen thousand men, with a hundred and fifty guns mounted. A Burman was found to carry a dispatch to general Campbell, which reached him when he was two marches beyond Sarawâ. Returning to that place, he crossed the river by means of canoes he found on the bank, and marched down to Danubyu.

February 11, A.D. 1825. 1st March. 4th March. 7th March. 10th March 25th March.

On reconnaisance, the strength of Bandula's fort was evident, and an attack in form was necessary.[1] Trenches and batteries were constructed about three hundred yards distant from the north-west angle. General Cotton,

[1] A plan and section of the fort as evidence of Bandula's skill is added. It is taken from the work of Captain T. A. Trant, 95th Foot, Assistant Quartermaster-General.

who had dropped down the river, came up with his column; mortars and heavy guns were landed and placed in battery; fire was opened, and continued with little intermission for several hours. All was ready for the assault early in the day, when it was found that the fort had been evacuated during the night. Mahâ Bandula had been killed, and his brother, the second in command, could not keep the garrison together. Guns, powder, and immense stores of rice fell to the victors.

Siege of Danubyu.

2d April.

Death of Bandula.

Alarm of the Burmese court.

This disaster struck the king and his court with intense terror. Hpagyîdoa, naturally a man of mild disposition, had been led on to the aggressive acts which produced the war, chiefly by the ambitious prompting of Mahâ Bandula. He was encouraged to persevere by the court faction, of which the queen and her brother Menthagyî were the leaders. War with the British had indeed at first been popular, with all parties and all ranks of the nation. But constant defeat had tamed the spirit of many, and it was known that the prince of Tharâwadi advocated peace. The queen, who was of humble birth, had gained such entire influence over the king, that she was called by the members of the royal family "the sorceress." It was seriously believed that she had acquired and retained her power by witchcraft. Her brother, originally a retailer of fish at a bazaar stall, now took precedence of every one in the kingdom except the king's brother. He was hated by the royal family for his haughty bearing, and by the people generally for his rapacity and cruelty. The king, even before the defeat of Bandula at Rangoon, had become convinced of the error he had committed in provoking war; but his pride, and the influence of the war faction, kept him from negotiating with the invaders. He was heard to remark that he was in the predicament of a man who had got hold of a tiger by the tail, which it was neither safe to hold nor

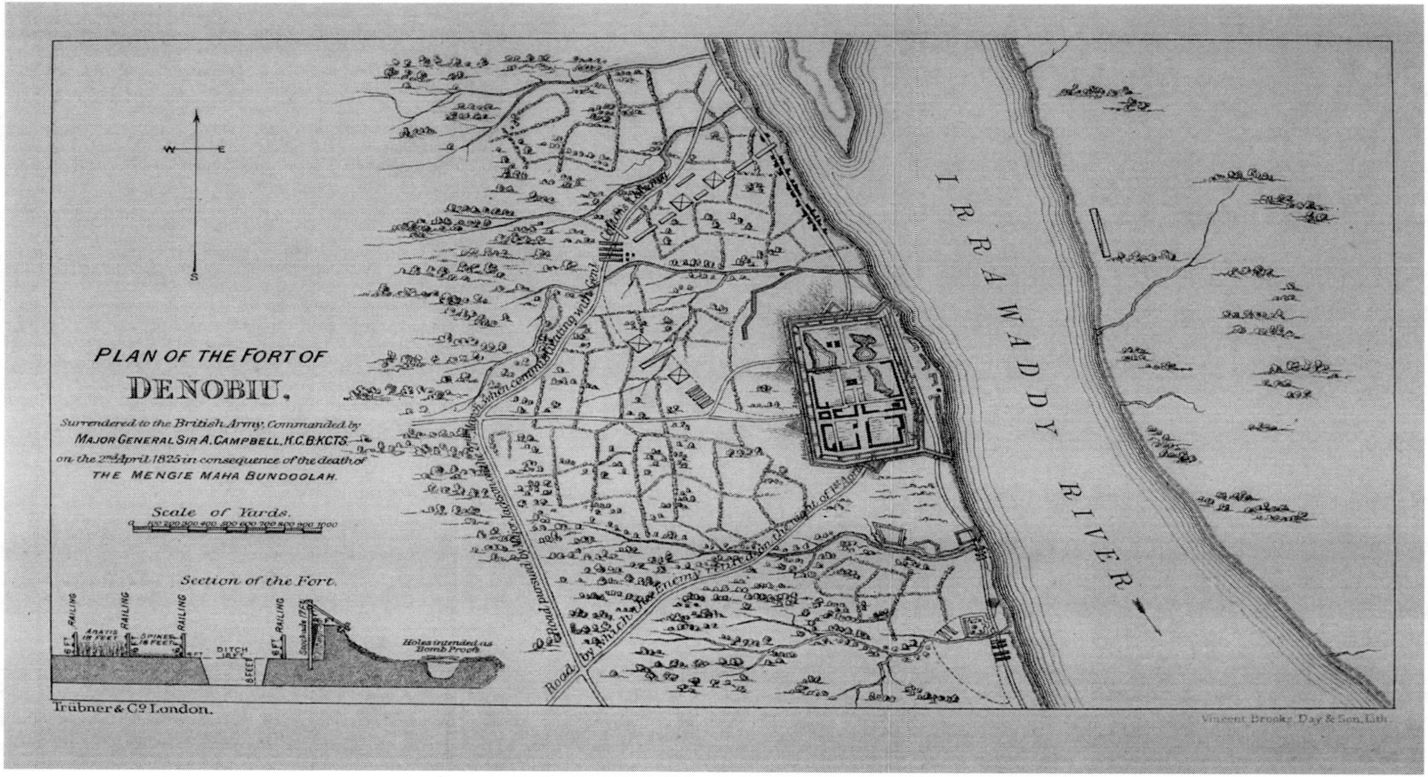
PLAN OF THE FORT OF
DENOBIU,
Surrendered to the British Army, Commanded by
MAJOR GENERAL SIR A. CAMPBELL, K.C.B. K.C.T.S.
on the 2nd April, 1825 in consequence of the death of
THE MENGIE MAHA BUNDOOLAH.
Scale of Yards.
0 100 200 300 400 500 600 700 800 900 1000
Section of the Fort.
RAILING
ABATIS
RAILING
SPIKES
RAILING
DITCH
RAILING
Stockade
Holes intended as Bomb Proofs
W
E
S
IRRAWADDY RIVER
Road by which the Enemy Retreated
Trübner & Co. London.
Vincent Brooks, Day & Son, Lith.

to let go. Menthagyî feared the loss of his own power if peace were made. The court astrologers, probably under his influence, continued to predict success. All Europeans at Ava, including the American missionaries, had been put into prison as suspected spies, and were treated with the barbarity used towards those accused of treason. On the death of Bandula, the king accepted the offer of the Pukhân Wungyî to lead an army against the invaders. This functionary had formerly served in Asâm and commanded in Manipur. Lately he had been in disgrace, and was for some time in prison along with the Europeans. He was a man of relentless cruelty. On being appointed commander-in-chief, he determined to inaugurate the assumption of his high office by putting the European prisoners to death, as a sort of sacrifice to the infernal powers—a horrible superstition, altogether outside and opposed to, the national religion. The prisoners were sent out to Aungpenglè, where this dreadful act was to be perpetrated. But the Pukhân Wungyî had many enemies. Having been twice punished by the king, it was suggested that he designed to raise himself to the throne. The dark deed he meditated seems to show a deeper design than that of success in the field. His house was searched, and it was said that royal insignia were discovered therein. He was trodden to death by elephants. The king's half-brother, Mengmyatbo, was next appointed commander-in-chief, being probably selected as one likely to be subservient to the war faction. The prince of Tharâwadi was in command of a corps, with his headquarters at Mengyî; but when general Campbell retraced his steps to cross the river to Danubyu, the prince had made no effort to interrupt him. He had become convinced of the hopelessness of continuing the war, and recommended negotiations for peace. As the British force advanced, he retired to Myèdè, and soon relinquished his command. Mengmyatbo established his headquarters at Malwun with his advance at Prome under an Atwenwun; while his second in command, the Kyîwungyî, who once more appeared in command, cautiously remained on the right bank of the river.

April 4. Prome occupied by the British.

General Campbell recrossed the Irâwadi, and pursued his march by the left bank, regulating his progress by that of the flotilla. Arrived at Prome, he found it deserted by the inhabitants. The Atwenwun in command before retiring had fired the town, and more than half of it was burnt. By a miracle two hundred barrels of powder in the arsenal did not explode. One hundred guns and jingals of various calibre were found mounted on the walls. The inhabitants soon began to return, and the Burmese civil officers of this and the neighbouring towns resumed their duties under the orders of the general.

The British field force went into cantonment at Prome for several months. Though the rainy season is there much lighter than in the delta, yet the river, swollen by rain in the mountains of Asâm, has a rise of forty feet above its lowest level; overflows its banks, and the country becomes impassable for military operations. This interval was employed in resting the men, establishing hospitals, collecting cattle, and bringing up from Rangoon stores of all kinds. The Burmese government found a difficulty in raising another army. The ancient plan of forced service no longer sufficed. A bounty was now offered for each recruit, and this politic measure was extended to the Shân states, where the chiefs by ancient custom had been wont to furnish contingents in war-time to the kings of Burma. While a new army was being formed, the invaders remained unmolested. In the middle of August general Cotton proceeded up the river in the steamer. At Myèdè he observed the Burmese army ranged in line, and judged the number he saw to be from sixteen to twenty thousand men. Some days later, a Burmese war-boat

September 6.

appeared with a flag of truce, and a written proposition to treat. An armistice of forty days was agreed to. Conference was held at Ngyaungbengzaik, twenty miles above Prome, between the general and commodore, and the Kyî Wungyî, who appeared as the Burmese chief commissioner. The object of the king of Burma in sanctioning this conference was to ascertain the terms upon which the British invaders might be induced to retire. Hope was entertained that an arrangement similar to that entered into with the Chinese generals during the reign of Hsengbyusheng might now be made. The terms declared by the British commissioners included the cession of Arakan, Tavoy, and Mergui, and payment of two millions pounds sterling. The Burmese commissioners could not have expected these conditions to be accepted by their government, but to allow of reference to the court, the armistice was prolonged to the 3d of November. Hpagyîdoa had no intention of complying with the British demands. Towards the end of October the Kyî Wungyî changed his tone of politeness, and wrote to the British general that yielding territory and paying money was contrary to Burmese custom. Hostilities were forthwith resumed. The Burmese army closed around Prome. The centre, said to consist of thirty thousand men under the Sâdoa Wun, who had distinguished himself in repelling the attack on the Kyaikkalo stockade in the previous year, was entrenched ten miles to the north of Prome. On the right bank of the river, as before the position of least danger, was the Kyî Wungyî with a division; and at Wettîgan, twenty miles to the north-east, was a body of eight thousand Shâns, with two thousand six hundred Burmese under Mahâ Nèmyu.

Negotiations for peace.

A.D. 1769.

The British general determined first to dislodge the latter force, which, in a forward movement, might act on his right flank. Five regiments of native infantry under colonel McDowall, one being kept as a reserve,

War resumed. British advance on Myèdè.

November 15. were ordered on this duty. The march was made by night in three columns, proceeding by different routes, which were to converge on the point of attack. The country was still deep with mud, and the movement was thereby retarded. The columns did not succeed in uniting according to arrangement, and colonel McDowall, arriving in front of a breastwork thrown up by a Shân corps, was killed. The several columns were forced to retreat with heavy loss in killed and wounded. The Burmese army now drew closer to Prome and occupied Shwêdaung in the British rear. A detachment stockaded at Padaung, on the right bank of the river, was surrounded by a part of the Kyî Wungyî's division. The force at Shwêdaung was driven off by a detachment of the 87th regiment, which arrived at the moment on its way from Rangoon, and the attack at Padaung was repulsed.

In a few days, general Campbell, with two thousand five hundred Europeans and fifteen hundred native in-
1st December. fantry, marched from Prome to attack the main body of the Burmese army. It was posted in a strong position on heights, from eight to ten miles north of Prome, with its right resting on an abrupt precipice overlooking the river, called Natpadî or Fairy-bead. The position was well stockaded and defended with guns. The flotilla, under commodore Brisbane, proceeded up the river to support the operations. Before attacking the main position, a stockade on the Naweng river, to the right of the line of march, was carried by assault, and Mahâ Nèmyu, a brave old man,
2d December. was there killed. The following day the troops advanced against the Burmese position, where Sâdoa Wun commanded. From the nature of the ground the artillery could not be brought near enough to afford material aid in the attack, but the whole position was carried by the infantry regiments, with the loss of twelve officers and one hundred and sixty men killed and wounded.

The Burmese loss during these actions was between two and three thousand men. The Shâns marched off to their own country. The Burmese troops on the west bank of the river were driven off three days later, and 5th December. followed their main army northwards. General Campbell, leaving two regiments of native infantry in garrison at Prome, pursued his march on Myèdè, at the head of four thousand five hundred men, with twenty-eight guns. The flotilla kept pace with the land force. The advance of the army entered Myèdè without opposition. 7th December.

The British government, still desirous of negotiating for the settlement of peace, had appointed Mr. Thomas Robertson, of the Bengal civil service, as joint commissioner with the commander-in-chief for that purpose. He had arrived, and brought with him the brahman already mentioned as Râj Guru, who had been deputed on a secret mission to Bengal by Hpagyîdoa, and was there detained as a prisoner. The Râj Guru was now sent to the Burmese general with a document announcing the terms of peace, which, it was hoped, he would be able to communicate personally to the king. The army continued its march, and reached Patanago with- 20th December. out opposition. On the opposite side of the river was 29th December. Malwun. Here was a stockade, with a garrison of four thousand five hundred men, commanded by Prince Mengmyatbo. The Burmese Government having now appointed Kaulen Mengyî, with the Kyî Wungyî and two other colleagues, to negotiate, the Râj Guru came across to the British camp, and it was arranged that the commissioners of the two powers should meet on board a boat anchored in mid-stream. After two or three meetings a treaty was signed by both parties, and a truce for January 3, A.D. 1826. fifteen days agreed upon to allow of the ratification by the king. The time expired, and no communication from the Burmese commissioners had been received. The batteries from the British side of the river now 19th January. opened on Malwun, which was completely commanded from the eastern bank, the stream being about nine hundred yards wide. After a destructive cannonade the British troops crossed the river in gunboats, and stormed the stockade. The Burmese fled, although the garrison had been considerably increased, leaving guns, powder, a great store of grain, and numerous documents, including the signed treaty, which had not been forwarded to the king for ratification. The British army pursued its march northward. When near Yènangyaung, Dr. Price, an American missionary, appeared, accompanied by a subordinate Burmese officer and some British officers, who had been taken prisoners. The object was to ascertain the ultimatum of the British general. They were informed that the British army would march on to Pugân, and there await the ratified treaty.

Malwun taken by the British.

25th January.

1st January.

The war party at Ava even now had not abandoned the hope of retrieving the disasters of the past. Menthagyî had come some distance from the capital down the river, but did not trust himself where fighting might occur. Prince Tharâwadi again strongly recommended peace. The queen was for flying to Mutshobomyu, the city of Alaunghprâ. An obscure officer, Letyâthura, with reckless ambition, offered to collect an army of thirty thousand men and drive back the invaders. The king, clutching despairingly at any chance to be rid of the invaders, appointed the applicant commander-in-chief, designating him Nê Weng Bureng, lord of the setting sun, antithetical to his own title of, lord of the rising sun. The new general does not appear to have gathered more than half the force he asked for. He took up a position at the ancient capital, Pugân. Leaving a part of his force within the walls of the ruined palace or citadel, he drew up the remainder extended in the form of a crescent. The selected battlefield was the "Burmese Thebaid," amidst the ruins of temples and pagodas, which in the time of their splen-

Action at Pugân.

dour had beheld the tumultuous march of the hordes of Kublai Khan. Prince Mengmyatbo and the other men of rank, now deprived of authority, withdrew to an adjoining village and waited the issue of the battle. General Campbell had sent out detachments to collect cattle and grain, and on reaching Pugân, had with him only nine hundred Europeans and about the same number of native infantry. Without hesitation he attacked the Burmese army, and defeated it with slight loss to his own. The unfortunate lord of the setting sun fled to Ava, and was forthwith ordered to execution. Loyal to the last, he bowed down to the palace-spire and submitted to his fate. The British general halted at Pugân to allow the detachments to rejoin, and then marched on. He reached Yandabo, and encamped four marches from the capital. The king was prepared to fly northward, but at last authorised a treaty to be concluded. The American missionaries, Messrs. Price and Judson, were sent down with the senior Wungyî and an Atwenwun. The Burmese commissioners brought with them one-fourth of the million sterling now required as payment towards the expenses of the war, and announced their readiness to accept the general terms before proposed. The treaty was now signed without discussion. By its provisions, Asâm, Arakan, and the coast of Tenasserim, including the portion of the province of Martaban lying east of the Salwìn river, were ceded to the British Government; and the king of Burma agreed to abstain from all interference in Kachâr, Jyntîa, and Manipur. Provision was also made for the future conclusion of a commercial treaty. The British army then retired to Rangoon, which was held until the second instalment of the sum due for the expenses of the war was paid, towards the end of the year. The town of Maulmein was rebuilt on the ancient site, and became the headquarter station and chief port of the province of Tenasserim.

February 8.

February 16.

British army at Yandabo, February 22.

Treaty signed, February 24.

The Burmese soldier.

Let justice be done to the Burmese soldier, who fought under conditions which rendered victory for him impossible. The peasant is taken from his village home, and brought into the field as a combatant, without having gone through drill or any suitable instruction. He is supposed to know how to load and fire a musket, which he probably does; but up to the end of the war, the musket given him, generally much worn by use and neglect in a damp climate, would have been condemned in every army of Europe. Many in the ranks were armed only with the native sword or spear. The gunpowder, made in the country, would not have been accepted as serviceable in the armies of the princes of India. After the large stores of that material had been lost at Danubyu and Prome, even the rude powder used became scarce; and at Malwun, before the assault, the Kaulen Wungyî, who was second in command to Mengmyatbo, but knew nothing of war even after the Burmese fashion, was seen measuring out the powder in a niggardly way to the soldiers. Cartridges were issued to few, and the soldier had to load as he best could. The artillery branch of the service was even more inefficient than the infantry. There were a great number of guns in different parts of the country, and these were mounted in the stockades, but they were mostly old ship-guns of diverse calibre, and some of them two hundred or more years old. Round shot was not plentiful; grape or canister there was none. Even at Danubyu, before the death of Bandula, the guns were so ill-served that any one piece was not fired oftener than once in twenty minutes. Generally, the Burmese officers never lead their men except in flight. Yet, with all these disadvantages, the Burmese ill-armed peasant never feared to meet Asiatic troops, though these were well armed and led by European officers. It was only to the European soldier that he succumbed. After the first few months of the war, he found himself over-matched, and no longer fought with hope of success.

A commercial treaty was signed at Ava by Mr. John Crawfurd, envoy from the governor-general, and by two Atwonwuns for the king of Burma. It was not of a nature calculated to place the trade between the two countries on a satisfactory footing. The old haughty reserve of the court was still maintained. The letter delivered by the envoy from the governor-general was not noticed. The behaviour of subordinates to the envoy was sometimes insolent. The demand for some British-Indian subjects who were detained against their will, was evaded. Hpagyîdoa was left with a kingdom equal indeed to that of Anoarahtâ in the eleventh century, and with more tributary Shân states than that monarch possessed, but he brooded over his misfortunes, and was no longer the joyous, affable prince of the early years of his reign. The loss of Arakan and of the southern provinces, from which many of his family and dependants derived their incomes, restricted his means and soured his temper. The country, after the struggle of two years, was exhausted, and the numerous inmates of the palace could no longer be supported with the wonted profusion. Some years elapsed before a British resident was appointed under the treaty. At first his presence was regarded by the king as a mark of degradation, and the ministers urged that an embassy once in ten years from one court to the other, similar to their arrangement with China, would be more suitable. But during a residence of seven years colonel Burney gradually acquired a salutary influence. Burmese envoys were sent to India, and for the first time the king of Burma wrote a letter to the governor-general. The resident supported the Burmese government when he considered it had been hardly dealt with. He successfully urged its claim to the Kubo valley, which in the adjustment

Commercial treaty, November 23.

A.D. 1830.

of the boundary after the war had been given to Manipur. As time passed, Hpagyîdoa became subject to fits
A.D. 1831.
of melancholy. He no longer attended to public affairs, and had to be kept in strict seclusion. A commission of regency, presided over by the prince of Tharâwadi, with the Menthagyî and others as members, was appointed. The president for a time attended the meetings at the royal council chamber, but the influence of the queen and of her brother was predominant, and he ceased to act. The prince was deeply incensed at being excluded from power in the name of the king, his brother. He secretly engaged followers, collected firearms, and kept robber chiefs in his pay in different parts of the country. He prepared for a struggle in the event of his brother's death. A chance event precipitated the crisis. By order of Menthagyî and the other ministers, his house was searched for a notorious bandit said to be concealed there. The prince suddenly left
February, A.D. 1837.
the city and fled to Muthsobomyu. He rapidly gathered round him the desperate men whom for years he had retained. The force at the disposal of the regency could not cope with the prince's determined followers. He marched down to Ava, and the city
April.
surrendered to him. He announced that he did not mean to dethrone his brother, but to rescue him from evil counsellors. Before many days he proclaimed that
Hpagyîdoa dethroned. May.
king Hpagyîdoa had abdicated, and he took possession of the palace. The deposed king lived as a prisoner, but well treated, for several years.

Though king Hpagyîdoa was less blameworthy than any of his dynasty, yet every friend of humanity must rejoice that a power which conquered only to destroy, was, in retribution for its own misdeeds, driven from nearly all the countries which it had overrun and ruined, and in another generation was restricted to the land which history shows was the ancient home of the Burmese race.

CHAPTER XXII.

EARLY EUROPEAN INTERCOURSE WITH BURMA.

Information in Ptolemy's Geography—Marco Polo—Narrative of Nicoli di Conti—Athanasius Nikitin, a Russian traveller—Hieronimo di Santo Stefano—Ludovico di Varthema—Portuguese in Pegu—Ferdinand Mendez Pinto—Cæsar Fredericke of Venice—Gasparo Balbi—Ralph Fitch—Nicolas Pimenta—Peter Williamson Floris—Sebastian Manrique in Arakan—Dutch and British traders in Pegu.

THE earliest notice in western authors of the countries which afterwards formed the Burmese empire is to be found in Ptolemy. Mention is therein made of cities in the interior and on the sea-coast. The delta of the Irâwadi appears as Chrysê Chersonêsus, the Suvarna Bhumi, or golden land of ancient India; a term corresponding in meaning to Thatun, the Burmese form of the Talaing name for the ancient port and capital of the country. Argyre is identified by Colonel Yule with Arakan.[1] After a long interval comes Marco Polo, who may have entered upper Burma with the Mongol invading army coming from Yunnan in the last quarter of the thirteenth century. He gives some graphic sentences on the country, mingled with grave inconsistencies as to the power of the king. In one chapter he terms him "a very puissant prince, with much territory, and treasure, and people," who fought bravely against the Tartars. In another he states that the

Information in Ptolemy's Geography.

Marco Polo.

[1] See "Notes on the Oldest Records of the Sea Route to China from Western Asia." Proceedings of the Royal Geographical Society, November 1882.

great khan conquered the country with a set of "gleemen and jugglers," having only a captain and a body of men-at-arms to help them. There were, however, two expeditions, at an interval of several years. In the last there was no fighting, and possibly Marco Polo's story of the gleemen and jugglers referred to it. But there are chronological difficulties in assuming that Marco was in the country during the latter period.

Narrative of Nicolo di Conti.

The first authentic narrative of travel in the countries of the Irâwadi is by a Venetian, Nicolo di Conti.[1] This traveller resided during the first quarter of the fifteenth century at Damascus as a merchant. He proceeded to Bussorah, and thence by sea, in company with some Persian merchants, to Cambay and Ceylon. He next went to the port of Tenasserim, then a place of importance, and from that to Bengal. After having sailed up the river Ganges, he returned to the coast, and took ship, apparently at a port on the Megna, for Arakan. He arrived at the estuary or mouth of the river, which he calls Racha, and which foreigners still call the Arakan river, though that is not the native name. He proceeded to the capital, which, he correctly states, has the same name as the river. He then went eastward across the mountains, still apparently accompanied by some of his Persian friends, until they reached the river Irâwadi, which he calls Dava, no doubt from the name of the capital. He proceeded up to Ava, where he arrived probably during or about A.D. 1430, when Monhyin Mengtarâ was king. He names the country Macinus or Mahâchin, a term he learnt from his Persian or Indian companions. He describes two methods of trapping and taming wild elephants as practised by the natives, the white elephant kept by the king, the rhinoceros, and other animals. He mentions some customs characteristic of the people. Nicolo returned to the

[1] India in the Fifteenth Century, by R. H. Major, F.S.A. Printed for the Hakluyt Society. London, 1857.

sea-coast by the Taungu route, and speaks of the city of Pegu, the capital of the province of the same name.

Athanasius Nikitin, a Russian traveller.

The next traveller whose narrative of a visit to Burma or Pegu has been preserved, is Athanasius Nikitin of Twer.[1] He travelled in Asia between the years 1468 and 1474. He went to the city of Pegu, but only mentions the Indian traders there. He does not note the difference of race between them and the Burmese or Talaings.

Hieronimo di Santo Stefano.

The Genoese merchant Hieronimo di Santo Stefano went to India from Egypt with Hieronimo Adorno. From Coromandel[2] they came to Pegu, and arrived at the city of that name in the year 1496. This was during the reign of Binya Rân, king of Pegu. He mentions Ava, where grow rubies and many other precious stones. "Our wish was to go to this place, but at that time the two princes were at war, so that no one was allowed to go from the one place to the other." The native histories do not mention any actual war between the kings of Pegu and Burma at this time; but Binya Rân attacked Dwârawati, a city or fort belonging to Taungu, which was very likely to bring about war with Ava. Hieronimo Adorno died in Pegu on St. John's day. The property of the deceased was seized as a forfeit to the king, according to the law of Burma and Pegu in the case of foreigners dying in the country. The property was, after much delay, restored to the survivor, but the traveller was detained in the country for a year and a half.

Lewes Vertomannus (Ludovico di Varthema), of Rome, went from Pulicat, north of Madras, to Tenasserim about the year 1503 or 1504, also in the reign of Binya Rân.[3] In his narrative, as translated in Hak-

[1] See "India in the Fifteenth Century." Nikitin's narrative is translated from Russian by the Count Wielhorsky.

[2] This may mean a port on the Krishna, or Godaveri, or Karimanal, a few miles north of Madras, or even Nêgapatam, to the south.

[3] His travels have been edited by the Rev. S. Percy Badger, for the Hakluyt Society, vol. xxxi.

Ludovico di Varthema.

luyt, he remarks: "The king useth not such pomps and magnificence as doth the king of Calicut, but is of such humanity and affability that a child may come to his presence and speak with him. It is in a manner incredible to speak of the rich jewels, precious stones, pearls, and especially rubies which he weareth, surmounting in value any great city. Not long after news were brought that the king of Ava was coming with a mighty force, whom the king, with an innumerable army, went to resist." This army probably was the force which Binya Rân took up the Irâwadi to Prome, and thence on to Pugân. This expedition may have been made to resist an anticipated attack; but in the Talaing history it is represented as a pilgrimage with an armed escort to the pagodas of those cities. No collision with a Burmese army is recorded. Ludovico presented to the king some coral, and received in return about two hundred rubies, of about one hundred thousand ducats in value, "whereby he may be considered the most liberal king in the world." He mentions Armenians and Nestorian Christians as being in Pegu.

Portuguese in Pegu.

Communication between Europe and India by the Cape of Good Hope had been opened by the Portuguese navigator Vasco de Gama, who reached Calicut on the Malabar coast in May 1498. A few years later Albuquerque built a fortress at Cochin, formed a settlement at Goa, and in 1510 occupied Malacca. In the following year he sent Ruy Nunez d'Acúnha to Pegu, but there is no detailed account of his proceedings. In 1517 John de Silveyra, with four sail, went to Chittagaon, then subject to Arakan, and was invited to the latter country. In 1519 Anthony Correa concluded a treaty at Martaban with the king of Pegu. From this time the Portuguese established a factory or trade depôt at that port. Twenty years later Ferdinand de Morales was sent by the viceroy at Goa with a great galleon to Pegu. He was in the river at the time of the invasion of Pegu by Tabeng Shwêhtî. He took part in the defence of the king of Pegu and was killed.

Ferdinand Mendez Pinto.

The next traveller to Pegu is one whose name has become, though unjustly, a byword for untruthfulness.[1] Ferdinand Mendez Pinto, who, though he evidently wrote his narrative of travels in Burma under the influence of a certain degree of glamour, does not make himself a hero of adventure, nor does he exaggerate the wealth and splendour of the kings in Indo-China, and the numerical strength of their armies, more than other European travellers of the sixteenth century do; on the latter point they merely repeated what they were told by the natives. His geography of the interior of the countries he passed through, is certainly difficult to be reconciled with what is now known; but that is no reason for attributing to him wilful falsehood, in the description of his journey from Burma through a part of Laos. The historical events he narrates, which can be compared with the native and other accounts, are correctly told. Pinto came by sea from Malacca, being sent by the governor of that place as an envoy to the viceroy of Martaban. Passing Tenasserim, then a Siamese port, where Portuguese merchants were settled, he mentions Mergui and Tavoy, and arrived at the mouth of the Martaban river (the Salwîn), according to his statement, in March 1545. The city was being besieged by Tabeng Shwêtî. In the Burmese history this event is stated to have occurred in 1540–41. At the time of his arrival at Martaban the siege had lasted more than six months. The surrender occurred about a month later. His estimate of the number of men in the besiegers' camp as being seven hundred thousand is no doubt a great exaggeration.

Pinto having come accredited as an envoy to the

[1] Congreve, in "Love for Love," act ii. scene 5:—"Ferdinand Mendez Pinto was but a type of thee, thou liar of the first magnitude." Translation of the travels of Pinto. 3 vols. London, 1663.

viceroy of Martaban, incurred thereby the displeasure of the Burmese king. He was detained as a prisoner, and sent over to Pegu under the charge of the treasurer of "Bramaa," so he styles king Tabeng Shwêhtî. He afterwards accompanied the Burmese army to the siege of Prome, which city surrendered, according to the Burmese history, in June, A.D. 1542.[1] His narrative of this event, while greatly exaggerating the numerical strength of the army and the numbers of killed and wounded, may be accepted as proving his presence. He mentions that the city gates were opened by the treachery of one of the commanders in the city. He now for the first time mentions Bureng Naung as the foster-brother of king Tabeng Shwêhtî under the title of Chaumigrem; the attempted relief of Prome by the Shân king of Ava, and other incidents recorded in the Burmese and Talaing histories. His exaggerations consist in stating that the Bramaa king had eighty thousand men killed and thirty thousand wounded. His statement that five hundred Portugals were killed and wounded at the siege is possibly correct, as it would include their native followers.

Pinto then relates how the king followed up the Shân army to Ava. Here he has confused events which happened in 1545 with those of 1542. In the former year there was a combination among the northern Shân chiefs to retake Prome. The allied army was commanded by the chief of Unbaung whom Pinto apparently mentions as the "Siamon," a corruption of "Shân Meng." As the northern Shân chiefs had entered into an alliance to resist the designs of Tabeng Shwêhtî upon Ava, the account by Pinto of a Burmese officer of high rank being sent by the claimant to the throne of Burma, to secure the good-will or active support of the eastern Shân states and the king of Zimmè, is credible and probable. Pinto accompanied the envoy, and though

[1] See chap. xii.

there is no reason for doubting the general truth of the story, the description as to the mode of travel, partly by land and water, is confused; and the geography of the country as described or inferred, altogether impossible. But he was still with the Burmese as one detained against his will, and probably could not keep notes.

The envoy and his escort proceeded by boat up the Irâwadi, and somewhere above Ava avoided the country of the "Siamon," and branched off to the east. But the narrative is so worded as to imply that after leaving the Irâwadi they proceeded the whole way by water. They came to a great river—no doubt the Salwîn—in the territory or under the control of a chief of Laos or the king of Zimmè, who is called the Calaminham. The envoy was received in great state by this potentate, who pledged his friendship to King Tabeng Shwêhtî, and agreed to support him against the "Siamon." The party then made their way back to the Salwîn, and came down by water to Martaban. Pinto, together with other Portuguese who were detained by the Burmese king of Pegu as useful servants, at length made his escape and reached Bengal. As he could scarcely have been in a position to keep notes of his journey, he may be excused for the confusion he has made in the means of transit by land and water, as well as in the geography of the country.[1]

Cæsar Fredericke of Venice.

After Pinto, the next traveller whose narrative deserves notice is that of Cæsar Fredericke of Venice, translated in Purchas. This traveller arrived in Pegu in 1567, when king Bureng Naung was absent on his expedition to Siam. He is truthful in his statements, yet he exag-

[1] The notion among the Burmese of there being a continuous interior communication by water between Ava and Martaban is mentioned by Dr. Francis Buchanan (Hamilton) in a paper on the geography of Burma (Edinburgh Philosophical Journal, vol. v. for 1821). Mention of this is also made in Dalrymple (vol. i. p. 113); the communication being over a tract of low land overflowed in the floods.

gerates in some respects. Thus he states that the invading army numbered one million four hundred thousand men; and of the reinforcements sent to the army in Siam six months later, he states that he saw "when that the officers that were in Pegu sent five hundred thousand men of warre to furnish the places of them that were slaine and lost in that assault." Cæsar was again in Pegu when Bureng Naung returned with the captives taken on the surrender of Ayuthiâ.[1] He describes the new city of Pegu, which was completed while he was in the country. It was surrounded by a wall, a complete square, with five gates on each face. There was a broad moat, having water in which were crocodiles. The streets were spacious, crossing at right angles, and perfectly straight from one gate to another. The king's palace was in the centre. It consisted of many pavilions of wood, gilded all over. Cæsar Fredericke, after stating that the king of Pegu can bring a million and a half of men into the field, observes, that "for people, dominions, gold, and silver, he far exceeds the power of the Great Turk in treasure and strength." He describes also how the king "sitteth every day in person to hear the suits of his subjects, up aloft in a great hall, on a tribunal seat with his barons round about;" while on the ground, forty paces distant, are the petitioners "with their supplications in their hands, which are made of long leaves of a tree, and a present or gift according to the weightiness of their matter. If the king think it good to do them that favour or justice they demand, then he commandeth to take the presents out of their hands; but if he think their demand be not just or according to right, he commandeth them away without taking their gifts or presents." The traveller relates the consideration shown to foreign merchants. "If any Christian dieth in the

[1] By the Burmese history this was in August 1570. See chapter xiii.

kingdom of Pegu, the king and his officers rest heirs of a third of his goods, and there hath never been any deceit or fraud used in this matter. I have known many rich men that have dwelled in Pegu, and in their age have desired to go into their own country to die there, and have departed with all their goods and substance without let or trouble."

Of Arakan Cæsar Fredericke reports: "The king of Rachim hath his seat in the middle coast between Bengala and Pegu, and the greatest enemy he hath is the king of Pegu. And this king of Rachim may arm two hundred gallies or fasts by sea; and by land he hath certain sluices with which, when the king of Pegu pretendeth any harm towards him, he may at his pleasure drowne a great part of the country."

These sluices were for the defence of the capital, and proved to be efficient when required to be used.

Gasparo Balbi, jeweller of Venice, came to Pegu in 1583, when Nanda Bureng, the son of Bureng Naung, was on the throne. He relates that the king was at war with his uncle the king of Ava, because the latter had refused to pay him homage. Suspecting that some of his nobles secretly supported the king of Ava in his disobedience, he had them, their wives, and children, burnt alive in a great temporary building. Balbi states the number thus put to death at four thousand, and that he was present at the time. The incident, except as to the number executed, which must be exaggerated, corresponds with what is related in the Burmese history. He mentions the battle between the two kings, in which the king of Pegu, though victorious, lost two hundred thousand men. Gasparo Balbi.

Ralph Fitch, an English merchant, came to Pegu in 1586–87, during the reign of Nanda Bureng. He describes the country as being then in a prosperous state, and the foreign trade of great extent. The capital he describes as being of great magnificence, and the streets Ralph Fitch.

"the fairest that ever I saw." He mentions the great pagoda near the modern town of Rangoon, known as Shwè Dagun. Near it was a Buddhist monastery or great hall of assembly for religious purposes, "gilded with gold within and without." Fitch vaguely says of the king that he keeps great state, and "at my being there he went to Odia (Ayuthiâ) with three hundred thousand men and five thousand elephants."

Fitch was for some time at Chittagaon, then subject to Arakan, and there gathered much information regarding that country. He observes, "The Mogon, which be of the kingdom of Recon and Rame, be stronger than the king of Tippara."[1] The name Ramu is applied to the country of Chittagaon in a general description of Bengal which is found in Purchas.[2] These instances probably explain the name of Ruhmi, Rahma, or Rahmaa given to a kingdom on the seacoast of the Bay of Bengal by the Arabian voyagers in the ninth and tenth centuries of the Christian era.

It has been supposed to refer to Ramrî in Arakan, or to Ramanyâ, the classic name of Pegu.[3] There is now a village called Ramu in the southern part of the Chittagaon district, which is a police-station. It probably represents the name by which the territory in question was known to the Arabs, and which we may now conclude extended from the north bank of the river Nâf to the confines of Bengal. Fitch heard the name when in Chittagaon, and the king of Arakan then held the country north of the Nâf.

Nicolas Pimenta. Nicolas Pimenta, a Portuguese priest, who came to the country in 1598, relates the terrible condition to which Pegu was brought, by the long wars carried on for nearly half a century. The famine was so great

[1] See Purchas, vol. ii. p. 1736.

[2] See vol. v. p. 508.

[3] See remarks on the Indian Balharâ, by Mr. E. Thomas, F.R.S., in Numismata Orientalia, vol. iii. part i.; and a review of the same in the Athenæum for Sept. 30, 1882.

"that they did eat each other; and in the city of Pegu there were not of all ages and sexes above thirty thousand remaining." He quotes from the letters of two Jesuit fathers of a later date as follows: "It is a lamentable spectacle to see the ruins of temples and noble edifices, the ways and fields full of skulls and bones of wretched Peguans killed and famished, and cast into the river in such numbers that the multitude of carkasses prohibiteth the way and passage of any ship."

Peter Williamson Floris, a Hollander, was in Arakan in the year 1608, and for several years afterwards in Pegu and the neighbouring countries. He gives a sketch of the transactions of the time, including the story of Philip de Britto at Syriam, and observes of the desolate state of Pegu consequent on the long wars: "In this manner came this mighty empire to ruin, so that at this day there is no remembrance of it." He returned to Europe in 1615. Peter Williamson Floris.

Sebastian Manrique, a friar of the order of St. Augustine, was sent from Goa, in company with others of the same order, to Bengal in the year 1612.[1] Manrique was instructed to proceed to Arakan, where there was a mission. He sailed from Chittagaon to Dianga, the Portuguese settlement, situated on the coast, apparently towards the Sungu river, to the south of the Kurnaphulî. From thence he went by land to the city of Arakan, and describes the great difficulties encountered in crossing the steep mountain-ranges. It must have been at the commencement of the rainy season, when the storms of wind are very severe. From what is said of the "roar of tygers and other wild animals," it is probable that he heard the loud deep-toned cries of the hoolook ape, which resound dismally in those dark forest solitudes, and startle the traveller to this day. The doleful Sebastian Manrique in Arakan.

[1] Historical Account of Discoveries and Travels in Asia, by Hugh Murray. Edinburgh, 1820. Vol. iii. pp. 96–114.

sounds would alarm those who did not know the source of it, for the animal generally keeps hidden from view. Arrived at the city of Arakan, Sebastian describes the king's palace, having "gilded columns of such immense magnitude as to make it quite astonishing that they should be composed of a single tree. It also had a hall covered all over with the purest gold." The rubies and other riches in the palace are mentioned as being of wonderful size and beauty, and of immense value. Manrique appears to have witnessed the ceremony of a Rahan's or Phungyi's funeral. He apparently mistook the lofty car or catafalque on which the body is placed, and burnt, for an idol car like that of Juggernáut; and states that people met death by throwing themselves under the wheels. This must have been a mistake of his, though accidentally some persons may have been killed on the occasion; for there is at such funerals ardent struggling between two sides or rival companies of men, to have the honour and merit of dragging the body to the place where it is to be burnt. He likewise describes the splendour of the ceremonial of the king's coronation or consecration; but when he mentions that thousands of human beings were put to death to avert a predicted evil, it is probable he merely repeated tales which from time to time arise among the people even at the present day, without any more foundation than the tradition of an ancient pre-Buddhistic custom. The king of whom these horrors are told is Meng Khamaung, the darling of the Arakanese people.

Dutch and British traders in Pegu.

The Portuguese settlement at Syriam had been destroyed. Other Europeans now appeared in Pegu.

Towards the close of the sixteenth century the Dutch had, in spite of opposition, gone round the Cape of Good Hope, and supplanted the Portuguese in the spice trade. They took possession of the Moluccas, and formed establishments in Java and Sumatra. Early in the seventeenth century they had possession of the island of Negrais. The first English East India Company had sent ships to the eastern seas under Lancaster, who appeared at Acheen in 1602, and established a factory. By the year 1612 the company had factories at Surat and other places on the coast of western India. About the same time they had agents and factories at Syriam, Prome, Ava, and, there is reason to believe, at Bamoa. A dispute between the Burmese governor of Pegu and the Dutch, caused the expulsion of the merchants of both nations from the country before the middle of the seventeenth century. The Dutch never returned. After this there is no record for many years as to British intercourse with Burma. Occasionally private traders may have gone to the ports, but the East India Company had no agents in the country. British merchants were settled in Siam; among other places at Mergui, then a Siamese port. In the account of the East Indies by Captain Alexander Hamilton,[1] it is related that the company was so jealous of the number of free merchants residing there, that in A.D. 1687 Captain Weldon was sent in a ship from Madras to drive them out. He threatened the governor of the port, ordering him to expel the private traders, and in a scuffle that occurred, killed some Siamese. In revenge, seventeen Englishmen who were in the town were massacred. After this British subjects were long excluded from Siam. The mission of M. de Chaumont, sent by Louis XIV., had arrived in 1685, and Englishmen had fallen into disrepute.

The first proposal for a renewal of commercial intercourse between Burma and the British factories in India came from the former. In 1688 a letter was received at Fort St. George (Madras) from the Burmese governor of Syriam, the only port to which foreign ships were admitted. The letter contained an invitation for

[1] Vol. ii. chap. xxxviii. London, 1744.

British merchants to settle in Pegu. Nothing was done at that time, but in 1698 Mr. Higginson, the governor of Madras, sent Mr. Fleetwood to be the commercial resident at Syriam. He proceeded to Ava, and had an audience with the king. Some trade privileges were granted, and permission to build a factory at Syriam. Two years later Mr. Bowyear succeeded as resident. In 1709 Mr. Allanson went as envoy to Ava with a letter from governor Pitt. The British continued to trade at Syriam until 1740, when the Talaing rebellion began. The company's resident was withdrawn in 1744.

APPENDIX.

A.

List of the Kings of Burma as entered in the Mahâ Râjâweng.

No. 1.—*List of Legendary Kings supposed to have reigned in Tagaung.*

No.	Names.	Relationship to each Preceding King.	Remarks.
1	Abi Râjâ	...	First of the dynasty; came from India.
2	Kan Râjângè . . .	Son	
3	Jambudîpa Râjâ . .	Son	
4	Thenggatha Râjâ . .	Son	
5	Wippanna Râjâ . .	Son	
6	Dewata Râjâ . . .	Son	
7	Munika Râjâ . . .	Son	
8	Nâga Râjâ . . .	Uncle	
9	Inda Râjâ . . .	Brother	
10	Thamuti Râjâ . . .	Son	
11	Dewa Râjâ . . .	Son	
12	Mahinda Râjâ . . .	Son	
13	Wimala Râjâ . . .	Son	
14	Thîhabânu Râjâ . .	Son	
15	Denggana Râjâ . .	Son	
16	Kantha Râjâ . . .	Son	
17	Kâlingga Râjâ . . .	Son	
18	Thengdwè Râjâ . .	Son	
19	Hîhala Râjâ . . .	Son	
20	Hantha Râjâ . . .	Brother	
21	Wara Râjâ . . .	Son	
22	Alaung Râjâ . . .	Son	
23	Koalaka Râjâ . . .	Son	
24	Thîrîra Râjâ . . .	Son	
25	Thengyî Râjâ . . .	Son	
26	Tainghkyît Râjâ . .	Son	
27	Padun Râjâ . . .	Son	
28	Menghlagyî Râjâ . .	Son	
29	Thanthuthîha Râjâ . .	Son	
30	Dengga Râjâ . . .	Son	
31	Hinda Râjâ . . .	Son	
32	Moariya Râjâ . . .	Son	
33	Binnaka Râjâ . . .	Son	

NO. 2.—*List of Legendary Kings supposed to have reigned at Mauroya and Tagaung.*

No.	Names.	Relationship to each preceding king.	Remarks.
1	Daza Râjâ	...	Came from India.
2	Thado Taingra Râjâ .	...	
3	Thado Rahtâra Meng .	...	
4	Thado Tahkwunra Meng.	...	
5	Thado Hlanbyanza Meng	...	
6	Thado Shwè Meng . .	...	
7	Thado Galunra Meng .	...	
8	Thado Nagâra Meng .	...	
9	Thado Nagânaing Meng .	...	
10	Thado Rahoala Meng .	...	
11	Thado Paungshè Meng .	...	
12	Thado Kyaukshè Meng .	...	
13	Thado Hsenglauk Meng .	...	
14	Thado Hsengtin Meng .	...	
15	Thado Tainghkyît Meng .	...	
16	Thado Menggyî Meng .	...	
17	Thado Dhammâ Râjâ, or Mahâ Râjâ Meng	...	Dethroned by invaders.

No. 3.—*List of the Kings of Burma who reigned at Tha-rê-khet-ta-râ and at Pugân, as entered in the Mahâ Râjâweng.*

No.	Names of Kings.	Commencement of Reign.			Length of Reign. Years.	Relation-ship of each Succeeding King.	Remarks.
		Year of Religion.	B.C.	Burmese Era.			
1	Ma-há-tham-ba-wa	60	483	...	6		Dynasty established at Tha-rê-khet-ta-râ.
2	Tsú-la-thám-ba-wá	66	...	...	35	Brother	Son of Thado Dhamma Râjâ Meng, king of Tagaung.
3	Dwot-ta-baung	101	...	...	70	Son of No. 1.	
4	Dwot-ta-ran	171	...	...	22	Son	
5	Ran-baung	193	...	...	50	Son	
6	Ran-mhán	243	...	...	50	Son	
7	Rek-khan	293	...	...	31	Son	
8	Khan-loung-meng	324	...	...	38	Son	
9	Lek-khaing	362	...	...	34	Son	
10	Thi-ri-khan	396	...	...	28	Son	
11	Thí-rí-rit	424	...	...	9	...	
12	Nga-ta-bá	433	110	...	51	...	A change of dynasty. Nga-ta-bá was the adopted son of Thí-rí-rit.
13	Phá-pe-ran	484	...	...	66	Son	
14	Rán-muk-khá	550	A.D. 7	...	15	Son	

No.	Names of Kings.	Commencement of Reign.			Length of Reign. Years.	Relationship of each Succeeding King.	Remarks.
		Year of Religion.	A.D.	Burmese Era.			
15	Ran-thun-khá	565	...	...	3	Son	
16	Ran-mú-tsa-lein-da	568	...	...	15	Son	
17	Be-rin-da	583	...	...	12	Brother	
18	Mú-tsa-la	595	...	...	5	Son	
19	Pún-na	600	...	...	3	Son	
20	Thá-kha	603	...	...	3	Brother	
21	Thá-khi	606	...	...	3	Son	
22	Kán-nú	609	...	...	1	Brother	
23	Kán-tek	610	...	...	3	Brother	
24	Bits-tsá	613	...	...	4	Brother	
25	Shú-mun-da-ri	617	...	...	7	...	Relationship not stated.
26	A-de-tya	624	...	...	3	Son	
27	Thú-pi-nyá, or Na-ga-ra-tshein-na	627	84	...	11	Brother	At the death of this king in A.D. 95, the kingdom of Tha-rê-khet-ta-râ ends. There is an interval of thirteen years before the new dynasty begins to reign at Pugân.
1	Tha-múg-da-rit	651	108	...	45	...	This king, said to be a nephew to Thú-pi-nyá, established a dynasty at Pugân, which is also called Pauk-gán, Pu-gú-rá-ma, Thí-ri-

							pits-tsa-rá, Ari-mád-da-ná, Tám-pa-di-pa, and Tám-pa-wa-ti.
2	Ra-the Kyúng	696	...	...	15	...	
3	Pyú-meng-tí, or Pyú-tsau-tí	711	...	...	75	...	**Supposed descendant of the ancient kings of Mau-re-ya and Upper Pugân.**
4	Hti-meng-yin	786	...	...	57	Son	
5	Yin-meng-baik	843	...	...	25	Son	
6	Paik-theng-lay	868	...	...	20	Son	
7	Theng-lay-gyúng	888	...	...	43	Son	
8	Kyúng-du-rit	931	...	...	25	Son	
9	Thay-htán	956	...	...	23	Son	
	Several Usurpers	979	...	...	55	...	
10	Tha-ra-mwun-byá	1034	...	...	22	...	Grandson of Thayhtan.
11	Thaik-taing-meng	1056	...	...	7	Son	
12	Theng-lay-gyúng-ngé	1063	...	...	9	Son	
13	Theng-lay-paik	1072	...	...	15	Brother	
14	Khán-lúng	1087	...	...	10	Brother	
15	Khán-lat	1097	...	...	12	Brother	
16	Htwun-taik	1109	...	...	13	Son	
17	Htwun-byít	1122		...	16	Son	
18	Htwun-Khyí	1138	...	...	15	Son	
19	Thengá Rá-dzá, or Pup-pá-tsaú Ra-hán	1153			27	...	Usurper.
20	Shwe-ún-thí	1180	637	...	12	...	The existing Burmese era, though said to have been established by Thenga Rádzá, commences A.D. 639, in the month of March.

No.	Names of Kings.	Commencement of Reign.			Length of Reign. Years.	Relationship of each Succeeding King.	Remarks.
		Year of Religion.	A.D.	Burmese Era.			
21	Peit-thun . . .	1192	649	11	8	Brother	
22	Peit-túng . . .	1200	657	19	50	Son	
23	Nga Khwe . . .	1250	...	...	6	Brother	
24	Myín Kywe . . .	1256	...	...	10	...	Usurper.
25	Theing-khá . . .	1266	...	...	8	...	Relationship not stated ; said to be of the royal race.
26	Thein-tswun . . .	1274	...	...	6	Son	
27	Shwe-laung . . .	1280	...	...	9	Son	
28	Htwun-dweng . .	1289	...	...	9	Son	
29	Shwe-mhauk . .	1298	...	...	23	Son	
30	Mwun-lwut . . .	1321	...	...	17	Brother	
31	Tsau-kheng-nhít . .	1338	...	...	27	Son	
32	Khai-lú . . .	1365	...	...	17	Son	
33	Pyín-byá . . .	1382	...	...	32	Brother	
34	Tan-net . . .	1414	...	...	28	Son	
35	Nga Khwe . . .	1442	...	...	9	...	Grandson of a younger brother of No. 26, Thein-tswin.
36	Thein-kho . . .	1451	...	...	16	Son	
37	Ngyaung-ú-Tsau Rahán	1467	...	...	33	...	Usurper.
38	Kwon tshau Kyúng Phyú . . .	1500	...	...	22	Son of No. 34, Tannet	Dethroned.

39	Kyí-tso	1522	...	...	6	Son of No. 37	
40	Tsuk-ka-tá	1528	...	...	25	Brother	
41	Anoa-ra-htá-soa	1553	1010	372	42	Son of No. 38	The history places the commencement of this reign in 379 B.C., but this does not agree with the date deduced from the length of previous reigns.
42	Tsau-lú	...	1052	...	5	Son	
43	Kyan-tsit-thá	...	1057	...	28	Brother	A supposed son of Anoa-ra-htâ-soa.
44	A-lúng-tsí-thú	...	1085	...	75	Grandson	
45	Meng Sheng-tsau	...	1160	...	...	Son	Reigned one day.
46	Na-ra-thú, surnamed Ku-lá Kyá Meng	...	1160	...	4	Brother	
47	Mengyín-na-ra-thun-khá	...	1164	...	3	Son	
48	Na-ra-ba-dí-tsí-tsi-thú	...	1167	...	37	Brother	
49	Dze-ya-thein-khá	...	1204	...	23	Son	
50	Kyá-tswá	...	1227	...	16	Son	
51	U-za-ná	...	1243	...	5	Son	
52	Na-rá-thí-ha-pa-té, or Ta-ruk pye-meng	...	1248	...	31	Son	
53	Kyau-tswá	...	1279	...	12	Son	Deposed, and afterwards killed by three Shân brothers. End of the Pugân monarchy.

No. 4.—*List of Kings of Burma of Shân Race who succeeded the Pugân Kings, and reigned at Myin-saing and Pân-ya.*

No.	Names of Kings.	Commencement of Reign.		Length of Reign. Years.	Relationship to Preceding King.	Remarks.
		Burmese Era.	A.D.			
	A-theng-kha-yá Rá-dzá-theng-gyan Thí-ha-thú Ta-tsí-sheng	660	1298	14	...	Three brothers of Shân race, who usurped authority and governed with equal power.
1	Thí-ha-thú Ta-tsí-sheng	674	...	10	...	The youngest brother reigned alone at Pánya.
2	U-za-ná	684	...	20	...	Son of Kyau-tswá, the deposed king of Pugân, adopted by No. 1.
3	Ngá-tsí-sheng Kyau-tswá	704	...	8	Half brother	Son of Thí-ha-thú Ta-tsí-Sheng.
4	Kyau-tswá	712	...	9	Son	
5	Na-ra-thú	721	...	5	Brother	
6	U-za-ná byaung	726	1364	3 months	Brother	Dethroned by Tha-do-meng-bya, A.D. 1364.

No. 5.—*List of Kings of Shân Race who reigned at Sagaing contemporaneously with the Kings of Pánya.*

No.	Names of Kings.	Commencement of Reign.		Length of Reign. Years.	Relationship to Preceding King.	Remarks.
		Burmese Era.	A.D.			
1	A-theng-kha-yá Tsau Ywon	677	1315	7	...	This prince was the son of Thí-ha-thú Ta-tsí-sheng, who reigned at Myin-saing and Pánya.
2	Ta-ra-bya-gyí	684	...	14	...	Stepson of Thí-ha-thú Ta-sí-sheng.
3	Shwé-daung-tet	698	...	3	Son	
4	Kya-tswá	701	...	10	Son of No. 1	
5	Nau-ra-htá Meng-rai	711	...	7 months	Brother	
6	Ta-ra-bya-ngai	711	...	3	Brother	
7	Meng byauk Thi-ha-pa-té	784	1352	2	Brother-in-law	This prince was driven from Sagaing by an army of northern Shâns and put to death by his stepson Tha-do-meng-bya in the year 726=A.D. 1364.

No. 6.—*List of the Kings of Burma from the foundation of the City of Ava.*

No.	Names of Kings.	Commencement of Reign.		Length of Reign. Years.	Relationship to Preceding King.	Remarks.
		Burmese Era.	A.D.			
1	Tha-do-meng bya	725	1364	3	...	Founder of the city of Ava. This king, said to be descended from the ancient kings of Tagaung, was on his mother's side grandson of Atheng-kha-yá Tsau-ywon, the Shân king of Tsa-gaing.
2	Meng kyí Swá Tsau-kai or Ta-ra-ra-bya	729	...	33	...	Elected to the throne as a descendant of the kings of Pugân, and of the family of the three Shân brothers.
3	Hseng-phyú Sheng, Ta-ra-bya	762	...	7 months	Son	
4	Pyin-tsing-meng-tswé, or Meng Khaung	763	...	21	Brother	
5	Thí-ha thú, Hseng-phyú-Sheng	784	...	4	Son	
6	Meng-hla-ngai	...	...	3 months	Son	
7	Ka-lé kyé-taung-ngyo	...	...	7 months	...	Usurper.

8	Mo-nhyin Meng-ta-rá or Meng-nan-si	788	1426	13	...	A chief of Shân descent, who enforced his claim to the throne, as a descendant of the kings of Pu-gân, and of the family of the three Shân brothers.
9	Meng-rai-kyau-swá	801	1439	3	Son	
10	Thí-ha-thú or Bhureng Na-ra-pa-tí	804	...	26	Brother	
11	Ma-há-thí-ha-thú-ra	830	...	12	Son	
12	Thí-ri-thu-dham-má Rá-dzá-dhi-pa-ti, or Duti-ya Meng Khaung	842	...	21	Son	
13	Má-há Rá-dzá, Dhi-pa-ti, or Shwé-nan-sheng, Nara-pa-ti	863	...	25	Son	Killed by Tho-han-bwá, who succeeded to the throne.
14	Tho-han-bwá	888	...	16	...	Son of Tsa-lun, the Shân chief of Mo-nhyin, who conquered Ava.
15	Khun-mhaing-ngai	904	...	3	...	Shân chief of Un-boung, who was elected king. He was related to Shwé-nan Sheng.
16	Mo-byé-meng Na-ra-pa-ti	907	...	6	Son	Abdicated.
17	Sa-gaing Tsí-thú-kyau-hteng Na-ra-pa-ti	913	1551	3	...	A chief of Shân descent, who seized the throne; conquered and deposed by Bau-reng Naung.

No. 7.—*Kings of Burma of the Taungu Dynasty who reigned at Ava and at Hansâwadi.*

No.	Names of Kings.	Commencement of Reign. A.D.	Length of Reign. Years.	Relationship to Preceding King.	Remarks.
1	Ngyaung Râm Meng	1599	6		Son of Bureng Naung. Died in Momeit.
2	Mahâ Dhammâ Râjâ, surnamed Anaukphet lwun Mengtarâ	1605	23	Son	Reigned in Pegu from A.D. 1613.
3	Mengrê Dippa	1628	1	Son	This king, not having succeeded in establishing himself in Ava, is not included among the kings in the Mahâ Râjâweng.
4	Thalwun Mengtarâ, or Thado Dhammâ Râjâ	1629	19	Uncle	The seat of government established at Ava.
5	Bengtalê, or Ngâ Htâp Daragà	1648	13	Son	
6	Pyî Meng, or Mahâ Pawara Dhammâ Râjâ	1661	11	Brother	
7	Narâwara	1672	...	Son	Reigned a few months.
8	Thiri Pawara Mahâ Dhammâ Râjâ	1672	26	Brother	
9	Thiri Mahâ Thihathura Thudhammâ Râjâ, *Mar Aung Ratana Daragâ*	1698	16	Son	
10	Thiri Pawara Mahâ Dhammâ Râjâ Dibati Hsengphyusheng	1714	19	Son	
11	Mahâ Dhammâ Râjâ Dibati	1733	18	Son	Taken prisoner when Ava was captured by the Talaing army, A.D. 1751. Taken to Pegu, and there put to death.

No. 8.—*Kings of Burma of the Dynasty of Alaunghprâ.*

No.	Names of Kings.	Commencement of Reign. A.D.	Length of Reign. Years.	Relationship to Preceding King.	Remarks.
1	Alaunghprâ	1753	7	...	Founder of the dynasty capital Muthsobomyu.
2	Naungdoagyî	1760	3	Son	Capital at Sagaing.
3	Hsenghpyusheng	1763	12	Brother	Capital at Ava.
4	Singgu Meng	1775	6	Son	
5	Maung Maung	...	...	...	Son of No. 2, Naungdoagyî ; reigned only a few days.
6	Badun Meng, Bodoahprâ	1781	38	...	Son of Alaunghprâ ; built Amarapura as the capital.
7	Sagaing Meng or Phagyîdoa	1819	18	Grand-son	Capital at Ava ; dethroned by his brother, Tharâwadi Meng.
8	Tharâwadi Meng	1837	9	Brother	Capital at Amarapura.
9	Pugân Meng	1846	7	Son	Capital at Amarapura; dethroned by his half-brother.
10	Mengdun Meng	1853	25	Brother	Built Mândalè as the capital.

B.

Kings who Reigned in Pegu.

No. 1.—*List of the Kings of Suvarna Bhumi or Tha-htun, from the Native Chronicles.*

1 Thi-ha-Rá-dzá.[1]
2 Thiri Dhammá Thauka.
3 Titha.
4 Dhammá Pá-la.
5 Dham-ma dhadza.
6 Eng-gu-ra.
7 Uba-de-wa Meng.
8 Thí-wa-rít.
9 Dzau-ta-kummá.
10 Dham-má Thau-ka
11 Uttara.
12 Ká-tha-wun.
13 Mahá-thá-la.
14 A-ra-ka.
15 Na-ra-thú-ra.
16 Ma-há-Bad-da-ra.
17 A-da-ra.
18 An-gu-la.
19 U-run-na-ta.
20 Mahá Thuganda.
21 Thuganda Rádzá.
22 Brahmadát.
23 Manya Rádzá.
24 A-di-ka.
25 Ma-rá-di Rádzá,
26 Tha-du-ka.
27 Dham-ma bi-yá.
28 Thu-da-thá.
29 Dip-pa Rádzá.
30 A-thek-ka Rádzá.
31 Bhum-ma Rádzá.
32 Man-da Rádzá.
33 Ma-hing-tha Rádzá.
34 Dham-ma tsek-ka-ran.
35 Thu-tsan ba-di.
36 Bad-da-ra Rádzá.
37 Na-ra-thú Rádzá.
38 Tsam-bú-dí-pa.
39 Ke-tha-rít Rádzá.
40 Wi-dza-ya Kum-má.
41 Ma-ni Rádzá.
42 Tek-ka meng.
43 Ku-tha Rádzá.
44 Dip-pa Rádzá.
45 Na-ra Rádzá.
46 Rá-dzá Thúra.
47 Tsit-ta Rádzá.
48 Di-ga Rádzá.
49 Ut-ta-ma Rádzá.
50 Thì-ri Rádzá.
51 Dham-ma Rádzá.
52 Má-há Tsit-ta.
53 Gan-da Rádzá.
54 Dzé-ya Rádzá.
55 Thu-ma-na Rádzá.
56 Mad-da-ka Rádzá.
57 A-min-na Rádzá.
58 U-din-na Rádza.
59 Ma-nú-ha Meng.[2]

[1] The first king. He died the year Goadama entered Nirvana, B.C. 543. Came from India.

[2] Manúha (No. 59) was king of Tha-htun when the city was taken and destroyed by Anoarahtá, king of Pugân, about the year A.D. 1050.

No. 2.—*List of the Kings of Pegu from the Foundation of the City of Hansáwadi.*

No.	Names of Kings.	Commencement of Reign.		Length of Reign in Years.	Relationship of each Succeeding King.	Remarks.
		Year of Religion.	A.D.			
1	Mahimu Thamala Kumára	1116	573	12	...	**Came from Thahtun to build the city of Pegu.**
2	Wimala	...	585	7	Brother	
3	Kathá Kum-má	...	592	7	Nephew	
4	Mahimu Arinda Rádzá	...	599	7	Son	
5	Mahintha Rádzá	...	606	17	Son	
6	Geinda Rádzá	...	623	12	Brother	
7	Mahimu Mig-ga-dib-ba Rádzá	...	635	15	Son	
8	Gits-tsa-wi-ya	...	650	10	Son	
9	Kara-wi-ka Rádzá	...	660	12	Son	
10	Tsan-da-la Rádzá	...	672	13	...	**Relationship not stated.**
11	At-ta-thá Rádzá	...	685	15	...	Ditto ditto.
12	Anuma Rádzá	...	700	12	Son	
13	Mahimu Mig-ga-dib-ba-ngé	...	712	10	...	Usurper.
14	Mahimu Egga Thamanda Rádzá	...	722	12	Brother	
15	Uba-ma-la Rádzá	...	734	12	Son	
16	Pun-na-ri-ka Rádzá	...	746	15	...	**Relationship not stated.**
17	Thamin Tik-tha, Titha, or Tissa Rádzá	...	761	20	Son	**From this time a blank of about five hundred years occurs in the annals of Pegu, during which the names of no native kings are entered. The two last kings in this list probably represent two periods, the religious ascendancy or religious strife of Brahmanists and Buddhists, extending over about three hundred years. The close of Titha's reign would then synchronise with the conquest of Pegu and Thahtun by Anaurahtá about A.D. 1050, when Pegu became subject to Burma for about two hundred and thirty years.**

No. 3.—*List of the Kings of Pegu of Shân Race who Reigned after the Re-establishment of the Kingdom under Warêru*, A.D. 1287.

No.	Names of Kings.	Commencement of Reign.			Length of Reign in Years.	Relationship of each Succeeding King.	Remarks.
		Year of Religion.	A.D.	Burmese Era.			
1	Wa-rê-ru	...	1287	649	19	...	A Shân chief, who established the dynasty, but had his capital at Muttama.
2	Khun-láu, or Tha-ná-ran-bya-keit	...	...	668	4	Brother	
3	Dzáu-áu, or Theng-mháing	...	...	672	13	Nephew	
4	Dzáu-dzip, or Binga-ran-da	...	...	685	7	Brother	
5	Binya-é-láu	...	...	692	18	Cousin	Son of No. 2, Khun-láu.
6	Binya-ú, or Tsheng-phyú-sheng	...	...	710	37	Cousin	Son of No. 4, Dzáu-dzip. This king restored the ancient capital, Pegu or Hansâwadi.
7	Binya-nwé, or Rá-dzá-di-rít	...	...	747	38	Son	
8	Binya Dham-má Rá-dzá	...	...	785	3	Son	
9	Binya Rán-kit	...	...	788	20	Brother	
10	Binya Wa-rú	...	...	808	4	Nephew	
11	Binya Keng	...	...	812	3	Cousin	
12	Mháu-dáu	...	...	815	...	Cousin	Reigned seven months.
13	Sheng-tsáu-bu, Binya-dáu (queen)	...	...	815	7	...	Daughter of No. 7, Rádzá-di-rit.
14	Dham-ma Dzé-di	...	...	822	31	...	Not of royal race.
15	Binya Rán	...	...	853	35	Son	Son-in-law of No. 13, Sheng-tsáu-bu.
16	Ta-ká-rwut-bi	...	1526	888	14	Son	Conquered and deposed by Tabeng Shwéhtí, king of Táungu, A.D. 1540.

No. 4.—*List of the Kings (or Emperors) of Pegu from the Accession of the Táungu Dynasty, called by Europeans the Brahma or Barma Kings.*

No.	Names of Kings.	Commencement of Reign. Year A.D.	Length of Reign. Years.	Relationship of each Succeeding King.	Remarks.
1	Tabeng shwé htí	1540	10	...	King of Taungu, of Burmese race; conquered Pegu; assumed the title of emperor, having subordinate to him the kings of Ava, Prome, Taungu, and Martaban.
2	Thamin-dwut	1550	3 months	...	Styled by the Portuguese writers Ximi de Zatan.
3	Thamin-htáu	1550	1	...	Styled Xemindoo by the Portuguese. He was a son of Binya Rán, No. 15 of the kings of Pegu, descendants of Wareru.
4	Bureng Naung	1551	30	...	Styled Branginoco by the Portuguese; was the general of the armies of Tabeng Shwéhtí, and claimed to be his lawful successor.
5	Nanda Bureng, or Ngá tsú dá-ra-ga	1581	18	Son	Dethroned and put to death by the king of Taungu.

NO. 5.—*Kings who Expelled the Burmese and Reigned in Pegu.*

No.	NAMES OF KINGS.	Commencement of Reign. Year A.D.	Length of Reign. Years.	Relationship of each Succeeding King.	REMARKS.
1	Buddha ke thî Gwe meng	1740	6	...	Abdicated voluntarily.
2	Ḅinya Dala	1746	11	...	Conquered by Alaunghprâ.

C.

CHRONOLOGICAL TABLE OF THE KINGS OF ARAKAN.

Dhy-nyga-wa-ti Dynasty.

No.	Name of Sovereign.	Date of Accession.		Reign.		Relationship of each Succeeding Sovereign.
		B.C.	Ar. Era.	Yrs.	Ms.	
1	Ma-ra-yo	2666	...	62	0	
2	Ma-ra-dzi	...	...	32	0	Son.
3	Ma-ra-on·leng	...	...	53	0	,,
4	Ma-ra-rway-leng	...	...	48	0	,,
5	Ma-ra-bengh	...	...	55	0	,,
6	Ma-ra-dzi	...	...	33	0	,,
7	Ma-ra-keng	...	...	32	0	,,
8	Nga-tshap-o	...	...	21	0	An usurper.
9	Dwa-ra-tsan-dra	...	...	40	0	Son of Má-ra-keng.
10	Tho-la-tsan-dra	...	...	33	0	Son.
11	Tsan-da-thu-ri-ya-tsan-dra . .	...	...	37	0	,,
12	Ka-la-tsan-dra	...	...	40	0	,,

No.	Name of Sovereign.	Date of Accession.		Reign.		Relationship of each Succeeding Sovereign.
		B.C.	Ar. Era.	Yrs.	Ms.	
13	Ti-tsan-dra	...	...	31	0	Son.
14	Ma-dhu-tha-tsan-dra	...	...	20	0	"
15	Dze-ya-tsan-dra	...	...	40	0	"
16	Mok-kha-tsan-dra	...	...	26	0	"
17	Gun-na-tsan dra	...		12	0	"
	Three nobles reigned for seven days, three months, and eight months successively	...	... ...	0	11	Usurpers.
18	Kan-Ra-dza-gyi	...	...	41	0	Grandson of Gun-na-tsan-drá.
19	Kan-Ra-dza-ngai	...	...	36	0	Brother.
20	In-da-thu-ri-ya	...	...	35	0	Son.
21	A-thu-rin-da-thu-ri-ya	...	...	30	0	"
22	Tha-ra-me-ta	...	...	28	0	"
23	Thu-ri-ya	...	...	31	0	"
24	Meng-thi	...	...	22	0	"
25	Meng-ba	...	...	22	0	"
26	Tsi-oung	...	...	28	0	"
27	Ta-taing-theng	...	...	31	0	Brother.
28	Kyau-khoung-weng	...	...	31	0	Son.
29	Thu-ri-ya-nan-da-mit	...	...	21	0	"
30	A-thu-rin-da-bha-ya	...	...	31	0	"
31	Let-ya-tsi-thu-kyi	...	...	32	0	"

32	Thi-ha-ka	...	...	43	0	„
33	Meng-bhun-than	...	...	31	0	„
34	Tha-ret-hmwe	...	...	49	0	„
35	Dze-ya-nan-da-thu	...	...	51	0	„
36	Tek-ka-thu	...	...	46	0	„
37	Lek-kha-na	...	...	37	0	„
38	Gun-na-rit	...	...	48	0	„
39	Thi-wa-rit	...	...	41	0	„
40	Meng-hla-hmwe	...	...	31	0	„
41	Ma-rin-da	...	...	62	0	„
42	Thi-dhat-kum-ma-ra	...	...	22	0	„
43	Meng-hla-kyi	...	...	47	0	„
44	Meng-hla-ngay	...	...	24	0	Brother.
45	Nga-tsa-rit	...	...	38	0	Son.
46	Myet-hna-wun	...	...	31	0	„
47	Let-thut-kyi	...	...	27	0	„
48	Thi-ri-kam-ma-thun-da	...	...	31	0	„
49	Nan-da-ko-ta-bha-ya	...	...	27	0	„
50	Meng-nan-hpyu	...	...	20	0	„
51	Meng-ma-nu	...	...	28	0	„
52	Meng-khoung-ngay	...	...	19	0	„
53	Louk-khoung-ra-dza	...	...	40	0	„
54	Meng-ngay-pyau-hla-tsi	...	...	6	0	„
	Three nobles usurp the throne	...	...	6	8	

Dhi-ngya-wa-ti Second Dynasty.

No.	Name of Sovereign.	Date of Accession.		Reign.		Relationship of each Succeeding Sovereign.
		B.C.	Ar. Era.	Yrs.	Ms.	
1	Kan-Ra-dza-gyi	825	...	37	0	
2	Thi-la-Ra-dza	...	...	48	0	Son.
3	Wa-tsa-thu-ra	...	...	31	0	"
4	Nan-da-wi-thu-ra	...	...	40	0	"
5	Pu-na-thu-ri-ya	...	...	32	0	"
6	Thu-ran-da	...	...	23	0	"
7	Tsan-di-ma	...	...	37	0	"
8	Thi-ri-tsan-da	...	...	40	0	"
9	Thi-ha-ran	...	...	46	0	Brother.
10	Thi-ha-nu	...	...	20	0	Son.
11	Pa-ya-ka	...	...	31	0	"
12	Ne-la-gun	...	...	41	0	"
13	Roha-ha-gun	...	...	31	0	"
14	Thi-ri-gun	...	...	24	0	"
15	Tha-ma-dza	...	...	35	0	Nephew.
16	Kum-ma-ra	...	...	20	0	Son.
17	Thek-hteng-hypu	...	...	40	0	"
18	Tha-bheng-u	...	...	42	0	"
19	Te-dza-wun	...	...	36	0	"
20	Mun-dza-ya-ba	...	...	34	0	"

21	Kum-ma-ra-wi-thud-dhi . .	...	...	87	0	„
22	Wa-thu-mun-da-la	...	...	34	0	„
23	Thu-rin-da	...	...	31	0	„
		A.D.				
24	Ra-la-ma-yu	15	...	22	0	Brother.
25	Na-la-ma-yu	37	...	31	0	Son.
26	Wa-dha-gun	68	...	22	0	„
27	Wi-thu-ra-dza	90	...	21	0	„
28	Thi-ri-ra-dza	111	...	35	0	„

Dhi-ngya-wa-ti Dynasty of the Religion of Goad-a-ma.

29	Tsan-da-thu-ri-ya	146	...	52	0	Son.
30	Thu-ri-ya-di-ti	198	...	47	0	„
31	Thu-ri-ya-pa-ti-pat . . .	245	...	53	0	„
32	Thu-ri-ya-ru-pa	298	...	15	0	„
33	Thu-ri-ya-man da-la . . .	313	...	62	0	„
34	Thu-ri-ya-wan-na	375	...	44	0	„
35	Thu-ri-ya-na-tha	418	...	40	0	„
36	Thu-ri-ya-weng-tha . . .	459	...	9	0	„
37	Thu-ri-ya-ban-da	468	...	6	0	„
38	Thu-ri-ya-ka-lya-na . . .	474	...	18	0	„
39	Thu-ri-ya-muk-kha . . .	492	...	21	0	„
40	Thu-ri-ya-te-dza	513	...	31	0	„
41	Thu-ri-ya-pu-nya	544	...	8	0	„

No.	Name of Sovereign.	Date of Accession.		Reign.		Relationship of each Succeeding Sovereign.
		A.D.	Ar. Era.	Yrs.	Ms.	
42	Thu-ri-ya-ku-la	552	...	23	0	Son.
43	Thu-ri-ya-pa-bas	575	...	25	0	"
44	Thu-ri-ya-tsi-tra	600	...	18	0	"
45	Thu-ri-ya-the-tha	618	...	22	0	"
46	Thu-ri-ya-wi-ma-la	640	...	8	0	"
47	Thu-ri-ya-re-nu	648	...	22	0	Brother.
48	Thu-ri-ya-geng-tha	670	...	16	0	Son.
49	Thu-ri-ya-thek-ya	686	...	8	0	Paternal uncle.
50	Thu-ri-ya-thi-ri	794	...	20	0	Son.
51	Thu-ri-ya-ke-thi	714	...	9	0	"
52	Thu-ri-ya-kut-ta	723	...	23	0	"
53	Thu-ri-ya-ke-tu	746	...	42	0	"
	Dynasty of the City We-tha-li.					
1	Ma-ha-taing-tsan-dra	788	150	22	0	Son.
2	Thu-ri-ya-taing-tsan-dra	810	172	20	0	"
3	Mau-la-taing-tsan-dra	830	192	19	0	"
4	Pau-la-taing-tsan-dra	849	211	26	0	"
5	Ka-la-taing-tsan-dra	875	237	9	0	"
6	Du-la-taing-tsan-dra	884	246	19	0	"
7	Thi-ri-taing-tsan-dra	903	265	32	0	"

8	Thing-gha-tha-taing-tsan-dra	935	297	16	0	"
9	Tsu-la-taing-tsan-dra	951	313	6	0	"
10	A-mya-thu	957	319	7	0	A chief of the Myu tribe.
11	Pai-phyu	964	326	30	0	Nephew.
12	Nga-meng-nga-tum	994	356	24	0	Son of Tsu-la-taing-tsan-dra.
	Dynasty of Ping-tsa City.					
1	Khet-ta-theng	1018	380	10	0	Grand-nephew to Tsu-la-taing-tsan-dra.
2	Tsan-da-theng	1028	390	11	0	Brother.
3	Meng-reng-phyu	1039	401	10	0	Son.
4	Na-ga-thu-ri-ya	1049	411	3	0	"
5	Thu-ri-ya-Ra-dza	1052	414	2	0	"
6	Pun-na-ka	1054	416	4	0	"
7	Meng-phyu-gyi	1058	420	2	0	"
8	Tsi-tha-beng	1060	422	1	0	Usurper.
9	Meng-nan-thu	1061	423	5	0	Son of Meng-phyu-gyi.
10	Meng-la-de	1066	428	6	0	Son.
11	Meng-ku-la	1072	434	3	0	"
12	Meng-Bhi-lu	1075	437	3	0	"
13	Theng-kha-ya	1078	440	14	0	Usurper.
14	Meng-than	1092	454	8	0	Son.
15	Meng-pa-di	1100	462	3	0	"
	Dynasty of the City Pa-rin.					
1	Let-ya-Meng-nan	1103	465	6	0	Grandson of Meng-Bhi-lu.
2	Thi-ha-ba	1109	471	1	0	Son.

No.	Name of Sovereign.	Date of Accession.		Reign.		Relationship of each Succeeding Sovereign.
		A.D.	Ar. Era.	Yrs.	Ms.	
3	Ra-dza-gyi	1110	472	2	0	Son.
4	Tha-ki-weng-gyi	1112	474	3	0	”
5	Tha-ki-weng-ngay	1115	477	18	0	”
6	Gau-li-ya	1133	495	20	0	”
7	Da-tha-Ra-dza	1153	515	12	0	”
8	A-nan-thi-ri	1165	527	2	0	”
	Dynasty of the City Khyit.					
1	Meng-Phun-tsa	1167	529	7	0	Brother.
2	Pin-tsa-ka-wa	1174	536	2	0	Son.
3	Gan-na-yu-bau	1176	538	3	0	”
4	Tsa-leng-ka-bo	1179	541	1	0	Usurper.
	Second Dynasty of the City Ping-Tsa.					
1	Mi-dzu-theng	1180	542	11	0	Son of Pin-tsa-ka-wa.
2	Nga-ran-man	1191	553	2	0	Son.
3	Nga-pug-gan	1193	555	2	0	”
4	Nga-ra-khoing	1195	557	3	0	”
5	Nga-kyun	1198	560	3	0	”
6	Nga-tshu	1201	563	4	0	”

7	Nga-tswai-theng	1205	567	1	0	„
8	Meng-koung-gyi	1206	568	1	0	„
9	Meng-khoung-ngay	1207	569	1	0	„
10	Kam-bha-loung-gyi	1208	570	·1	0	„
11	Kam-bha-loung-ngay	1209	571	1	0	„
12	Let-ya-gyi	1210	572	8	0	„
13	Let-ya-ngay	1218	580	11	0	„
14	Tha-na-beng	1229	591	3	0	„
15	Nga-na-thin	1232	594	2	0	„
16	Nga-na-lum	1234	596	3	0	„

Dynasty of the City Loung-Kyet.

1	H-lan-ma-phyu	1237	599	6	0	Son.
2	Ra-dza-thu-gyi	1243	605	3	0	„
3	Tsau-lu	1246	608	5	0	„
4	Uts-tsa-na-gyi	1251	613	9	0	„
5	Tsau-mwun-gyi	1260	622	8	0	„
6	Nan-kya-gyi	1268	630	4	0	„
7	Meng-Bhi-lu	1272	634	4	0	„
8	Tsi-tha-beng	1276	638	3	0	Usurper.
9	Meng di	1279	641	106	0	Son of Meng-bhi-lu.
10	Uts-tsa-na-ngay	1385	747	2	0	Son.
11	Thi-wa-rit	1387	749	3	0	Younger brother.
12	Thin-tse	1390	752	4	0	„ „
13	Ra-dza-thu	1394	756	1	0	Son.

No.	Name of Sovereign.	Date of Accession.		Reign.		Relationship of each succeeding Sovereign.
		A D.	Ar. Era.	Yrs.	Ms.	
14	Tsi-tha-beng	1395	757	2	0	Usurper.
15	Myin-tsoing-kyi	1397	759	0	5	"
16	Ra-dza-thu (restored) . . .	1397	759	4	0	
17	Thing-ga-thu	1401	763	3	0	Brother.
	Dynasty of the City Myouk-u.					
1	Meng-tsau-mwun	1404	766	2	0	Son of Ra-dza-thu
	Interregnum	...	...	24	0	
	Meng-tsau-mwun (restored) . .	...	792	4	0	
2	Men-kha-ri	1434	796	25	0	Brother.
3	Ba-tsau-phyu	1459	821	23	0	Son.
4	Dau-lya	1482	844	10	0	"
5	Ba-tsau-nygo	1492	854	2	0	Uncle, a son of Meng-kha-ri.
6	Ran-oung	1494	856	0	6	Son of Dau-lya.
7	Tsa-leng-ga-thu	1494	856	7	0	Uncle by the mother's side.
8	Men-ra-dza	1501	863	22	0	Son.
9	Ga-dza-ba-di	1523	885	2	0	"
10	Meng-tsau-o	1525	887	0	6	Brother to Tsa-leng-ga-thu.
11	Tha-tsa-ta	1525	887	6	0	Son of Dau-lya.
12	Meng-beng	1531	893	22	0	Son of Men-Ra-dza.

13	Dik-kha	1553	915	2	6	Son.
14	Tsau-lha	1555	917	9	0	,,
15	Meng-Tsek-ya	1564	926	7	0	Brother.
16	Meng-Pha-loung	1571	933	22	0	Son of Meng-beng.
17	Meng-Ra-dza-gyi	1593	955	19	0	Son.
18	Meng-Kha-moung	1612	974	10	0	,,
19	Thi-ri-thu-dham-ma . . .	1622	984	16	0	,,
20	Meng-Tsa-ni	1638	1000	...		Son reigned only 28 days.
21	Na-ra-ba-di-gyi	1645	1000	7	0	Great-grandson of No. 11, Tha-tsa-ta.
22	Tha-do	1638	1007	7	0	Brother's son.
23	Tsanda Thudhamma	1652	1014	32	0	Son.
24	Thiri Thuriya	1684	1046	1	0	,,
25	Wara Dhamma Rádzá . . .	1685	1047	7	0	Brother.
26	Munithu Dhamma Rádzá . .	1692	1054	2	0	,,
27	Tsanda Thuriya Dhamma Rádzá .	1694	1056	2	0	,,
28	Naurahtá Dzáu	1696	1058	...		Son, reigned 15 days.
29	Mayuppiya	1696	1058	1	0	Usurper.
30	Kalamandat	1697	1059	1	0	,,
31	Naradhibadi	1698	1060	2	0	Son of No. 27, Tsanda Thuriya.
32	Tsanda Wimala	1700	1062	6	0	Grandson of No. 22, Thado.
33	Tsanda Thuriya	1706	1068	4	0	Grandson of No. 23, Tsanda Thudhamma.
34	Tsanda Widzaya	1710	1072	21	0	Usurper.
35	Tsanda Thuriya	1731	1093	3	0	Son-in-law.
36	Naradhibadi	1734	1096	1	0	Son.
37	Nara Pawara Rádzá	1735	1097	2	0	Usurper.
38	Tsanda Widzala	1737	1099	0	8	Cousin.

No.	Name of Sovereign.	Date of Accession.		Reign.		Relationship of each Succeeding Sovereign.
		A.D.	Ar. Era.	Yrs.	Ms.	
39	Katya	...	...	...		A foreigner; held the palace for three days.
40	Ma-da-rit	1737	1099	5	0	Brother to No. 38.
41	Na-ra-a-pa-ya	1742	1104	19	0	Uncle.
42	Thi-ri-thu	1761	1123	0	3	Son.
43	Pa-ra-ma-Ra-dza	1761	1123	3	0	Brother.
44	Ma-ha-Ra-dza	1764	1126	9	4	Brother-in-law.
45	Thu-ma-na	1773	1135	4	0	" "
46	Tsan-da-wi-ma-la	1777	1139	...		Usurper, reigned forty days.
47	Tha-di-tha-dhamma-yit	1777	1139	5	0	A chief from Raṁ-byi.
48	Tha-ma-da	1782	1144	2	0	A chief in whose reign the Burmese conquered the country.

INDEX.

U

PRINTED BY BALLANTYNE, HANSON AND CO.
EDINBURGH AND LONDON.

MAP OF THE
BURMESE EMPIRE,
Showing the
Present Approximate Boundary with
BRITISH INDIA & BRITISH BURMA.
BAY OF BENGAL
Gulf of Martaban
Gulf of Siam
PEGU
MARTABAN
TENASSERIM
SHAH STATES
TRIBUTARY to SIAM
PROME
RANGOON
MARTABAN
MAULMAIN
TAVOY
Bangkok
PITSALAUK
C. Negrais
Trubner & Co. London.
Vincent Brooks Day & Son lith.

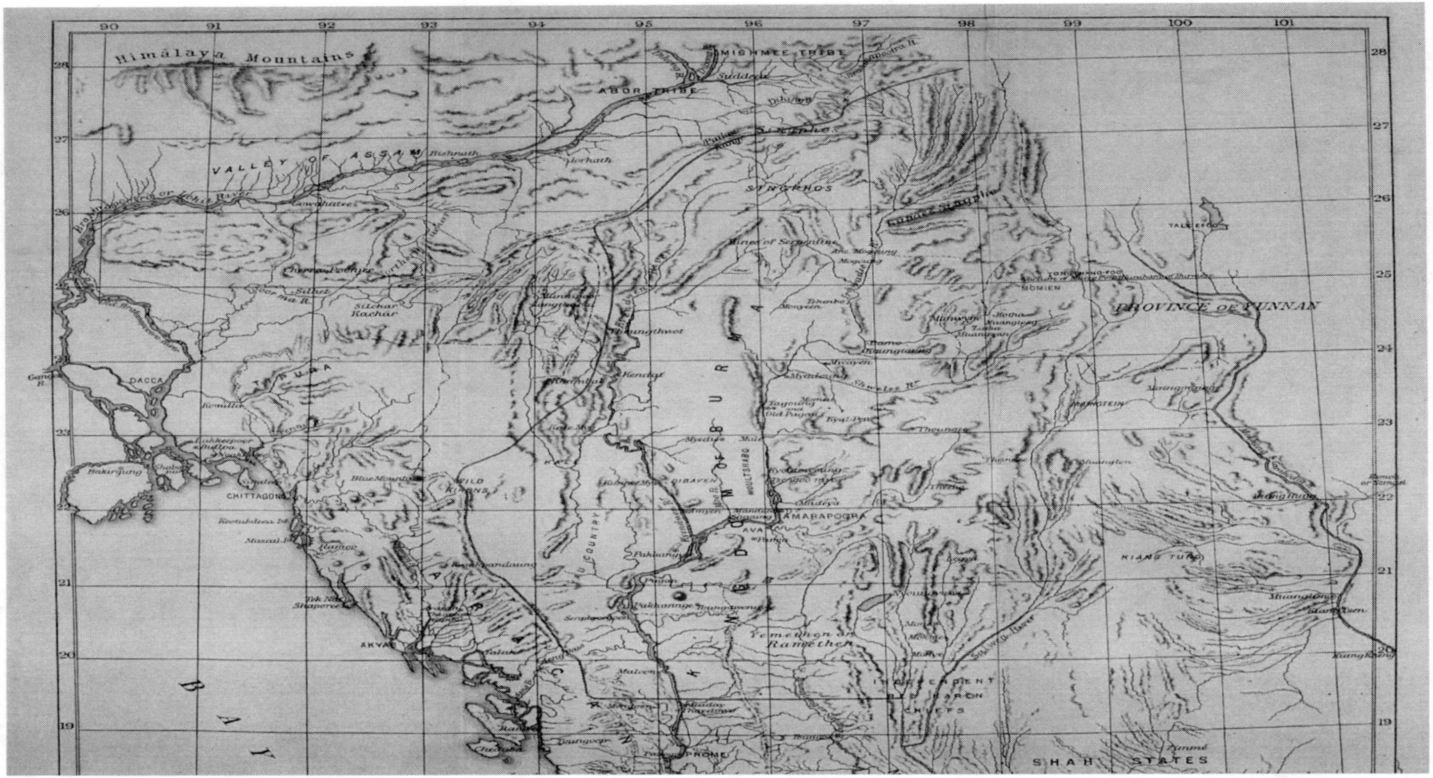
Himâlaya Mountains
MISHMEE TRIBE
ABOR TRIBE
VALLEY OF ASSAM
SINGPHOS
PROVINCE OF YUNNAN
MOMIEN
DACCA
CHITTAGONG
AKYAB
PROME
AVA
AMARAPOORA
KIANG TUNG
SHAN STATES
B A Y